CRACKING THE BRO CODE

Labor and Technology

Winifred Poster, series editor

Madison Van Oort, *Worn Out: How Retailers Surveil and Exploit Workers in the Digital Age and How Workers Are Fighting Back*

Sofya Aptekar, *The Green Card Soldier: Between Model Immigrant and Security Threat*

Margaret Jack, *Media Ruins: Cambodian Postwar Media Reconstruction and the Geopolitics of Technology*

Coleen Carrigan, *Cracking the Bro Code*

CRACKING THE BRO CODE

COLEEN CARRIGAN

The MIT Press
Cambridge, Massachusetts
London, England

The MIT Press would like to thank the anonymous peer reviewers who provided comments on drafts of this book. The generous work of academic experts is essential for establishing the authority and quality of our publications. We acknowledge with gratitude the contributions of these otherwise uncredited readers.

This book was set in Stone Serif and Stone Sans by Westchester Publishing Services. Printed and bound in the United States of America.

Library of Congress Cataloging-in-Publication Data

Names: Carrigan, Coleen, author.
Title: Cracking the bro code / Coleen Carrigan.
Description: Cambridge, Massachusetts : The MIT Press, [2024] | Series: Labor and technology | Includes bibliographical references and index.
Identifiers: LCCN 2023028854 (print) | LCCN 2023028855 (ebook) |
  ISBN 9780262547055 (paperback) | ISBN 9780262377164 (epub) |
  ISBN 9780262377157 (pdf)
Subjects: LCSH: Women computer industry employees—United States. |
  Sexual harassment of women—United States. | Sex discrimination against
  women—United States. | Male domination (Social structure)—United States.
Classification: LCC HD6073.C65222 U533 2023 (print) | LCC HD6073.C65222
  (ebook) | DDC 331.4/80040973—dc23/eng/20230817
LC record available at https://lccn.loc.gov/2023028854
LC ebook record available at https://lccn.loc.gov/2023028855

10 9 8 7 6 5 4 3 2 1

For my grandparents Dorothea and John Moran

CONTENTS

PROLOGUE: A VISIT TO THE VERSAILLES OF SILICON VALLEY

The shuttle drops me off in a large courtyard. Dotting the walkways are nine sculptures; three are busts of women, including oceanographer Sylvia Earle. I take a moment to walk through a beautiful garden with flowers and edible plants. Next to the garden is a brightly lit cafeteria offering a smorgasbord of fruits, vegetables, and grains. I stop in my tracks at the sight of a life-sized skeleton of Tyrannosaurus rex that is being set upon by flamingos. Dozens of bikes painted in primary colors are lined up outside the building. Much like polytechnic universities such as MIT, buildings are assigned numbers instead of names. Upon entering No. 43, I am greeted by a troupe of corporate representatives in bright blue golf shirts. They check my identification, direct me to wear a badge, and head upstairs. Looming above the stairs hangs a huge replica of a space shuttle with Paul Allen's name inscribed on it. Colorful, comfortable couches are around every corner. I pass by outdoor patios adorned with plants and more sculptures and kitchens stocked with espresso machines, fruit, and candy. Individuals are hard at work on their laptops.

Everywhere I turn there is a "No Visitors" sign in bright red. Security guards in the same bright blue shirts stand closely together in a wide-legged stance, forming a perimeter around the conference room. Their presence restricts my movement so that I cannot walk more than 10 feet without being asked: "Can I help you find something?" At first, I feel conspicuous as an outsider and disconcerted at being so closely watched and surveilled. But then I remember I am here to do the same. I ask one of the guards, Terrance, what he and the other guards are doing. He says their job is to help to guide visitors and treat medical accidents. Apparently, lots of people fall off the communal bikes that the employer provides to help expedite trips across the large headquarters. I smile and say "Okay. Why security guards and not medics?" He shrugs and says, "I'm just doing this gig until I graduate from school and enter law enforcement."

Men roam the halls in packs, wearing jeans, hooded sweatshirts, and t-shirts and carrying MacBooks. During this long first day of the conference, I see more male security guards than women employees. I speak with two of the women I see working here, both from human resources. Through closed glass doors, I see three meetings with over 15 people in each one and not a single woman!

At the end of the day, on a different floor, I search for a bathroom and observe a fourth meeting. One woman is present among nine men.

I see a woman running frantically through a hallway. She looks at me anxiously. Here is another woman . . . I smile. She replies by shaking her head and mumbling: "Meetings, meetings, meetings." Then I find myself lost. The air has shifted, buzzing with energy. People are working closely in groups and individually. Whiteboards are covered in a programming language foreign to me. A poster of Napoleon Dynamite is trimmed in red tinsel. Cubicles are packed, and the conference rooms and offices are small and transparent. The space is dense with people and offers little privacy. I am out of my element and getting more lost, so I retrace my steps. Once more on secure footing, I realize I have accidentally wandered past a "No Visitors" sign.

I discover a few private phone rooms within the visitors area, and I use one of them for some moments unobserved (or so I hoped) to check in with colleagues at my university. In the bathroom, the toilet seats are heated and the tampons are free. In every stall, there is a laminated poster with tips on how to code more efficiently. Each stall proffers different coding tips. Apparently, this place wants every moment of your "free" time.

Later, as I wait outside for my hotel shuttle to take me back to my accommodations, I peer inside building No. 34. An entire wall of the first floor, at least 2,000 square feet, is a large screen, lit up by the corporation's name bouncing across the room—a screensaver to fill a room. With my nose pressed up against the glass, I see in the middle of the room a stairwell that is also lit with screens. There are also screens on each stair's riser, illuminated with the names of cities where the corporation's offices are located.

I am incredulous at the sight—the screens have taken over the room. My shuttle arrives to take me back to my hotel, and I climb onboard in a daze, overwhelmed by the culture at the Versailles of Silicon Valley.

This book is an ethnography of women knowledge workers in sites of computer science and engineering, fields that focus on the design and building of computer systems. In these pages, I share the stories of technologists in US computing workspaces that confer preferential treatment to men from dominant racial groups. Such favor in these lucrative, prestigious jobs has societal impacts that need further investigation. These technologists and their stories help us to understand how this occupational injustice is a danger not only to disenfranchised workers but to broader society as well. I examine the intellectual challenge that women face navigating and persisting in computing culture, despite the contradictions between their lived experiences and the performative philanthropic heroism performed by their bosses, who are prominent computing figures. I argue that technologists have the potential to provide leadership critical to ameliorating these harms.

Sexism stubbornly persists in computing culture, as does technocracy, a dogmatic belief that computer technology is always needed and always munificent. The cultural means by which these problems entwine and fortify one another in computing is the crux of this book's inquiry. I am especially curious because other scientific fields have been yielding to broader social movements for justice and public criticisms of computational machinery are proliferating these days. What is special about computing culture that makes it seemingly impervious to desegregation? By spotlighting this potent combination of sexism and technocracy, we can learn how digital bosses have come to operate in our society imperiously, dodging taxes and oversight with impunity, and how some programmers who look like them, serving at their right hands, are enchanted with a sense of divine right. In the context of the powerful influence of computers, we may also do some divination of our own and speculate on how the cultural mechanisms sustaining sexism and technocracy in computing workspaces affect society.

Technological acumen in this cyber era is a form of social power, and yet access to acquiring such acumen is reserved for a select few. My field memo in the beginning of this Prologue describes the context in which computing labor takes place, exhibiting themes significant to this book, including gender, surveillance, privacy, labor practices, and wealth. The rest of this book will explore relations of power inside these citadels. A highly segregated workforce produces computing knowledge and products. How and why this segregation happens in computing workplaces is important to understanding regressive politics in the context of computing labor, artifacts, and the digital economy. High technology's dependence on sexist culture calls into question the socially revolutionary narrative promoted by the computing industry. Further, it also challenges us to think about the costs of society's growing dependence on computers and the consequences of trusting those who own the means of their production and their vision for the future of humanity.

In this book, I bring together feminist anthropology, feminist science and technology studies (STS), and Marxist feminism to frame how a fusion of reproductive, economic, and knowledge politics shape and are shaped by computer technology. I draw on two years of ethnographic research with cisgender and transgender women who persist in computer science organizations at all stages of a technical career. *Cracking the Bro Code* is in chorus with other scholars who are working to foment the social and intellectual movement to transform barriers to women's opportunities in computing—which, I hope, may also have a salubrious effect on the kinds of technology that are developed and adopted.

INTRODUCTION

I dropped out of Big Tech. It was more than I could bear—a potent mix of sexism and harassment that corroded my health. Now, I work to understand how women and nonbinary people persist in computing to contribute their labor and hard-won expertise to one of the most influential fields on the planet. While I am concerned with justice in all science and technology fields, sexism in computing workspaces has proved most difficult to ameliorate, even though successful efforts for transformational change in this occupation would have wide impacts. One of my inspirations for leadership in this regard is Dr. Maria Klawe, former president of Harvey Mudd College. Klawe gave a distinguished lecture at the University of Washington in which she shared how she participated in a 2012 White House Forum on Women in the Economy. She was discussing gender politics in science with Valerie Jarrett, senior adviser to President Barack Obama, and believed a finer point needed to be made about calls to action. As Klawe tells it (Klawe 2012; Obama 2012), she said, "'Valerie, you've got it wrong. We need more women in engineering and computer science, not in STEM fields. That's just the wrong message.' And she argued with me and I argued back. And then President Obama came in to address us, and I was so happy because he said, 'We need more women in STEM fields. Especially in engineering and computer science where they're really needed.' And I'm going, 'Yay!'"

Science, technology, engineering, and mathematics (STEM) is too broad an aggregate these days, since many other STEM fields are having some success with representational parity. Big Tech companies now admit they need to hire and welcome more technologists of color and women. Feminist

activism like the #MeToo movement has galvanized public support for combating gender violence, and predators in computer science and engineering
are under more scrutiny. Similar to President Obama, who welcomed senior
women's expertise on complex scientific problems, some men in leadership
positions are helping to advance the cause of justice in the computing labor
force.

Has, however, #MeToo ended sexism and harassment in computing
education and workplaces or, at least, significantly curbed it? My students'
experiences and my own in recent years leave me doubtful. Every year, I
teach an introductory course in cultural anthropology in which I assign
mini-ethnographic projects on culture at our university. The good news is
that white students and male students care about acts of racism and sexism and their systemic outcomes. The bad news is that, year after year, this
assignment yields much evidence that opportunities are being denied to
people who have faced steep barriers to technical education. Worse, while
navigating these institutions, scholars of color, queer scholars, and women
scholars are being harmed by bias, discrimination, and harassment.

The people you will meet in this ethnography also confirm that computer
science and engineering has a serious cultural problem. From senior leaders in the field to undergraduates navigating their first year of college, the
participants in this book's study will tell you how sexism and harassment
manifest in computing through values, norms, behaviors, evaluations, and
policies. While other STEM fields are making strides in recruiting, retaining,
and respecting women workers, computing fails, year after year, to do so.

Just before the COVID pandemic and many years after leaving high-
tech to pursue anthropology, I attended a professional dinner in honor of
a renowned scholar who is doing cutting-edge work on ethics in computational machinery. The rock star guest and I were the only people at the table
who were neither cisgender men nor in the fields of computing or philosophy. A sixth man joined late and sat next to me. I knew he was in computing but we had not yet met. "Hi, I'm Dick," he said, introducing himself.
"You must be Jason's wife." "Hi, I'm Coleen," I responded. "I am a faculty
member." An awkward silence descended on the table. Dick stammered an
apology as I rearranged my silverware. "You were sitting next to Jason, so
I assumed you were his wife." "Yes, because I am married to everyone I sit
next to," I responded with a smile. Nervous laughter broke the tension.

Early in my career in Big Tech, at a company I will heretofore refer to as *Colossus*, I would not have had the experience or confidence to respond to a peer's sexism like this. Now that I have benefited from hearing similar stories from hundreds of other women and nonbinary technologists, this incident did not affect my confidence or my sense of belonging. It confirmed however, that there is still a pressing need to transform a culture that keeps technologists from imagining their women peers in roles other than those traditionally associated with providing goods and caring labor, like secretary, sex object, or wife.

Dick is not a bad apple. He is an adherent of the Bro Code, a cultural problem (not an individual one) in a field that flounders in efforts to welcome a critical mass of women (as opposed to mere tokenism) to ameliorate sexist divisions of labor in traditionally male-dominated fields (Carrigan, Quinn, and Riskin 2011). Anthropologists study the powerful process of enculturation, and here, I hold up to scrutiny a particular culture with much power to justify and enforce its values and worldview. The reach of computing science and engineering is vast and its coffers deep, which affords the field significant means by which to succeed in its bid for self-regulation and claim to know what is best for all of humanity, both present and future. I want to inoculate my students from the harms of the Bro Code. I want to repay my research participants' generosity by amplifying efforts to hold technological organizations accountable for fair and just workplaces. First, I must convince you, esteemed reader, to see the Bro Code as your problem, too. It everyone's problem—together, let's crack it.

1 GENDERED LABOR IN COMPUTING

The #MeToo movement, feminist activism with strong public support to end gender violence, has positioned us at a critical juncture in research on broadening participation in computing. We must better understand why, when it comes to access, some science, technology, engineering, and mathematics (STEM) disciplines (e.g., biology) are examples of gender parity while other disciplines—computer science and engineering, for example—remain stubbornly segregated (Cheryan et al. 2017; Gibbons 2009; Wajcman 2009). While others argue that the answer lies in women's lack of experience, self-efficacy, and comfort with computing culture, I contend that computing culture reinforces gender violence. Not only are individual women harmed in computing workplaces through a combination of bias, discrimination, and harassment but the failure to rectify the occupational segregation in the field undermines feminists' efforts to increase women's earning capacities, access to power, and our political and bodily sovereignty in broader culture. Further, due to a combination of massive wealth accumulation and masterful branding that suggests a cosmological power to which it is in our best interests to submit, computing workplaces are bathed in a halo of exceptionalism and thus shielded from regulation and inoculated from ill-repute more than other fields.

Gender in the world of computing is an advantageous standpoint from which to demystify the power of this technology and its owners and outputs. My feminist ethnography unearthed several core values driving culture in computing production, including precision, abstraction, aggression, a love of machines, and a disdain for behaviors or ideas that may threaten the marriage between masculinity and technical competency. I call these values and the ways they are policed in technological work the "Bro Code," and I use the term to refer to the performance and norms of gender enacted by straight cisgender men from dominant racial groups in computing organizations and values that privilege masculinist identities, instrumental rationality, and binary thinking. It is influenced by norms in broader society governing technology, race, and gender and also exports its values to help shape society. It's the secret to why computing remains stubbornly sexist and uneven in its distribution of opportunity, resources, and regard.

THE SIGNIFICANCE OF THE BRO CODE

Why is "bro culture" in the computing industry particularly important to study? I am often asked, "What about white men's shitty behavior in finance, for example?" My answer is threefold. First, "every company wants to be a tech company" (Tarnoff and Weigel 2020, 8). JPMorgan employs more software engineers than most Big Tech corporations, blurring the boundaries between the finance sector of the economy and computing domains (Tarnoff and Weigel 2020). Given how the solvency of many industries now rely on algorithmic infrastructure, the Bro Code permeates many other influential fields beyond the major Big Tech corporations, and thus cracking it will have wide impact.

Second, computer technology companies tolerate discrimination and harassment more than non-tech companies (Scott, Klein, and Onovakpuri 2017). Women of color in technical fields experience the greatest amount of mistreatment, including being blocked from advancing into leadership and targeted by sexual harassment and stereotyping (National Academies 2022). In this way, the Bro Code impedes racial justice and the accumulation of generational wealth in communities of color.

Finally, since technical skills are in demand in many arenas in the US economy, denying women the opportunity to develop and perfect the skills required for leadership in the twenty-first century stands to roll back decades of progress toward a more just, egalitarian society.

Computing is a field that floods the market with unregulated commodities with seismic social impacts. This is why, in addition to studying technological things and their social impact, the conditions under which computing artifacts are made are important to examine, too. Who produces computing knowledge affects what is made and toward what ends it is used. Workplace values become encoded in computing commodities. Given the vast domains on which computers have influence, their reach makes the Bro Code a problem of global proportions. Along with digital artifacts and infrastructures, the Bro Code may be considered another significant output of computing, one of the factors contributing to extreme disparities of wealth and opportunities in the US, especially along vectors of gender and race.

In the 1940s and 1950s, women made up the ranks of computer programmers, a fact that has been erased or downplayed in computing lore (D'Ignazio and Klein 2020; Abbate 2012; Hicks 2017; Ensmenger 2010b). Once the level of intellectual demand and skill required for this labor were recognized, software programming, like other scientific fields, followed a pattern that devalued women's contributions as the discipline inversely rose to prominence (Etzkowitz 2008). Computer programming was redesigned as men's work (Kraft 1979; Daub 2021). The erasure of computing pioneers contributes to the exclusion and harassment of the women who persist in computing today. This radical swing in labor value in the field also contributes to a peremptory form of fragility that, according to my experience, characterizes the attitudes of Bro Coders. In other words, the mendacious myth that the computer's origins are solely patrilineal stems from a gender politics that fashions and fortifies the Bro Code.

All-male cabals are nothing new. They are cornerstones of societies that reproduce patriarchal structures of power (e.g., Western science, the Catholic Church, and the nerve center of global finance—Wall Street). Here I advance a theory of the Bro Code built on five arguments related to its unique characteristics and why it is worth exploring. First, women who navigate, resist, and subvert male hegemony to persist as workers in computing have a unique standpoint in US society and the potential to transform, institutionally and interpersonally, unjust social relations. Second, interview protocols, long hours, precision questioning, combative work styles, and the logical and abstract approaches to knowledge production prized over creative ones reproduce the ideological union between masculine ideals and competency in the field. These rituals also serve to indoctrinate computing workers to the core values in computing commodity production, including constant observation, intense evaluations of others, and the devaluation of sociality. Third, participants' emotions allowed me to locate and interpret the conflicts and contradictions in women's lives. Many of these contradictions signal a rupture as women struggle to navigate the bifurcated nature of their workplace role, feeling at once privileged to be agents in a powerful field and marginalized as members of this field (Smith 1990). These sites of rupture are areas ripe for social change activism. Fourth, the majority of my participants have social change aspirations. They want to use their computing skills to make the world a better place. These aspirations correlate with a commitment to support other women in computing, both on an interpersonal level and in congress with others. Navigating the experience of rupture, combined with a yearning for social justice, may ignite feminist consciousness in women computer scientists, which can lead to collective action in pursuit not only of equality in computing but in broader cultural domains. Finally, I argue that social change aspirations are a collective form of reproductive aspirations—shared yearning to contribute to the collective well-being of society around which computing workers can effectively organize.

What makes patriarchal culture in computing unique can be found in the stories of my ethnographic participants—stories of navigating a work culture dominated by the Bro Code. In these pages, you will learn how these values manifest in daily work relations and how they can result in unjust labor relations and stubborn segregation.

Cracking the Bro Code offers portraits of technologists who in one way or another oppose the Bro Code and persist in one of the most powerful, influential workforces in the world. You will meet a white transgender woman and early-career scholar whose nonplussed attitude toward her male peers and the incivility of advisers is a master class on handling white male fragility. You will meet a Black cisgender woman who off-ramped from software engineering in industry into academia in order to align her career with her altruistic values to make the world a better place. You will meet a cisgender woman from Russia in the high-tech world of finance with a shrewd take on reproductive politics in the computer science workforce. You will meet a cisgender man from Ghana who takes special care in his dress and associations at his software engineering job to mitigate racism.

The technologists who participated in my study generally respond to workplace exploitation, including stereotyping, discrimination, and sexual and gender harassment, in four ways, which I list in order of high to low risk of attrition from computing: they internalize, desensitize, criticize, or collectivize, and some employ a combination of these strategies. In the chapters ahead, you will meet people who respond to the Bro Code by *internalizing* its hostility, which manifests in the impostor syndrome and the sense that one does not belong. Others respond by *desensitizing*, which means acting as "gender agnostics," people who care not to see sexism or gender in computer engineering. Only white cisgender women computer scientists exhibited these desensitization tactics. These participants avoided considerations of gender at work as a persistence mechanism, one predicated on the privileges of whiteness and heterosexuality. However, many of this study's research participants *criticize* inequitable labor relations in computing. Critical interlocutors in this study also tended to *collectivize*—that is, they organize in groups to fight for, support, and advance women in computing and destabilize the imposition of the Bro Code. In the chapters ahead, I will share evidence of these four types of responses and explain how they illuminate the connections between technology, gender, and race, thus perpetuating segregation within computing organizations. In addition, I explore efficacious pathways for developing collective oppositional perspectives to address these complex injustices.

Technological workers have unique standpoints that can help us understand how power operates within its cybernetic citadels. Their stories suggest a connection between sites of computing production and the further enclosure of social life within the digital economy. As important, some of these computer scientists and engineers have values that directly contradict the corporate, technocratic values of their organizations. People inside the exclusive domains of computer production provide essential checks and balances for those of us who are operating from outside these fields as we endeavor to reshape technology cultures and determine the societal purposes for which computers will be used.

THE BRO CODE: WHAT DO WE KNOW? WHAT DO WE NEED TO LEARN TO CRACK IT?

This book is concerned not only with sexism in technoscience but also with how it creates unjust labor conditions for workers and students historically disenfranchised from US computing. I reckon with the social inequities inside computing classrooms and workplaces that are made possible by the Bro Code. Enacting justice inside the walls of my field sites may help to advance justice in the realms of human health, social justice, as well as state and global politics. I ask two questions: (1) How do gender and race intersect to influence outcomes in the production of computer technology? (2) How can we transform computing sites of knowledge production and fairly distribute their power and influence on our world?

I am conflicted about asking more women to lend their talent to computing organizations dominated by the Bro Code because I know, from both my own professional experience and years of ethnographic research into computing culture, just how hard it is and how much resiliency it takes to persist and thrive. On the one hand, we need women working from within computing to make change. Representation does matter; a *critical mass* of women in STEM influence design outcomes and organizational culture, resulting in more egalitarian outcomes (Carrigan, Quinn, and Riskin 2011; Margolis and Fisher 2003; Etzkowitz, Kemelgor, and Uzzi 2000). On the other hand, given that technocracy—the pervasive belief that more technology is better and technology always benefits the social good—how can I advocate for women to make machines that do harm to historically disenfranchised groups for the enrichment and advancement of a powerful elite?

I make no claim that women's inclusion is a good idea for corporate profit or shareholder value because I care not for capitalists' enrichment but for the well-being of women in computing who exercise their right to participate in shaping the future of digital life, often at great costs.

I center the lives and voices of group members marginalized in a powerful field because they bring a new and different perspective on power relations. Their perspective can generate new knowledge and applications of existing tools. Computational machinery can be tools of social control. In order to interrupt and destabilize the reproduction of unregulated algorithmic artifacts and obedient participants in the technocratic neoliberal order, the folks marginalized in the field must have their say.

Women's persistence and achievement in high-tech has broader economic implications. Economic independence hinges on women's ability to earn a living wage, something that is made infinitely easier as a technologist. Denying women jobs in computing or harassing them out of these positions are forms of economic injustice that disenfranchise both individuals and generations to come. The accumulation of disadvantages resulting from such exclusions is also a form of reproductive injustice. Systematic denial of access to high wages, steady employment, wealth, and leadership opportunities causes women to become more vulnerable to poverty and

patriarchal demands that coerce many into the provision of nonrecipro-
cated, morally coded goods and caring labor to male-dominated institutions. The people who took the time to share their experiences with me for
this research are trailblazers with more courage and grit than I have. Unlike
my research participants, I leaned out. I did not persist.

In this study, I represent myself in two ways. First, as a narrator who
interprets participants' experiences through a prism refracting my lived
experiences as a white woman and a feminist scholar. My whiteness influenced my relations in the field and what I learned from participants who are
and are not white. Given the legacies of white supremacy in the academy
and white women's role in upholding these relations today, my whiteness
likely impeded trust with some participants of color. Also, my feminism
was sometimes an impediment in the recruitment phase of the study, turning off gender agnostics who feign not to see gender in their classrooms or
workplaces. Second, I also represent myself as a woman worker who has
experienced and resisted gender and sexual harassment and wage exploitation in Big Tech. Gender harassment is a form of sexual harassment, but
the disparaging conduct is not intended to elicit sex. Instead, it consists in
verbal, physical, and symbolic behaviors that convey hostile and exclusionary attitudes toward women. I use legal documents and journal entries that
I wrote while employed as a project manager and acting senior manager at
Colossus to demonstrate how interpersonal and structural sexism operated
in order to contribute to and reproduce patriarchal relations in corporate
high-tech.

Cracking the Bro Code thus examines phenomena that contribute to the
reasons that women's attrition in technical fields is 50 percent higher than
men's (Fouad et al. 2017). The Bro Code is not just about repelling any
infiltration of femme-identified programmers; it is also about preserving
a particular kind of sanctuary—a Geek temple, as it were. The book moves
upstream from corporate or nationalist logics common in gender equity
scholarship to explore how the reign of the Bro Code in high-tech workplaces and classrooms is simply cultural, and culture is nothing but in flux.
My aim is to use this fact to destabilize harassment in the field and shine
a spotlight on people who historically made computers possible and continue to do so today.

DISENFRANCHISEMENT

According to the National Center for Women & Information Technology (NCWIT), "women's proportional representation in STEM disciplines at the bachelor's level has generally risen since the mid-1990s—except in computer and information sciences (CIS) and mathematics" (DuBow and Gonzalez 2020, 4). In 2019, women earned only 21.5 percent of the bachelor's degrees in computing in the US compared to 37 percent in 1985 (Zweben and Bizot 2020). The year before, 2018, was the first time in 33 years when the number of women earning bachelor's degrees in computing "had exceeded the 1985 historic peak of 13,733" (DuBow and Gonzalez 2020, 5). In contrast, the number of bachelor's degrees awarded to men has more than doubled since its 1987 historic peak of 25,887 (DuBow and Gonzalez 2020). Only 9 percent of all computing degrees are awarded to African Americans, with only 2 percent of those being African American women (Hamrick 2019).

Such stark underrepresentation permeates the workforce as well. Women make up only 25 percent of the computing workforce at large (Ashcraft, McLain, and Eger 2016). Only 21 percent of computer programming positions are held by women (Ashcraft, McLain, and Eger 2016). Of that 21 percent, only 2 percent are African American, and only 1 percent are Latina (Ashcraft, McLain, and Eger 2016); furthermore, 50 percent of women in technology have felt discriminated against in their job because of their gender, and African American women and Latinas with degrees in computing are hired less often and paid significantly less than their white peers (Urwin 2023). During the COVID-19 pandemic, women in computing were twice as likely to be furloughed or fired compared with men. They are also 65 percent more likely than their male peers to be impacted by mass layoffs in the computing industry (Urwin 2023). Those who did retain their jobs found remote work challenging. For example, women of color in tech were far more likely than white women to report that the pandemic took a serious toll on their work-life balance and to express dissatisfaction with their managers' efforts to connect and communicate with them (Awad et al. 2022). These dismal trends are especially disturbing in light of the fact that computer science and engineering is one of the degrees with the highest earnings (Hess 2019), allowing degree holders to accumulate economic and cultural capital. Even when women gain entry to these prestigious worksites, they are paid less than their male peers. For example, "an audit of Google's pay practices by the Department of Labor found six to seven standard deviations between pay for men and women in nearly every job category" (West, Whittaker, and Crawford 2019, 9). Across commercial tech firms, women coders of color earn less than their male peers and white women (West, Whittaker, and Crawford 2019). Understanding how discrimination in computing is maintained and reproduced stands to contribute to closing the gap between what computer science leaders say computers do for society and the field's actual application, outputs, and outcomes.

In this lucrative field with enormous influence on wealth creation, women's perspectives are missing to the detriment of many (Chang 2018; Margolis and Fisher 2003). The consequences of the segregated high-tech workforce invite further scrutiny of computing artifacts, which can threaten people's safety and well-being. For example, popular search engines stereotype and demean people of color, especially women of color, while reproducing whiteness and maleness as normative (Noble 2018). Google's search algorithms mislabel Black people as gorillas (Simonite 2018), and corporate systems using artificial intelligence (AI) significantly misgender women and darker-skinned individuals (Buolamwini and Gebru 2018). Suzanne, a white, mid-career executive at Facebook who participated in this study, described how she was at a design team meeting tasked with developing a tracking device for a mobile phone application that would allow users to meet up with friends while out on the town. She was the only woman on the team, and she became frustrated that the men on the team were all extremely enthusiastic about the potential of this feature, without reservation or ethical considerations. She finally interjected and asked the men: "Have you ever been stalked, harassed, or afraid for your life? Women deal with fear of male violence every day, and we need to give our users a sense of security. We must make privacy paramount." If she had not been in that planning meeting, millions of women worldwide who participate in Facebook's platform would have been put at greater risk. Segregation in technology is not only a matter of justice for workers in computing fields; it is also a matter of life and death for users of computer technology.

TECHNOCRACY AND TECH FETISHISM

Scholarship is now proliferating on how racism and sexism are encoded in computing artifacts and disseminated widely through "user experience" with digital platforms.[1] This ethnography, like Sareeta Amrute's 2016 book *Encoding Race, Encoding Class*, focuses on the computing workplace and its disenfranchised workers forced to either uphold exploitative relations or contest them at great cost. *Cracking the Bro Code* decenters the artifacts of technology to interrogate instead the social architecture of labor involved in creating and making computing technology. I also prioritize producers of technology over consumers because the conditions of computing workplaces matter in our society. If these workplaces can become more just, fair, and equitable in terms of who is welcomed, celebrated, and compensated in technological creation, then these creations may better serve society. The voices of my participants (and my own) may not have been worthy of consideration at the lab benches and boardroom tables in our worksites. Here, we offer our stories and perspectives to those who seek to challenge the Bro Code.

Computing culture prizes objectivism, and yet computer scientists love mythologizing and spinning fantastical stories about its contributions to society. Technocratic ideals are as ubiquitous as computing commodities, cultural fabrications that both engender and buttress Big Tech's power in the world. But beyond the noisy rhetoric on the "revolutionary" power and promise of "magical" technology lay hidden abodes of exploitation. To understand what work this rhetoric does in the world, I analyze it in relation to labor conditions described by my research participants in computing workplaces, classrooms, and labs. In other words, I mind the gaps between what computer scientists say they do for society and their actual impacts. I begin with the ways that computing leaders influence the knowledge workers who create their products and generate profits for them. This assessment requires opening the black box containing the matrix of intersecting structures of power governing labor in computer science education and Big Tech.

Big Tech's promulgations are no longer dogmatic, and studies on its negative effects on society—for example, exacerbating racist and sexist harms and expanding surveillance, privacy transgressions, wealth disparities, climate degradation, extremist ideology, and labor exploitation—are having wide uptake (Bender et al. 2021; Noble 2018; Roberts 2019; Hicks 2017; Benjamin 2019; Broussard 2018; Sadowski 2020; O'Neil 2017; D'Ignazio and Klein 2020). Activists, tech workers, and scholars are not only debating the sophisticated mechanisms of these harm but also forming coalitions to resist inequities in data science classrooms and workplaces (Costanza-Chock 2020). Extending earlier scholarship (Adam 1998), these critiques disrupt the ennobling discourse of the benevolent influence of data science in US society. Still, the munificence of computer technology and the speculative belief that computational machinery is a "magic" panacea to social problems are too often assumed.[2] Worse, sexual harassment in the computing workplace is unrelenting, perpetuated by a culture of "open secrets" and meritocracy that pervade the field (West, Whittaker, and Crawford 2019; Molina and Sussman 2021; Carrigan, Green, and Rahman-Davies 2021).

Technocracy and tech fetishism are two repertoires helpful to understanding the ways people are enchanted to think, act, and feel about computer technology and the opportunities and constraints it (unevenly) offers humanity (cf. Hess 2007). Technocracy is an ideology where technological progress is equated with human advancement (Davis-Floyd 1992). Technocracy is a concept similar to what Meredith Broussard (2018) coined as technochauvinism, in which technology is always the best solution.[3] Importantly, to technochauvinists, the adherents of technocracy, there is no alternative to the growth of computer systems. Any problems with technology are assumed to be social, a pollutant that can be purified through a more rigorous logical process—a technical fix—to eliminate it. The virtual is sacred; the material is profane. This reigning ideology is a source of power for the high-tech ruling class, foreclosing opportunities for transparency and public deliberations on and resistance to the incursions of technological forces. Further, the elite workers who look like their Big Tech bosses and help make their riches possible perform their power in US culture with such keen vigor as to deserve recognition. I have named these types of performances the *geek mystique* in order to excavate a subterranean postulate informing the practices and principles of technochauvinism.

The geek mystique is a halo effect around white geeks in hoodies created by the Bro Code, naturalizing their outputs as wholly benevolent and rigorous evidence of unfolding progress, divine and linear, which is always already manifesting a higher good. In this way, computing commodities are produced, circulated, and fetishized. The geek mystique is specific form of power and authority imbued not just in technological artifacts (Winner 2010) but also in those who created such artifacts. There is a common base note of fundamentalism in these principal logics undergirding the digital economy. This element makes the geek mystique a logical application of scientific rationalism in service of an economy that is oriented around principles aiming to reduce labor costs, externalize the costs of social reproduction to precarious workers, and financialize human behavior and relations. In the Age of Information, leaders believe themselves to be wizards or priests (Ensmenger 2010a). They lean into authoritarianism, prompted to repress complaints and resistance (Sadowski 2020; Bourdieu 2003). The wattage of the geek's halo has been obscuring an amalgamation of race, gender, technology, and economics at play in the making of computer technology. Through my participants' stories evincing the geek mystique, these intersecting structures of power will come into sharper relief, especially in chapter 4.

The second repertoire key to opening the black box of labor in computer science is tech fetishism. The Bro Code relies on not just the imposition of technocracy but also a myth-making process that involves the circulation and promotion of aggrandized narratives. Much like religious belief systems, technocratic dogma is seeded culturally using myths of cosmic scale. "We must incorporate communications, advertising and marketing in our analyses. The production of desire is its own big business—with complex links to culture, subjectivity and power" (Peterson 2003, 77). The hegemony of technocracy is enforced by this fetishism, the mythification surrounding a new form of commodity—the digital commodity—that I articulate from a feminist standpoint. Mythification is an implacable public relations campaign pushing a "grift . . . a presentation of civility that masks a politics of cruelty . . . and bloodthirsty capitalist intentions" (Dubal 2020).

Tech fetishism is a belief system, a force that envelops Big Tech with a mystical sheen that repels scrutiny and accountability, two elements that are crucial to the power it wields in society (Carrigan, Green, and Rahman-Davies 2021).

The tech fetish is predicated on two other long-standing myths. The first is the naturalization of reproductive labor as women's destined capacity for servility. I use the term "reproductive labor" to define labor in the realm of necessity—the work and relationships of social reproduction: attending to sustenance needs like food production, provision, and preparation;

providing care for others' physical, mental, and emotional well-being; maintaining kin and community ties; and reproducing the labor force, both on a day-to-day basis and generationally. This broadly defined definition of reproductive labor demands that we spotlight structures of power that deny people meaningful ways to subsist. Feminist anthropologists have long challenged the validity of the public/private binary and framed the family as an economic unit, thereby connecting reproduction to the economic relations of production (Rosaldo, Lamphere, and Bamberger 1974; Leacock 1981; Rapp 1979; Ginsburg and Rapp 1991; Moore 1988; Sargent and Browner 2005; Sanger 2003; Browner 2001; Bray 2007). Steep barriers to women of color, white women, and nonbinary people participating in computer science constitute both an economic *and* reproductive injustice because occupational segregation and sexual harassment deny people the opportunity to do meaningful work without harm or economic impoverishment.

The second myth at the heart of tech fetishism, one widely circulated in US society, is that it is not only *best* but inevitable to organize economic relations in society so that many are subjugated for the excessive enrichment of a few. If we are to hold computing bosses accountable to society, ethically and democratically, we must regulate them through civic channels, incentivizing them to care about public welfare.

The Age of Information is haunted by the absences of women. Susan Leigh Star encourages us to borrow a methodological tool from Mary Daly—spooking—to ameliorate these kinds of hauntings. Spooking means elucidating that which haunts certain forms of knowledge and culture so one can "spark" and make meaning from how these "absences or silences . . . creatively work together" (Bauchspies and Puig de la Bellacasa 2009, 335; Daly and Caputi 1987). To do this, I dig into three levels of violence that disappear women from full participation in public life. First, there is material violence, which is evident in the uneven distribution of resources. Second is epistemic violence, which excludes women and people of color from a system of knowledge and justifies these exclusions as "natural." Lastly, our society's dominant belief system is predicated on what anthropologists Faye Ginsburg and Rayna Rapp (1995, 4) call "euphemized violence"—the structures of power that efface the centrality of women to our society and fail to acknowledge the impact of this effacement on the lives of women, families, and communities. I hope these conceptual tools of spooking the

Bro Code and sparking significant connections between its comprising elements will further a collective "spinning," the creation of new meanings, the weaving of new modes on knowledge of technology and gender (Bauchspies and Puig de la Bellacasa 2009; Daly and Caputi 1987).

FEMINIST ETHNOGRAPHY

Feminist ethnographers spend time in communities to get to know research participants in-depth, and often, we unsettle the boundaries of insider/outsider and self/other in research (Abu-Lughod 1990; Davis and Craven 2016). Feminist ethnography involves putting oneself on the same plane as one's participants, taking part in and observing informal situations to make the familiar strange (Forsythe and Hess 2001). Finally, feminist ethnography transgresses the false binary between public and private spheres, dissolving preconceived notions that people's professional and personal lives are separate.

In accordance with these principles, I designed this study cross-sectionally to investigate the personal and professional aspirations of knowledge workers in computing at different points along a life course, including training initiation, labor market participation, and career advancement. This book offers portraits of people at various points of time in a computing career, bypassing the constraints of a longitudinal study, to compare different groups along markers of gender, race, and sexuality in order to understand the Bro Code in computing worksites.

Effective solutions to the entrenched problem of Bro Code culture require intersectionality, a Black feminist approach that forefronts the ways in which structures governing race, sexuality, and gender interweave and relate (Mullings and Schultz 2006; Cho, Crenshaw, and McCall 2013; Crenshaw 1991; Metcalf, Russell, and Hill 2018). The cross-sectional design (described above) buttressed my intersectional analytic strategy, thereby providing data for a systems-level analysis of the Bro Code and its differential effects on high-tech workers (Collins 2015). The analytics of intersectionality are essential to not only challenging inequitable power relations in technoscience but also understanding its multidimensional and far-reaching impacts (Subramaniam et al. 2017).

Because I once was an insider in high-tech and have since stepped out and trained as an anthropologist, I bring to this study both my "insider" experiences in computing and a structural analysis made possible from an outsider's perspective. Even though I did not persist in the field, my experience witnessing technical knowledge being practiced and performed from *inside* a Big Tech corporation is a perspective that I can offer the study of computer technology. Being a target of gender and sexual harassment in Big Tech elevated my critical capacities in this feminist project and also inspired me to care about the health of those disenfranchised in computer science and engineering. For example, I mapped women's mental, emotional, and physical well-being; paid close attention to signals in my dataset of women's strain and stress; and traced the implications. Unsettling the boundaries of insider/outsider helps me to understand how identity-based harassment in computing workspaces is a public health issue as well as a social, political, epistemic, and economic one.

My career as an anthropologist of science and technology has been motivated by the desire to contribute to efforts to regulate and desegregate computing (Hess 2007). I bring a feminist perspective to the social study of technoscience and a political economic perspective to gender equity theory on representational harms in computing. Finally, as an anthropologist, I bring a fascination with kinship and cosmology and a critical methodological approach forged in the crucible of anthropology's reckoning with colonialism and patriarchy.

During the time of this study, I was a member of the National Science Foundation's ADVANCE community, working to broaden women's participation in academic STEM careers in the US as part of a social and intellectual movement.[4] This group membership afforded me opportunities to attend conferences around the country hosted by academic and industry organizations and have informal conversations with hundreds of technoscientists about gender, race, and power in the field. I also performed participant observation at these conferences that are organized around the goal of transforming the social barriers that keep technoscience segregated. Of note are the National Center for Women & Information Technology (NCWIT); American Association of University Women; National Science Foundation ADVANCE PI (Principal Investigator) conferences; IEEE Women in Engineering and Google events; Society of Women Engineers; American Society for Engineering Education; Anita Borg Institute; Women in Engineering Pro-Active Network; and dozens of lunches, retreats, and conferences hosted by the center at which I worked for eight years—the University of Washington ADVANCE Center for Institutional Change.

This study also relies on lived experiences as told to me in 43 semi-structured interviews, conducted from 2011 to 2013, with people who work as technical professionals in elite corporations and universities. More than half of these participants had some association with the groups enumerated above, all of which are organized around efforts to broaden participation in US technoscience. Throughout this book, I use pseudonyms to refer to my research participants. My participants were extremely accomplished. When I decided to "study up," I decided to really go for it. Most of my academic participants were either trained in or working for computer science departments that *US News and World Report* deems the "most competitive" in the US, like the Massachusetts Institute of Technology, the University of Wisconsin at Madison, Carnegie Mellon, the University of Washington, Stanford, and the Georgia Institute of Technology, to name a few. My non-academic industry participants work for companies that most Americans recognize and solicit services from, including Intel, Microsoft, Amazon .com, Hewlett-Packard, Google, Adobe, Cisco, and Facebook. My sampling strategy is in no way aimed at reproducing the elitism that these institutions represent. Rather, I seek to critically examine the prestige and influence of these high-tech institutions:

> The "high-IT core" workforce includes computer programmers, computer scientists, computer engineers and systems analysts whose jobs are directly involved in the study, design, development, implementation, support or management of computer-based information systems, particularly software applications and computer hardware. (Tam and Bassett, as cited in Bystydzienski and Bird 2006, 108)

When I use the terms computer science and engineering, computing, and "high-tech," I am referring to these types of jobs. The high-tech workforce has seen the greatest increases in employment and wages of any occupation. When I use the term "Big Tech," I am referring the aforementioned companies that employ technologists in high-tech jobs to create software applications, algorithmic architecture, and computer hardware.

I also recruited participants from my social networks in the tech industry in Seattle and performed participant observation in computing classrooms, workplaces, and technology conferences. I oversampled women—93 percent of participants identified as either cis- or transgender women. I interviewed four African Americans, four Latinas, six Asian Americans, five foreign nationals from three continents, 22 white Americans, and two participants whose racial/ethnic identities I could not confirm. Four participants were out members of the LGBTQIA community. I chose this sampling strategy in order to solicit insights into computing technology from people who must navigate both privilege and marginalization to persist in their field of choice. These "outside within" standpoints (Collins 2004) give my participants a dual consciousness within computing classrooms and workplaces that generates a unique perspective on social arrangements, one that a dominant group member or entirely dispossessed member of society could not perceive.

On the one hand, inquiry into the working conditions and lived experiences of these highly educated and very privileged women can provide insights into the institutions that shape the structures of power governing gender, race, and technology in the US and how particular kinds of laborers are reproduced in a range of elite sites. On the other hand, focusing on elite workers may limit the imaginative possibilities of transforming computing technology because participants are embedded in structures erected to maintain status quo relations of power. My participants bear the responsibility of building the infrastructure of globalized capital, and while they do not always critique power asymmetries in this economic system, they signal to the rest of us the importance of the ruptures that technologists experience between the constraints of their positions and the contributions they want to make. Understanding *why* and *how* they are thwarted in using their expert technical skills for the public good can tell us much about human society and its prevailing structures of meaning and power.

The technologists who shared their stories with me are sharp-witted and dynamic. In general, they were quick to respond, not afraid to challenge me, and had strong opinions. I am grateful to have heard these stories. To open up about one's accomplishments, one's fears and failures, one's life course, and the web of relations that keep us alive and sometimes even allow us to thrive—this is intimacy. This intimacy allowed me to know my participants and share their stories with reverence and respect. Participants also had many interests outside of their jobs. I spoke with a marathon runner, a trapeze artist, a pilot, a sculptor, high-performing athletes, two poets, and two race car drivers.

Keeping in mind the disparity in social power between high-tech managers and technical workers, I am careful in this research to categorize my participants as "laborers." Technical intelligence and skill give high-tech workers a unique viewpoint into the cyber-optic infrastructure of institutions of power in the US. Therefore, one of the contributions of this book is to show how high-tech workers can be powerful allies to both the dominant class and those who challenge dominant class rule. When a marginalized member of computing offers her intellectual labor to workers' movements to challenge technologic conditions of profit and social control, it has the potential to bring about social changes. What kind of social change can happen? Possible answers to this question emerge in my participants' stories, which help explain the significant contradiction between the social power of computing and the social constraints of this "highly rational" field organized along industrial lines.

TECHNOSCIENCE ON THE CRITICAL EDGE OF CARE

Feminist anthropologists have created groundbreaking scholarship on the intersection between technology and the social dynamics of gender, race, and sexuality (Rapp 1999; Chapman 2003; Ginsburg and Rapp 1995; Martin 1992; Ginsburg 1998; Davis-Floyd 1992; Scheper-Hughes and Lock 1987; Jain 2007; Forsythe and Hess 2001). Because outdated norms and ideologies are shaping the social dynamics of how computers in the US get made, I followed in the footsteps of these trailblazers and placed reproduction at the center of my analysis of computing. I found a story as ancient as Father Time, a bifurcated culture with hierarchies of value. In fortresses guarded by police academy trainees moonlighting as guards in golf shirts, computing culture equates the realm of freedom with the virtual and mechanical. Of course, much like its economic equivalent, neoliberalism—the "free" market—this realm of freedom is only accessible to an elite group while the rest of us encounter surveilled borders. The virtual and the computational machine are rarefied elements more valuable than the material and social aspects of human life, and these values are powered by politics of race and gender that reflect US culture more broadly.

Making reproduction central in anthropological inquiries is an approach that also augments the analytical frameworks in feminist science and technology studies (STS), including "matters of care" (Puig de la Bellacasa 2011; Martin, Myers, and Viseu 2015). Matters of care invite action in knowledge politics. For example, a close examination of the historical and cultural roots of positivism and how this epistemic dimension of scientific values influences who gets to do science (Franklin 1995; Traweek 1988; Bauer 1990;

Rosner 2018a) is, for me, a matter of care. In feminist STS, care is a conceptual resource, a mode of attention with which to explore sociotechnical assemblages. It is not necessarily motivated by a nurturing affect. Care can also be a commitment toward action in the face of injustice or harm (Puig de la Bellacasa 2011; Viseu 2015; Martin, Myers, and Viseu 2015). In essence, sanctifying labor relations in computing as a matter of care seeks to correct undervalued labor and uncover the myths, exclusions, and deletions propagated by the Bro Code and its pernicious effects. Ironically, approaching science as a matter of care is *not* a feminine-coded activity in US culture and thus not rewarded like such activities. Care in the study of science sometimes comes at the cost of being labeled as aggressive, corrosive, unrigorously reflexive, and my favorite, oversensitive (a charge made at me more times than I can count when I interrupted bias and discrimination at Colossus).

This book addresses both dimensions of care: [1] "that which we, as STS scholars, teachers and feminists enact *in our relations with* the worlds we study, and [2] that which *circulates among the actors* in the technoscientific worlds we encounter throughout our studies" (Martin, Myers, and Viseu 2015, 626, *original emphasis*). The first dimension is motivation for this study, reflecting my care for the well-being of people underrepresented in computer science and engineering and to do no harm in this study. My research participants "gaze back," and I am accountable to them (Harding 2004). The second dimension of matters of care prompts me to investigate both representational harm and allocation harm in technoscience (Barocas et al. 2017). In this way, I am "studying up" (Gusterson 1997; Nader 1972)—that is, studying people who work in a highly prestigious field, one with much power in a US culture, and holding up to scrutiny its social inputs and outputs.

My citation politics in this book are also a matter of care. Technocracy dictates that all computer science and engineering advances are not only divine but also improvements on their predecessors. In this positivistic way of thinking, progress is always linear. Those of us who study scientists can sometimes reproduce its allegiance to positivism, and this is reflected in a citation politics that privileges recent scholarship. These politics remind me of a design principle in technoscience—planned obsolescence—a key element of information and communication infrastructure whereby upgrades render earlier ideas and products useless or meaningless. The theories that

I rely on are often historically groundbreaking and originate with early adopt-ers of a critical approach to computer technology. I seek to (1) honor the voices of those who are (or have been) marginalized in computing and (2) cite interdisciplinary scholarship from the past five decades. Women helped found the field of computing and have been erased from its celebrated lore (D'Ignazio and Klein 2020; Abbate 1999; 2012; Hicks 2017; Ensmenger 2010b). I refuse to reproduce the violence of erasing pioneers in computing and early adopters of tech critique and thus aim to be in conversation with both my peers and our predecessors.

CHAPTER MAP

In the chapters to follow, I explicate the cultural instructions assembling the Bro Code. The narratives that my participants shared with me tra-verse a wide terrain, from intimate portraits of moments of self-reckoning to bird's-eye views of interconnected systems of power. They suggest the possibilities of both grassroots and regulatory interventions for subverting dominant class rule in computing. In addition to recounting personal strat-egies of career persistence, I strive to capture the broader social dynam-ics that women must navigate in several formative stages of a computing career. I document the norms and values of three dimensions of technical knowledge and labor: (1) personal attributes, relationships, experiences, and emotions; (2) internal dimensions of computing; and (3) broader cul-tural domains.

Chapter 2 asks, "Why Care about Sexism in STEM?" Here, I canvas extant theories on mechanisms that enforce exclusion in technoscience. To do so, I weave together three bodies of literature—equity in STEM, feminist STS, and scholarship on sexual harassment—to explain barriers and constraints to women's full participation in powerful and influential technical fields and what changes we need to demand in order to desegregate computer science and engineering. I argue that sexual harassment is a significant reason why computing remains stubbornly segregated. Its enactment and tolerance are predicated on assumptions about who is a competent knowledge producer and who is not, and whose bounds of privacy and autonomy are respected and whose are transgressed. These assumptions are generated in a social matrix of structures of power and disempowerment along vectors of race, gender, and sexuality. I frame bias and sexual harassment as a matter of care

(Puig de la Bellacasa 2011) in order to undertake an analysis that will verify and fortify a theory on harassment in computing that "can be applied to innovating policy and practice" (Bowleg 2019, 418) and foster greater collegiality in technoscience. Selective incivility must end if we ever hope to transform computer technology into an egalitarian force that serves democratic ideals and social justice.

In chapter 3, "Contradictions of Care: Altruistic Aspirations and Reproductive Politics in Computing," I reorient occupational segregation in high-tech as a reproductive justice issue. This lens brings into focus two significant problems that may explain why the field of computing lags behind other technical fields in terms of workplace civility and representational justice. First, women of color and other disenfranchised technologists in this study claim that their collective reproductive aspirations—their altruism to make the world a better place—are being thwarted. Second, gender stereotypes constrain women's talents to feminine-coded caring services, which not only block pathways to leadership but also distract attention from the larger problems, like a culture of overwork and computing bosses' failures to significantly manifest their promises to serve the social good. I argue that these contradictions of care between the public welfare aspirations of some technologists and their bosses are a promising site for collective action to transform reproductive politics and tech and, potentially, US society more broadly.

In chapter 4, "Technically, 'You're Different, and Different Isn't Free,'" I walk through different organizational norms and disciplinary values that privilege male hegemony, as depicted through the stories of women who, both individually and collectively, navigate technical terrains of epistemic violence and gender harassment. I further explore geek mystique, a compulsory set of practices, norms, and identities in computing that reflect the new power held by computer scientists and engineers in US culture and the institutions in which they work. I analyze how it operates both symbolically and culturally as a rite of passage (Davis-Floyd 1992), which includes hazing in interviews, bragging, bullying, and eschewing social activities and socially relevant research. These rituals also serve to indoctrinate technical workers to the core values in computing knowledge production, including constant observation, combative work styles, and male hegemony. These rituals promote and fortify an exclusive brotherhood. How women navigate high-tech fields, marked and constrained by difference, and evaluate

their experiences of being in the minority can inform strategies that eradicate the barriers excluding them from these powerful, lucrative positions.
From the stories of my participants, I excavate the standpoint of dominant
group members, revealing how sexual harassment and its tolerance reveal
the fragility of the Bro Code and masculinity of its adherents.

Chapter 5, "Women Making Culture: Profiles of Persistence in Computing," features excerpts from my life history interviews and the lived experiences of those who persist in computing. These are workers on the front
lines in the fight to desegregate this powerful workforce. I pay particular
attention not only to women's vulnerabilities and resiliencies but also to
their skills, passions, and aspirations. I share life histories to painstakingly
document how research participants navigate through their career and
reproductive trajectories and negotiate the social dynamics within cultures
of computing across multiple levels of power. I connect altruism, computing, race, and gender to advance the theory that social purpose is an important factor to consider in working toward gender equity in computing. I
explore powerful themes that emerged from my data regarding emotions,
sponsorship, yearning for collective action, social aspirations, and intrinsic
resources that offer insights into the potential of transforming the use of
computing skills and technologies to advance social justice.

In chapter 6, "Transforming the Computing Workforce and the Social
Architecture of Its Labor Value," which forms the book's conclusion, I stress
the need to further organize around the issue of labor and gender harassment to disrupt the Bro Code. Based on participants' testimonies and the
demonstrable success of collective action by Big Tech workers, I make the
case that my participants' yearning for social justice could ignite a feminist
consciousness in technical workers, which can lead to collective action in
pursuit not only of equality in technical workspaces but also in broader
cultural domains. I stress how public welfare aspirations are a form of reproductive politics critical to collective leadership that demands and enacts
institutional change in high-tech. Centering reproduction engenders *Cracking the Bro Code* as a political economic critique, connecting sexism within
the field to power relations in the digital economy. In this way, the book
makes suggestions for interventions that blend feminist critiques of computing with political and economic ones, positioning the social movement
for equity in the computing field to fruitfully align with other organized
movements for justice.

CONCLUSION

The narratives of technical workers marginalized in cultures of computing knowledge production help us to analyze the co-construction of class, gender, race, and technology and the effects of living in a world mediated by ubiquitous technology created by an elite few. These elite operate according to the Bro Code, a white male hegemonic culture that draws its power from an amalgamation of structures of powers, including those governing gender, race, state, religion, and economics. I place the newly powerful geek and his imperial domains at the center of a critique of segregation in the US workforce. In the chapters ahead, I describe significant patterns in the trials that some women have endured in computing within the context of navigating inequitable structures of power pertaining to technology, gender, and labor value. Attracting and retaining women in computing is critical to ensuring a fair and just society—one in which women of all classes and races have the opportunity to influence the design and application of technology and use it toward ends that benefit many. However, it is not only insufficient but irresponsible to champion women's participation in the US computing labor force without studying the ways that high-tech corporations reproduce inequitable relations of power in their workplaces and, by extension, their domains of influence.

My central critique is focused on gender politics within the organizations of high-tech, which I use as a fulcrum from which to leverage a broader socioeconomic critique. I claim that Big Tech can be dangerous for women scientists and engineers, especially women of color, but also for broader populations of the globe, in terms of surveillance, erosion of civil rights, hoarding of wealth and opportunities, exploitation, and amplification of capital and its power. The Bro Code is a critical apparatus in divorcing the US from social realities and promoting the cultural acceptance of neoliberal austerity measures that shift the burden of social reproduction from the state to individual households, which differentially affects women. Set apart from the profanity of materiality of life and those assigned to care for this aspect of being human, the Bro Code, in its sanctity, sets its own rules and makes up its own myths that mask corporate activism as public welfare. I interrogate Big Tech's values within broader social priorities and practices governing not only computing but also modes of reproduction and economic labor relations. This book is a contribution to social movements reckoning with the costs of high-tech effects on human health, social relations, and state and global politics. I hope that by beginning with how the Bro Code operates within computer science and engineering work-sites, this book can support current and future efforts to debunk Big Tech's mythologies, combat its harmful practices, and uncrown its most favored beneficiaries.

2 WHY CARE ABOUT SEXISM IN STEM?

Feminists have long argued that women's overall underrepresentation in science, technology, engineering, and mathematics (STEM) is a serious problem. Computing knowledge, in particular, is produced in highly segregated classrooms, labs, and workplaces, and many of these sites are rife with exclusionary practices (Corbett and Hill 2015; Misa 2010; Barker, Garvin-Doxas, and Roberts 2005; Margolis and Fischer 2003; Cohen and Swim 1995). Theories abound as to why these injustices appear to be intractable. I argue that a cultural phenomenon, one I call the "Bro Code," operates in the production of computing knowledge to exclude women and denigrate their contributions to the field. To better understand the Bro Code and interpret this study's evidence of the influence it exerts in labs, classrooms. and workplaces, I review three bodies of literature on women's underrepresentation in computing science and engineering—and STEM more broadly. By reference to these literatures, I identify valuable theories about the barriers and constraints to women's full participation in powerful and influential technical fields and describe what must be further illuminated and reckoned with in order to end racist sexism in Big Tech. Not only do these studies hail from many different disciplines, but they use different analytical frames and offer unique conceptualizations to describe and explain similar cultural practices, behaviors, and values undergirding sexism in STEM. For example, gender bias, gender discrimination, gender harassment, gender inequity, and sexual harassment are all used in the feminist and anti-racist communities in which I work, and I see both parallels in these terms and meaningful differences that are important to understanding the Bro Code.

CURRENT SCHOLARSHIP

The first body of literature I engage here is what I call *equity in STEM*, and it includes scholarship from engineering education, social psychology, sociology, history and philosophy of science, and public policy. Equity in STEM scholars do not necessarily share common theoretical frameworks, methodologies, or strategies for outreach (Cech 2005), and I have taken liberties in grouping them and naming them. I have done so in the hopes of harnessing the vigorous spirit and rich insights that characterize this applied scholarship aimed at ending male dominance in technoscience.

Feminist science and technology studies (STS) is the second body of literature reviewed in this chapter. While equity in STEM literature focuses on policies and practices within STEM communities, often from a practitioner's point of view, feminist STS deconstructs social construction of science itself (Bystydzienski and Bird 2006). They argue both interpersonal and institutional dimensions of cultural norms operate at the level of the "collective social imagination" (Fricker 2007, 15) to exclude scholars of color and women of all gender and racial identities from cultural practices of power and denigrate their capacity as knowledge-producers (Margolis and Fisher 2003; Margolis 2008; Harding 1991; 2006).

Finally, the third body of scholarship we will consider in this chapter focuses on sexual and gender harassment. Though the prevalence and impacts of sexist oppression and exploitation go by many names and are understood differently across various fields, one commonality shared across academic research concerned with labor segregation in technoscience was a reluctance to confront the scope and harm of sexual harassment. This is changing, thankfully. A 2018 consensus report from the National Academies of Sciences, Engineering, and Medicine on *Sexual Harassment of Women* galvanized support in STEM communities to consider sexual harassment as a significant force that denigrates, harms, and excludes women from STEM fields, especially women of color and queer scientists. I have been collaborating with scholars in the social and intellectual movement to achieve equity in STEM for a decade and a half to convince the majority of STEM practitioners that the problem of representation relates to bias. The next horizon is to mainstream theories on the patterns of gender and sexual harassment, frames with which racialized gender violence in computing can be suitably reckoned with and prosecuted.

I will explain overlaps in these bodies of work in this chapter and highlight some important differences. As interdisciplinary collaborations between physical and biological scientists, technoscientists, and social scientists continue to grow, the need to share common concepts and frames becomes ever more important. It is also crucial to delineate our differences and how those differences affect the solutions we design and enact. A far-reaching theory of change in computer science and engineering requires bridging the gap between gender equity analyses and modern feminisms, particularly from critical race and STS orientations (Riley et al. 2009). This chapter builds this bridge by asking (1) Why do significant barriers to desegregating STEM persist? (2) Why should we care about racialized sexism in STEM, computer science, and engineering in particular, and how can we delineate between its myriad forms? Integrating this triad of analytics by feminist scholars with different disciplinary and epistemological commitments not only helps in building coalitions but also raises important considerations for people interested in cracking the Bro Code.

METHODOLOGY

In theorizing the Bro Code, I not only expand anthropological theories of reproduction beyond the physical and private sphere, I also join feminist STS scholars who extend theories of embodiment, labor, and the affective nature of care beyond traditional domains like health care and domestic labor (Martin, Myers, and Viseu 2015). In feminist STS, care is taken up as both a conceptual concern (*what do we care about?*) and a methodological one (*why do we care?*) (Puig de la Bellacasa 2011; Viseu 2015; Martin, Myers, and Viseu 2015). Embracing a methodology of care means that I choose to examine exclusionary practices maintaining the citadels of male cabals computing.

Bruno Latour (2004) theorized on matters of concerns in STS, urging STS scholars to "engage with the concerns that animate those who support" things (e.g., SUVs) whose utility is considered pernicious by some (Puig de la Bellacasa 2011, 90). He worries that social constructivist criticisms in this field are destabilizing belief in science and antagonizing technoscientists. To take up his call to understand the practice and applications of science through the eyes of its partisans here would mean pivoting away from the "thing politics" animating Latour's 2004 and Maria Puig de la Bellacasa's

2011 work (recognizing that objects have politics agency) to embrace a relational politics in computing. Relational politics from an STS approach could include the important discovery Jane Margolis, Allan Fisher, and Faye Miller (2000) made that women students of computing are interested in the context and connections that computers facilitate, which eschews a more myopic focus on the machines—the things themselves—that men students tend to exhibit. In the context of the Bro Code, it means caring about power relations in the spaces in which computer knowledge and artifacts are produced.

If the Bro Code includes relational politics predicated on bias and harassment to reproduce segregation in computing today, then taking up Latour's call would mean (for me) understanding harassers' motivations to defend Big Tech's bastions of white male privilege from the scourge of feminization and racial integration——as well as understanding the roles played by those who enable or support the harassers (Harding 1986). This is, in part, what I offer in this book: a spotlight on dominant group members' values and behaviors in an effort not to reproduce a "fix the woman" deficit theory of change in computer science and engineering. However, it has the dangerous potential to be an exercise in "himpathy," interpreting in the most generous way possible the motivations and context in which men exert entitlement, even when these exertions cause harm to others (Manne 2017).

Puig de la Bellacasa's (2011) critical reading of Latour's matters of concern detects a problematic opposition to the oppositional standpoints of marginalized members of science. Striking a balance between what Latour calls "corrosive critique" and pandering to the fragile identities of some dominant group members in science, Puig de la Bellacasa proposes treating sociotechnical phenomena as "matters of care." Matters of care is feminist. It means engaging with science with a commitment to doing something about the "persistent forms of exclusion, power and domination in science and technology" (Puig de la Bellacasa 2011, 91). How social relations in technoscience reproduce uneven distributions of power, access, and resources—the question that animates this book—is thus a matter of care and part of the lineage of feminist scholars who invoke(d) care as a conceptual tool to excavate, investigate, and valorize hidden labors, deleted from the individualistic, "heroic" myth building of technoscientific work (Martin, Myers, and Viseu 2015; Puig de la

Bellacasa 2011; Murphy 2015; Mol, Moser, and Pols 2010; Star 1991; Forsythe and Hess 2001).

Caring about bias, discrimination, and sexual harassment in technoscience requires more that measuring the prevalence of this violence, though this is very important. Caring also requires a commitment to listening to and documenting the ignored, silenced, and neglected experiences of marginalized group members of computer science and engineering. It requires rejecting meritocratic and objective assumptions about science and divorcing technical competency with masculinity, both of which will require reinventing the way in which we view science. No small task, indeed, and one not necessarily welcomed in either physical and biological science or STS (Bauchspies and Puig de la Bellacasa 2009).

Cracking the Bro Code invokes innovative methods and critical methodologies aimed at making the lived experiences of the dispossessed visible and uncovering systems of injustice in science (Kemmis and McTaggart 2000; Denzin, Lincoln, and Smith 2008). This choice of orientation could be read as prescriptive, and this gesture of speaking from an embodied, situated position risks a charge of "aggression" (Latour 2004). While I am mindful of Latour's concerns of "corrosive critique" in STS, I cannot ignore the overwhelming evidence of incivility and its vile offspring, sexual harassment, in computing worksites in technoscience. My concern is with discerning patterns in their cultural "modes of fabrication and . . . stabilizing mechanisms" (Latour 2004, 246).

THE MYTH OF MERITOCRACY

Although women of all classes make up the majority of the US workforce, they still remain segregated to low-paying, service-oriented professions (Shriver 2009; Greenberger et al. 2005; Nakano-Glenn 1992; Spaights and Whitaker 1995). Women workers are the reserve labor force of our current capitalist system, the shock absorbent when the system hits an inevitable crisis. For example, "employers cut 140,000 jobs in December. . . . Digging deeper into the data also reveals a shocking gender gap: Women accounted for all the job losses, while men gained 16,000" (Kurtz 2021). Extensive scholarship has documented the disproportionate barriers experienced by underrepresented groups in accessing opportunities in education and employment (e.g., Morley and Lugg 2009; Boice 1993; Heckman 1998; Massey 1990; Reskin, McBrier, and Kmec 1999).[1] Bias, discrimination, and harassment targeting women of color, queer people, and white women in higher education and the workplace takes many different forms, and inter-disciplinary theories explaining persistent segregation in the US labor mar-ket abound.

In this chapter, I recapitulate some of this research, specifically theories that relate cultural structures of power that marginalize and discriminate against women of color, queer people, and white women. First, however, to provide context, I begin by introducing and explicating a belief system with a firm grip on the American imagination. Meritocracy—the belief system that wealth, employment, and power are fairly distributed on the basis of hard work and innate abilities—is racism and sexism in modern form (Hing et al. 2011; Swim et al. 1995; Bonilla-Silva and Forman 2000). Meritocracy is a discourse that mythologizes the US as a postfeminist, color-blind soci-ety (Browne and Misra 2003; Bonilla-Silva and Forman 2000; Essed 2001; Moody 2004; Benokraitis 1998; Swim et al. 1995). By erasing prejudice as a cause of social inequalities, the ideology of meritocracy attributes the status of underrepresented group members to individual failings and group mem-bers' innate incompetence. Meritocracy can overpower scientists' powers of observation, obfuscating discrimination and harassment in professional settings, which burdens underrepresented group members with the task of educating their peers on hostile cultural practices and values and convinc-ing them that their lived experiences are indeed valid (Cech, Blair-Loy, and Rogers 2018).

In these ways, the ideology of meritocracy serves as a consistent and per-sistent barrier to building critical mass support for equity in STEM (Posselt 2020). This ideology is deeply embedded in our public consciousness. Its emphasis on individualism and personal responsibility reflects the political economic climate in the US, a system that favors the wealthy ruling class and fervently quells collective organizing. Meritocracy is an individual framework with which to view science and the labor force more broadly and serves to mask the uneven distribution of power, resources, and access in the US. This results in animosity when gender equity efforts challenge this ideology. Some scientists interpret criticism of power relations in STEM as an attack on their professional status and the means by which they acquired it.

Education and hard work are mythologized as the means by which anyone can succeed at reaching their goals in the US. This is well epitomized by the words of Bill Clinton, who, when asked to define the American Dream, said: "If you work hard and play by the rules, you should be given the chance to go as far as your God-given ability will take you" (Hing et al. 2011). However, the fact is that the "income achievement gap"—differences in standardized test scores and grade point averages—between children from families in the top 10 percent of the income distribution and children from families in the bottom 10 percent is growing rapidly: "The income achievement gap between children from the highest and lowest income deciles is roughly 30 to 40 percent larger among children born in 2001 than among those born in 1976" (Edsall 2012). Still, meritocracy is close to the hearts of some dominant group members in science and entwined with their beliefs about their abilities, their individual and social identities, and even the American Dream. The fact is that the mantra of meritocracy—*only the best and the brightest*—is a euphemism for "the blessed and the privileged" (Margolis 2008, 202). It is a justification of inequality, "a spurious story that people tell to protect themselves from the discomfort of acknowledging how their behavior and thinking may be part of the very problem they wish to solve" (Posselt 2020, 4).

The cultural dominance of meritocracy makes the racialized gender gap in STEM difficult to bridge. The continued reign of males from racially dominant groups in STEM reflects historical patterns of labor segregation in the US not yet fully understood. How do we continue reproducing such a pervasive system of disempowerment? Why are some fields less welcoming to underrepresented groups than others, and what are the consequences of these exclusionary institutions and practices? While women have gained access to higher education, the gains have only challenged segregation horizontally. In other words, gender equality can be declared in broad aggregates measuring representation, but "the stubborn persistence of gender segregation across fields and subfields of study masks deep gender inequalities rooted in traditional cultural values in US society" (Etzkowitz 2008, 409; Cheryan et al. 2017). Perplexingly, women have made gains in other male-dominated fields, such as medicine and law (Xie and Shauman 2003). Furthermore, a striking pattern of segregation *within* fields of study persists. For example, when women *do* enter STEM fields, they disproportionately choose the life sciences over the physical sciences and engineering (Mann and DiPrete 2013). Medical schools graduate 49 percent women while computer science and engineering doctoral programs graduate less than a third of that number (Misa 2010).

EXPLANATORY MODELS FOR UNDERREPRESENTATION IN STEM

The myth of meritocracy individualizes social problems and denies that injustice exists in the distribution of access, resources, and opportunities. This logic allows ample room for essentialist explanations to emerge. For example, in his keynote at the 2005 Conference on Diversifying the Science and Engineering Workforce, Larry Summers (2005), the former president of Harvard University, stated that women's underrepresentation in STEM is due to differential aptitude. Summers's gaffe was a galvanizing moment for women in STEM fields because it made visible what Pierre Bourdieu (1989) calls "symbolic violence," a means by which those in power justify their dominance and reproduce existing structures of inequality. Summers is just one in a long line of scholars who invoke biological reasons to explain women's exclusion from sites of STEM production, thereby naturalizing patterns of labor segregation and reserving occupations that bequeath wealth and cultural capital for members of dominant classes (Fine 2010). Naturalizing the pernicious segregation problem in computing is an effective way to nullify efforts to change it. This is unjust, given how lucrative engineering fields are (and computing ones especially), robbing women and women of color in particular, who are often the top earners in their immediate families and providers to their extended families, of individual and generational wealth (Ross, Hazari, and Sadler 2020).

In their 2010 summary report *Why So Few?*, the American Association of University Women (AAUW) identifies Summer's sexist logic, which Ben Barres (2006) coined as the "Larry Summers Hypothesis," as one of three significant reasons for women's underrepresentation in STEM:

> First, the notion that men are mathematically superior and innately better suited to STEM fields than women are remains a common belief. . . . A second theme revolves around girls' lack of interest in STEM. A third theme involves the STEM workplace, with issues ranging from work-life balance to bias. (Hill, Corbett, and Rose 2010, 19)

Ten years later, the Larry Summers Hypothesis still echoes through the halls of the networked towers, but its progenitors are no longer invited speakers but, instead, relegated to manifestos or op-eds. The second theme in the 2010 AAUW report gained some traction, most notably research on "ambient belonging" (Cheryan et al. 2009) and work on role incongruity (Diekman et al. 2010). The third theme—workplace culture—however, has had the most explanatory power in equity in STEM discourse over the last 10 years, until the resurgence of the #MeToo movement reignited public outrage on the prevalence of sexual harassment in American society. I will discuss this shift later in this chapter. Suffice to say, babies and bias were determined to be main culprits in women's underrepresentation in STEM fields and have been the subject of numerous academic studies (Barth et al. 2015; Bystydzienski and Bird 2006; Hill, Corbett, and Rose 2010; Correll, Benard, and Paik 2007).

Jacob Clark Blickenstaff's (2005) review of 30 years of literature address-ing women's absence from STEM augments the AAUW report with more explanations; as examples:

> girls' lack of academic preparation for a science major/career; girls' poor atti-tude toward science and lack of positive experiences with science; the absence of female scientists/engineers as role models . . . cultural pressure on girls/women to conform to traditional gender roles and an inherent masculine worldview in scientific epistemology. (Blickenstaff 2005, 371–372).

Note that the first two of these explanations are framed to spotlight girls' deficits. This approach puts the onus on girls and women for not entering STEM rather than on male scientists' exclusionary practices and a tendency for organizations to favor men's attributes and lifestyles. It also frames the social problem of occupational segregation as an individual prob-lem, which indicates the ideological influence of meritocracy. "Fixing the woman won't fix the problem" (Committee on Science, Engineering, and Public Policy 1998, 66). Instead, advocates for gender equity in STEM insist that we fix the scientific system. The deficit approach too often results in diversity, equity, and inclusion programs in STEM designed to help women assimilate to cultures formed by predominantly white male practitioners. This is the wrong approach. Ameliorating women's underrepresentation in STEM means a shift away from the "woman as deficit" model and toward policy interventions at the institutional level (Bystydzienski and Bird 2006; Rosser 2012). This shift is happening, and in recent years, equity in STEM scholarship has seen a proliferation of systems-level critiques that investi-gate racial and gender inequalities. Equity in STEM scholarship argues that sources of inequality originate not only in individual minds but also in institutional practices, norms, and values (Plaut 2010).

UNEXAMINED BIAS

As the Chilly Climate activism caught on in academic STEM, programmatic interventions to fix sexism in STEM relied on bias as a conceptual resource to combat gender segregation. Often called unconscious bias, implicit bias, or unexamined bias, bias in STEM research has received much attention both in academia and the US media. Bias is a form of stereotyping that is often unintentional and automatic and often contradictory to our conscious beliefs (Committee on Science, Engineering, and Public Policy 1998). Research demonstrates that threatening environments fostered through bias turn underrepresented groups away from majority domains (Chowdhury, Hoo, and Pasik-Duncan 2007; Valian 1999; Browne and Misra 2003; Adams et al. 2006; Cohen and Swim 1995), which is a critical reason why diversity eludes many STEM disciplines (Malcom 1999; Trower and Chaitt 2002; Ginorio 1995). These biases dictate that people from dominant groups, and white males in particular, inhibit the success of underrepresented scientists and deny scientific communities the talents and perspectives of diverse members. Bias can be perpetuated by highly educated, self-professed egalitarians in the course of making objective decisions. It is not always overt; nor is it conscious. It is coded in subtle ways to reproduce predictable patterns of structural inequality that privilege dominant groups (Moody 2004). Though we like to think that scientists are objective and able to impartially evaluate others' abilities and potential, it is important we acknowledge this is a myth (Posselt 2020).

Bias often comes into play in evaluation settings and leads to erroneous conclusions, most notably that women scientists and engineers are less competent than their male peers and less deserving of success, recognition, and accolades. For example, in a groundbreaking study published in the *Proceedings of the National Academy of Sciences* (PNAS), Corrine Moss-Racusin and her colleagues (2012) found that both female and male science faculty members harbor bias against female students. The faculty participants were given application materials from an undergraduate student applying for a lab manager position. All received the same exact materials, except that half the participants believed they were reviewing a male applicant's materials and the other half believed they were reviewing a female applicant's materials. Faculty participants rated the female applicant significantly lower than the male applicant in terms of competence, hirability, salary offers, and the faculty members' willingness to mentor women students.

These findings augment previous research by Rhea Steinpreis, Katie Anders, and Dawn Ritzke (1999), in which male and female faculty members evaluated a curriculum vitae that was randomly assigned a male or a female name. Both male and female evaluators rated the male applicant higher in research, teaching, and service experience and were more likely to hire the male than the female applicant. These two empirical studies confirm what I heard over and over from participants in this research on women in high-tech communities: women have to be twice as good as men to be considered half as competent. While Steinpreis and her colleagues show that bias plays a role in the faculty hiring process, Moss-Racusin and her colleagues demonstrate that bias affects women in STEM in the educational phase of their careers, a critical junction that serves as a launching pad for further opportunities.

These studies offer indisputable evidence that males pursuing STEM careers benefit from a presumed competence that gives them unearned advantages in the world of STEM production. The fact that both female and male scientists perpetuate sexist bias adversely affecting the career trajectories of female scientists helps to explain why diversity eludes many STEM disciplines in academia. Bias further helps to explain why underrepresented group members with comparable training drop out of STEM fields at greater rates than engineers from majority groups (Fouad et al. 2017; Seymour and Hewitt 1997; Bystydzienski and Bird 2006). Nadya Fouad and colleagues found alarmingly high rates of attrition among women in engineering fields and that their male colleagues enjoyed 50 percent higher rates of persistence. The authors concluded that this may indicate women's protest against the constraints of their subordinated positions within scientific institutions, voting with their feet, as it were (Fouad et al. 2017). Attrition has a ripple effect, with consequences for the next generation of scholars and their families. For example, a dearth of women faculty members adversely affects women students' persistence, as they have fewer role models to inspire and guide them (Eppes, Mialnoviv, and Snaborn 2010; Carrell, Page, and West 2010; Blickenstaff 2005). A dearth of underrepresented minority male faculty has negative effects on the persistence of women

students of color in computing (Domingo et al. 2020). Engineers who identify as lesbian, gay, bisexual, transgender, queer, intersexed, and asexual
(LBGTQIA) also turn down or step down from opportunities because of
homophobic discrimination and harassment (Nelson et al. 2017).

The trick to being an effective change agent is to examine our biases and
interrupt their application when they have been activated. Initially, this
requires deliberate acts of consciousness-raising, preferably in collective
settings (Carrigan et al. 2021), and then lots of practice. In essence, unexamined bias research claims that there are no bad apples—we all have to,
individually and collectively, examine our biases and interrupt them. This
premise undergirds both my past scholarship and collaborative efforts to
intervene programmatically in cultures of computing. I use the bias frame
when I want to meet majority computer scientists and engineers where
they are at, inviting them to take responsibility for interrupting bias in their
particular technical culture.

CULTURE IN STEM

In the 1970s and 1980s, feminist practitioners in STEM fields began to agitate, organize, and speak out against the constraints of their subordinate
status in their workplaces and disciplinary communities. Relying on their
dissonant experiences to inform their analyses of behaviors and social relations that privileged men and denigrated women's capacities and accomplishments (Wylie 2012), these activists named "culture" as a factor that
perpetuated systematic gender inequalities. Instead of culture, they used
the term "the chilly climate" (Sandler and Hall 1986). Chilly climate, an eco-
logical metaphor for a significant barrier to desegregating STEM, resembles
what anthropologists define as culture: "the collective behavior patterns,
communication styles, language, beliefs, concepts, values, institutions, standards, symbols, and other factors unique to a community that are socially
transmitted to individuals and to which individuals are expected to conform" (Strike et al. 2003). Culture serves as a mechanism that manufactures
social values and reproduces systems of power favoring the dominant class
(Smith 2005; Bourdieu 1989). Ethnographic studies of culture from this orientation, like this book, seek to question implicit assumptions and behavioral norms adopted as group values in a particular culture. Ethnographers
then interpret the meaning of these values and their role in shaping social

priorities and practices (Madison 2005). Science is a culture, one forged by "hundreds of years of active shunning of women," and to change it to welcome women of color, queer women, and white women will require "deep structural changes in the culture, methods and content of science" (Schiebinger 1999, 11).

A first step toward these institutional changes would be to raise a collective critical consciousness that recognizes how science incubates ideas within cultural spaces through the subjective standpoints of people and how its widely disseminated outputs both shape and are shaped by broader cultural values and power relationships (Franklin 1995). Building on the shrewd insights of Chilly Climate activists, the "science as culture" argument is vital to desegregating STEM, particularly highly technical fields like computing, and challenges the deeply entrenched belief that science is purely objective and created in meritocratic environments.

In the decades since Chilly Climate activists' achievement of hermeneutical justice—coining a term to name and define forms of male hostility toward women (Sandler and Hall 1986)—culture continues to be cited as a significant factor responsible for the persistent lack of diversity in STEM (National Academies 2018). Yet cultures in technoscience remain inadequately understood and theorized. On the one hand, women of color, queer people, and white women navigating STEM institutions know all too well that the institutions for which they work (and the people with whom they work) tolerate and even encourage inequitable labor relations. Quantitative studies, like those undertaken by Steinpreis, Moss-Racusin, and their colleagues, demonstrate the prevalence of racial and gender bias in STEM and the *need* for cultural change. On the other hand, cultural experts and qualitative methodologies can be marginalized in interdisciplinary efforts in science (Viseu 2015; Hackett and Rhoten 2011; Carrigan and Bardini 2021), and collaborations—both theoretical and programmatic—to warm the climate in STEM workplaces are no exception.

Victoria Plaut (2010, 82), in an attempt to valorize cultural research in STEM equity efforts, argues that it is important to pay "attention to historically rooted cultural and structural contours of human behavior and psychological tendencies . . . examining cultural ideas and beliefs prevalent in people's social worlds." The social and intellectual movement to end racialized gender discrimination in STEM is an extension of women organizing to contest a subordinated position in US society. In other words,

STEM equity efforts are a legacy of feminist activist in the US (hooks 2000). Dr. Nancy Hopkins, a biology professor at the Massachusetts Institute of Technology (MIT), is an example of a Chilly Climate scholar whose work was explicitly feminist. Hopkins and her colleagues gathered proof of a systematic reproduction of unequal distribution of labor roles and resources between female and male MIT faculty, and they garnered support to rectify this discrimination and achieve parity. In the course of this activism, Hopkins saw the value of organizing as women and for women. Soon after Hopkins and her coauthors published their report, MIT made a public, long-term commitment to analyzing resource and salary disparities and rectifying institutional and interpersonal gender inequalities at the faculty level (Rosser 2006). Perhaps inspired by this prestigious institution acknowledging and attempting to rectify institutional barriers against women in STEM, the National Science Foundation (NSF) initiated a new awards program called ADVANCE, with funding to create institutional, rather than individual, solutions to the problems of white male overrepresentation in STEM (Rosser 2006). In its call for proposals, the NSF encouraged this institutional transformation approach because women's underrepresentation in STEM is often a "systematic consequence of academic culture" (Rosser 2006, 70).

Even though feminism was integral to spotlighting culture as a significant barrier to just relations in science, Londa Schiebinger (2008) argues that feminist epistemologies and interventions have been mainstreamed into STEM and its frameworks, methods, and theories with little to no credit. I agree that even today, with some stellar exceptions, there is reluctance in gender equity studies to orient around feminist scholarship. Perhaps if interventions to recruit, retain, and advance women in STEM are perceived as overtly feminist, those advances may very well be scorned or ignored by faculty and administrators (Frehill 2007). In this way, feminism remains a specter in equity in STEM research, and risk aversion plays a role. Gender equity scholars concerned with justice in STEM must ask how much programmatic planning and knowledge production is constrained by peers' resistance and the threat of retribution. These fears are valid but can result in too much emphasis on "the individual processes of stereotyping and prejudice, which are less successful in changing these habits than lessons that highlight the systematic nature" of cultural oppressions (Plaut 2010, 83).

Relegating feminism to the sidelines of diversity in STEM scholarship and intervention strategies is akin to respecting the decision of LGBTQIA people to remain in the closet. It minimizes the risk of exclusion and other forms of violence to marginalized community members who are already vulnerable. However, the most promising efforts and ideas in equity in STEM research come from explicitly feminist centers like the Research Institute for Feminist Engineering at Purdue University and the Michelle R. Clayman Institute for Gender Research at Stanford University (Pawley 2011; Schiebinger 2008). Research on culture in engineering fields has grown out of feminist analyses of engineering education (Margolis and Fisher 2003; Godfrey and Parker 2010; Burack and Franks 2004; Pawley 2011). Since this scholarship is part of the legacy of Chilly Climate activism, it is no coincidence that it is some of the first STEM literature to investigate culture using qualitative methods that are uniquely suited to explore norms, values, symbols, and the lived experiences of group members from a range of standpoints (National Academies 2022).

SPOTLIGHTING DOMINANT GROUP CULTURE

One way to better understand inequities in STEM is to spotlight dominant group culture in these workplaces. For example, social scientists have identified male-dominant practices specific to computing, including jockeying for superior status, public criticism, impersonal communications, and competitive behaviors, especially in the classroom (Barker and Garvin-Doxas 2002, 2004; Margolis 2008; Margolis and Fisher 2003). Social psychology research finds that women are not drawn to computing because they do not fit the stereotypical norm of a male computer scientist (Cheryan et al. 2009). In an interview with the *New York Times*, Sapna Cheryan describes the stereotypical geek as "male, skinny, no social life, eats junk food, plays video games and likes science fiction" (Cain-Miller 2010, 2). Others note that underrepresented groups in STEM tend to be viewed as likable or competent but not both (Barnett and Rivers 2004). Just the fact of being a solo underrepresented group member in a white, male-dominated organization can create feelings of isolation that play a role in underrepresented group members' attrition from STEM disciplines (Greenwald and Banaji 1995; Nora and Cabrera 1996; Pewewardy and Frey 2002; Potter and Rosser 1992; Roos and Reskin 1984; Rosser 1995, 1998).

The stress of struggling to belong, in combination with discriminatory practices, lack of money and collegiality, slower promotions, and lower tenure rates, begins to explain the barriers to women's advancement in academic

STEM fields (Valian 1999, 220). Dissatisfaction with working conditions significantly influences women faculty's decisions to leave their institution (Committee on Science, Engineering, and Public Policy 2007). For example, women engineers make 90 cents for every dollar earned by their male colleagues (Society of Women Engineers 2021). White men are seen as the most qualified scientists and leaders, the most worthy of high salaries, and much more competent than other groups (Moss-Racusin et al. 2012). Women of color in STEM graduate programs found dominant group members' bias, microaggressions, and everyday racist slights, which revel in and reinforce white male superiority in technical matters, far more challenging than structural barriers (Ong et al. 2011).

THE CULTURAL IDENTITY OF ENGINEERS

Feminist cultural studies of science—an orientation that hails from a range of disciplines, including cultural anthropology, literary studies of science, STS, and studies of visual cultures (McNeil 2007)—needs to be in collaboration and conversation with equity in STEM scholarship. In order to locate my own research in these discourses, I draw attention to an issue that plays a key role in my project as a whole: the cultural identity of engineers. This focus also allows me to elucidate a methodological divide that must be acknowledged and debated if scientists and cultural feminists seeking diversity in STEM are to work together effectively. Efforts to sunder masculinity from the engineering identity must consider how the two were fused in the first place in order to better understand the legacies we have inherited in the current socioeconomic moment in which engineers labor today.

In their study, Cynthia Burack and Suzanne Franks (2004) discovered that dominant group members in engineering feel threatened by diversity efforts and defend their group identity in gendered interactions and discourses. To demonstrate a range of skills in a discipline that is not well understood by the general public, engineers point out that they "use two quite different kinds of skills: 'hard' and 'soft.'" Hard skills are "technical, mathematical and scientific; soft skills are interpersonal and communicative . . . their meanings are understood and shared, though left unspoken, by the community" (Burack and Franks 2004, 84). "Hard" also refers to "difficult," with the implicit assumption embedded in this linguistic framing that "soft" skills are really "easy" (Burack and Franks 2004). This reflects a sense of superiority among engineers, who believe they are smarter than their non-STEM peers (Carrigan and Bardini 2021; Burack and Franks 2004). The power of language and its ability to create inequality, bias, or exclusivity becomes apparent as unconscious understandings of "hard" and "soft" reflect gendered meanings. In engineering, rigor and "hardness" are glorified as are "performances of masculinity and assertions of male power" with phallic connotations (Riley 2017, 253). The double entendre of terms used to describe technical competence, or lack thereof—hard/soft and rigorous/easy—demonstrate how the ideological value system in STEM is a fusion of dominant norms governing both identity and epistemology.

These common forms of language, often used by engineers to tell stories of their profession, disadvantage certain groups along intersecting vectors of race and gender. For example, women of color are perceived as less competent than their white male peers and lack mentorship and encouragement (National Academies 2022; Ong et al. 2011; Espinosa 2011). Similarly, the technical/social divide that privileges technical skills and codifies them as masculine poses social challenges for women and LGBTQIA students in STEM (Cech and Waidzunas 2011).

Having worked with technoscientists closely for over 15 years, I can attest computer scientists and engineers generally agree that they have overarching characteristics that define them as a group. Jane Jorgenson (2002) refers to this phenomenon as "engineering identity," and Erin Cech (2005) refers to it as "engineering schemas." Broadly speaking, the engineering identity can be characterized as someone who enjoys and excels at problem-solving and getting one right answer (Chachra 2012). In a facilitated workshop, my colleague at the University of Washington ADVANCE Center for Institutional Change (UW ADVANCE) asked a large group of tenured engineering faculty members to name the top characteristics of engineers. Their answers included someone who is (in order of frequency) analytical; problem-solver; smart; designer/developer/builder; creative; logical; and visionary/innovative.

These characteristics may be idealistic or realistic; most likely, they are a combination of both. Regardless, they shape the evaluation criteria and culture of engineering fields, and this affects women engineers differently than their male colleagues. The long hours and laser focus of STEM fields operate to fit white male lives within the capitalist organization of labor, one in which bourgeois white men display their dominant position not only with unequal access to lucrative "hard skills" jobs but with stay-at-home wives caring for the household and children. Within the context of capitalist patriarchy, men's careers will fare better than their female peers who do not have the same access to free labor in their homes. The architecture of these modern patterns of labor segregation can be traced back to the Victorian era where, in white middle-class English society, domestic work became a sign of drudgery incompatible with class-climbing aspirations (Anne McClintock as cited in Lewis and Mills 2003). A white middle-class woman's vocation was not knowledge production but to make invisible domestic labor—the work of cleaning, cooking, and tending a home. Her labor promoted the prestige of male buying power without sullying it with evidence of female labor and, in the process, devaluated women's labor value and transformed wives' labor power into their husband's political power (McClintock as cited in Lewis and Mills 2003).

The historical dimensions of engineers' cultural identity helps to explain how everyday practices of exclusion are deeply woven into not only the group identity of individual members but also the class status of the field as a whole. A man's prowess with a machine is a source of pride, and tinkering is a form of male middle-class bonding in the US (Oldenziel 1999). The relationship between masculinity and machinery in the nineteenth and twentieth centuries is a symptom of a long-term cultural alliance between science and mechanistic paradigm. The core values of the Western world are a systematic objectification and mechanization of the human body and domination over nature (Merchant 1980). At the turn of the twentieth century, both elite engineers and those on the shop floor conspired to keep women out of the profession to "keep alive the promise, often unfulfilled, that upward mobility was still a viable option for middle-class men" (Oldenziel 1999, 43). The precarious position that engineers hold within the hierarchy of political economic organization, in a space between capital and labor, has shaped the collective identity of engineers and the defining characteristics of competency in this arena. In the professional culture of engineering, stereotypes about the social identity of group members are co-constructed with qualities and characteristics of competence (Cech and Waidzunas 2011). The confident, even peremptory, white male is the typical icon of scientific and technical competence (Carrigan 2018; Ong 2005). Ideologically, technology is canonized as the savior of the masses, and upper-middle-class white men have the privilege of interpreting and integrating this transformative force into society. These dominant group members go further to assert that their expert knowledge can be applied universally (Harding 2004). This posturing is what Maria Lugones (1989) calls "arrogant perception," being at ease in the world without challenging oneself or one's social position. Only dominant group members would assume that their knowledge claims should be applicable to all (Harding 2004). The role of hero that the engineer plays in our culture has not changed, but the identity of this hero has shifted from one who conquers the wild west frontier with dams, mechanical engines, mass agriculture, and (sub)urban planning to the stereotypical nerd who is a postindustrial hero storming the virtual frontier of cyberspace.

Women who do enter these domains are often coerced to perform the masculine ideals of engineering in order to be accepted as "one of the guys" (Carrigan 2018; Hacker et al. 1990; Faulkner 2000b). Some women navigate this pressure by denying any gender differences in both the scholarship and cultures of their fields. However, we must be careful not to naturalize social identities that make women choose between a gender identity and an engineering identity (Jorgenson 2002). Wendy Faulkner (2000b) recommends "pluralism" of style and identities, opening our minds and thinking beyond two popular themes—that women must act like men to succeed or that they must be different from men, which is a fixed identity difference. The fact is that when engineers hold high status in an organization, they dominate norms and exercise power that reaffirms a particular kind of masculinity, one that also reinforces class inequalities by affirming technical prowess and denigrating other kinds of work (Faulkner 2000b). Pluralism is an excellent orientation with which to frame ethnographic methodologies when studying cultures of STEM because it gives participants the opportunity to possess and perform multiple identities. For example, being perceived as a woman of color *and* a scientist is a complex and daunting negotiation of performance, social identity, and professional confidence, and female scientists of color operationalize multiple identities as a strategy of persistence (Ong 2005). To suss out the factors related to women's low participation in STEM fields, however, it is important to discuss dimensions of race, gender, and class identities within the context of a dominant engineering identity, cultivated and enacted to affirm a homosocial community of powerful professionals.

FEMINIST SCIENCE AND TECHNOLOGY STUDIES

Equity in STEM is well augmented with feminist STS. Feminist scholars of STS uncover historical and cultural foundations underpinning how and why modern technology is coded as the domain of white males (Harding 2004, 2006; Wyer 2009; McNeil 2007; Oldenziel 1999; Forsythe and Hess 2001; Harding 1991; Wajcman 2009, 1991; Hacker 1981; Franklin 1995; Faulkner 2000a; Riley 2014; Barker, Garvin-Doxas, and Roberts 2005; Suchman 2012; Lerman, Oldenziel, and Mohun 2003; Lohan 2000; Lie 1995, 1997; Frehill et al. 2009; Faulkner 2001; Margolis and Fischer 2003; Margolis 2008; Rosser 2004; Henwood 1996; Mayberry 1998; Kelly 1985). Feminist anthropologists have been prominent in this field of science studies, extending kinship studies to critique the cultural impact of new reproductive technologies and the ways in which women and our bodies are objectified and controlled (Rapp 1979; Davis-Floyd 1992; Martin 1994; Ginsburg and Rapp 1995).

A main vein of difference in feminist STS literature, as compared to equity in STEM literature, is an explicitly feminist stance that is reflected in different methodologies and arguments for problems and solutions to labor segregation in science. Also, feminist STS research expands the conversation beyond numbers—an important element, but one that needs to be placed in cultural contexts and historical legacies of systematic injustices (Malcom 2019; Harding 1986, 2008; Rossiter 1998). These injustices are the root causes of the lack of diversity and inclusion in STEM (Malcom 2011). Framing the low numbers of historically underrepresented group members in STEM as inequality and injustice is a political stance, one that allows for an intersectional critique of culture in STEM and the possibility of enacting transformational change in the halls of technical knowledge and power. Further, feminist STS asks: "How can the core epistemological presumptions of science be maintained when empiricism cannot recognize its own failures within the actual practice of science" (Grassie 1996, 286)? In other words, feminist STS destabilizes normative understandings of what constitutes the practices, inquiries, epistemologies, methodologies, cultural meanings, and applications of technoscience. Because of their interdisciplinary and critical approaches, scholars in feminist STS articulate an alternative yet comprehensive understanding of the social identities of technoscientists and the cultural production of technology (Reid and Traweek, 2000). Since

Donna Haraway's seminal intervention into probing the boundary between nature/culture (Haraway 1991), feminist STS has made many contributions to interrogating its epistemic and socially constructed grounds. The historical, cultural roots of positivist science are often masked and obfuscated (Franklin 1995; Traweek 1988; Bauer 1990). Although technology is a political activity in which women and men of various standpoints engage (e.g., by using cell phones), a small minority of the population decides what gets made and toward what end.

The study of culture in technoscience can be considered problematic given that scientific inquiry is often assumed to occur in a cultural vacuum—a "culture of no culture" (Traweek 1988, 162). Feminist STS scholars in particular argue otherwise, noting that objectivity is a cultural value in STEM and evolved out of scientific practices performed almost exclusively by white males (Haraway 1991; Harding 1986; Franklin 1995; Campbell 2009). Schiebinger (2008) argues further that many cultural practices in the sciences developed in opposition to women's participation. Therefore, naturalizing the epistemic knowledge of some and discrediting others for the purpose of reproducing institutional, historical inequalities must be rigorously scrutinized and combated (Collins 2000; Reid and Traweek 2000; Hess 2007).

This is why some STS scholars interrogate the production, distribution, and consumption of technoscientific knowledge as ethico-political processes (Puig de la Bellacasa 2011; Sismondo 2010). However, arguing that science is culturally contextualized and formed by unjust social norms strikes at the heart of the popular belief that scientific endeavors are separate from society (Nader 1996). Epistemological commitments of a moral and ethical nature in feminist STS are strongly resisted by both scientists and STS scholars alike because they do not want their allegiance to empiricism and achievements in this intellectual tradition to be criticized. "They find it intolerable to be positioned by feminist transformations of regulative ideals as less than fully ethically admirable" (Bauchspies and Puig de la Bellacasa 2009, 338). Thus, while STS as a field is becoming more comfortable with "scholarship that critically addresses the methods and practices that maintain oppressions within technoscience," mainstream STS scholars too often either resist critical scholarship or relegate it to the footnotes, especially work from a feminist orientation (Bauchspies and Puig de la Bellacasa 2009).

SEXUAL HARASSMENT

In the decades in between Chilly Climate activism and recent calls to action to fight sexual harassment in STEM, feminism, culture, and empiricism have been at the forefronts of debates led by scholars alarmed by violence in STEM. "Correcting biases drew attention to deeper, more pervasive problems" (Wylie 2012, 54), like women's subordinated position in broader society, structural racism, identity-based harassment in science, and the colonizing dimensions of objectivity in Western science—the hubristic "god trick," an infinite view from nowhere (Haraway 1988, 581). While unexamined bias is extremely important to catalyzing a critical mass of scientists and engineers to understand and interrupt barriers to desegregating their fields, we continue to reckon with this violence in both the STEM workforce and the fields' ties to militarism, capitalism, colonialism, and white male supremacy in broader society. An ethos of care, however, requires that praxis interrogating sexism in STEM to reckon with the harms and effects of gender and sexual harassment, both of which are, unfortunately, all too pervasive in academic science, technology and engineering fields (National Academies 2018).

Thanks to Anita Hill and the groundswell of feminist activism in the 1990s, sexual harassment has entered into US mainstream consciousness and public policy. Now, over 30 years later, gender and sexual harassment are being explicitly spotlighted and discussed in gender equity circles in STEM.[2] For example, a consensus study on *Sexual Harassment of Women: Climate, Culture, and Consequences in Academic Sciences, Engineering, and Medicine* called for cultural change in higher education to combat sexual harassment in STEM fields (National Academies 2018). Scientists and science policymakers are responding to this growing visibility of sexual harassment with decreasing tolerance for its effects and perpetrators.

Sexual harassment in science is multifaceted. Its enactment and tolerance are predicated on epistemological assumptions (rooted in institutional relations of gender and race) about who is a competent knowledge producer and who is not and whose bounds of privacy and autonomy are respected and whose are transgressed. These assumptions are generated in a social matrix of structures of meaning and patterns of power and disempowerment along vectors of race, gender, and sexuality. In *Cracking the Bro Code*, I am forging a path for moving forward at this critical juncture in research on broadening participation in STEM fields, arguing that sexual and gender harassment are significant reasons why some disciplines, like computer science and engineering, remain stubbornly segregated. This book is part of the lineage of anthropologists leading the groundbreaking study of sexual harassment in STEM (Howell 1988, 1990; Sharp and Kremer 2006; Nelson et al. 2017; Clancy et al. 2014, 2017). My perspective straddles anthropology and STS and the knowledge that I have gained working in interdisciplinary and cross-race collaborations to combat segregation and identity-based harassment in STEM. Ultimately, my vision is achieving the widespread adoption of gender harassment policies in academic STEM and enacting effective interventions that put a stop to this form of identity-based violence.

Sexual harassment takes three forms: unwelcome sexual attention; coercion, a sexual quid pro quo whereby professional advancement requires sex; and gender harassment (National Academies 2018). Gender harassment refers to disparaging conduct not intended to elicit sex. Instead, it is verbal, physical, and symbolic behaviors that convey hostile and exclusionary attitudes toward women. Examples of gender harassment include anti-female jokes, comments that women do not belong in computing or management, and crude terms of address that denigrate women. Gender harassment communicates hostility that is devoid of sexual interest but aims to insult and reject women (Leskinen, Cortina, and Kabat 2011).

Sexual harassment studies commonly rely on surveys and laboratory experiments to estimate "prevalence and determine correlates, antecedents, outcomes, and factors that attenuate or amplify outcomes from sexual harassment" (National Academies 2018, 30). Qualitative studies serve as complements to statistical ones because they are able to learn about minoritized members of scientific workplaces and offer intersectional insights into complex phenomena, the contexts in which they occur, and their consequences (National Academies 2022; Cho, Crenshaw, and McCall 2013). In this book, I am committed to moving beyond *describing* to *problematizing* a workplace culture that tolerates and "black boxes" the systemic problem of sexual harassment that reproduces oppressive relations in technoscience.

Sexual harassment rates in academic institutions (58 percent) are second only to the military (69 percent) when compared with industry, and the government (Ilies et al. 2003). The National Academies (2018) consensus study report makes important contributions to begin to address sexual harassment in academic STEM. The authors framed the problem not as an individual or interpersonal one but rather a cultural one. They go further to say that there are four elements unique to academic science, engineering, and medicine workplaces that make them more likely to tolerate sexually harassment, including

1) male overrepresentation;
2) hierarchies of power concentrated into the hands of a few individuals;
3) ineffective policies and procedures that perform concern for sexual harassment but hold zero consequence for noncompliance; and
4) lack of educated leadership being held accountable for preventing sexual harassment. (National Academies 2018)

This roadmap to potential interventions implores further research into cultures of STEM and their tolerance level for sexual harassment. While there is an abundance of research on unconscious bias in STEM, more research is sorely needed on the lived experiences of sexual harassment and how these experiences are either different or similar across racial identities and disciplines in STEM. Finally, we need to know more about what cultural attributes contribute the most to workplace environments that protect and even reward harassers.

The stakes of this issue are high—first, because the violence is so prevalent and second, because the effects of sexual harassment differentially affect highly marginalized women in STEM. For example, a groundbreaking study on fieldwork-based scientists found that 72 percent of their female respondents had been the target of gender harassment and 26 percent had survived sexual assault during the course of fieldwork, most often perpetrated by senior males on the research team (Clancy et al. 2014). A follow-up study by Kathryn Clancy and colleagues found that women of color scientists are targeted at higher rates than white female peers (Clancy et al. 2017). These findings support other scholarship on sexual harassment that the experiences of women of color in the US workplace differ from those of white women (Berdahl and Moore 2006; Buchanan, Settles, and Langhout 2007; Buchanan and Fitzgerald 2008; McGee and Bentley 2017; Raver and Nishii 2010; Richardson and Taylor 2009). Experiences of racial and gender discrimination also differ among Black, Hispanic, and Asian American women (Mohr and Purdie-Vaughns 2015). The manner in which race is gendered plays a significant role in a cultural matrix of power relations. For example, gendered racial stereotypes shape how "women in technical positions manage their gender and sexuality" (Alfrey and Twine 2017, 30–31). Furthermore, queer women experience higher rates of sexual harassment than their heterosexual peers (Rabelo and Cortina 2014).

Sexual harassment persists because it is tolerated through culturally normalized, daily acts of ignoring rather than mere ignorance (Quinn 2002). What we know so far about sexual harassment in STEM comes from a few rigorous descriptive studies and inductive hypothesizing by STEM education experts on findings from decades of sexual harassment research on workplaces *outside* academic STEM. Drawing on a knowledge politics informed by a de-colonial feminist STS, *Cracking the Bro Code* aims to make sense of the enactments and tolerance of sexual harassment in some of the most powerful laboratories and worksites in the world. Demanding an end to harassment in technoscience has a distinct advantage over a singular approach of combating bias in that sexual harassment is explicitly prohibited in government, university policies, and many professional societies in technoscience. Sexual harassment is a cultural phenomenon. To study it properly requires appropriate methods for studying culture—namely, qualitative methods.

A robust theory on sexual harassment in STEM is both timely and needed. We must more comprehensively understand not only the experiences of being sexually harassed but also the cultural phenomena that reproduce this violence in order to enact "effective, intersectional interventions, prevention strategies, and response models that are centered on the perspectives and needs of those who experience identity-based harassment" (Herbers, Metcalf, and Williams 2019, 4). In later chapters, I analyze my data intersectionally, looking to how women of color, queer women, and gender nonconforming people are disproportionately targeted by gender and sexual harassment (Clancy et al. 2017; Rabelo and Cortina 2014) and how this targeting then negatively affects their career, health, and persistence.

How might framing sexual harassment as a matter of care (Puig de la Bellacasa 2011) foster greater collegiality in technoscience and to what broader effects? In studying the traumatic effects and serial patterns of predation in science, how can one not only take care not to speak "for" others but also ensure that no further harm will come to research participants? In other words, how do I ensure that this research triggers no retributive responses toward those who are already targets of sexual harassment and discrimination in science?

CONCLUSION: TRANSFORMING GENDERED INSTITUTIONS

Caring about bias, discrimination, and harassment can illuminate workplace cultures that, through preferential treatment, support the persistence of some but not all members. Spurious forms of resistance to desegregation—bias, discrimination, and harassment—have too long been tolerated, especially in computing science and engineering workplaces, labs, classrooms, and professional society meetings. We must develop pathways of resistance where the people who produce computer technology are not just free of harassment and discrimination but also free to trouble the institutions they work for, to agitate not just for reform of exclusionary practices but for a transformation in how technology is produced, toward what ends, and for whose benefit. The end goal is not simply the vague concept of "inclusion" but rather that all have a voice at the table—one that is heard, respected, and supported. Further, the weight of responsibility should not fall on those targeted by bias, discrimination, and harassment to introduce and lead difficult conversations about the social dimensions of STEM production (e.g., racism, sexism, homophobia, and classism).

Too often, in their efforts to convince the public of the importance of diversifying STEM fields, STEM scientists argue that their fields are "critical to the national economy and America's global competitiveness," yet they leave these institutions unexamined (Hill, Corbett, and Rose 2010, 1). Commonly held reasons for equity interventions in STEM must be destabilized to reframe the exclusion of women and scholars of color from laboratories, faculty ranks, and boardrooms as a broader historical project of dispossession, the solutions to which require more than an "add and stir" approach to combating underrepresentation and carefully defined conceptualization of similarities and differences between discrimination and harassment.

I grounded this chapter's analysis in feminist STS methodological commitments to "matters of care" because I hope equity in STEM scholarship going forward will build on the 2018 National Academies report and inform activities and scholarship with an explicitly political stance against the tolerance and reproduction of harassment in STEM fields. My call to augment critiques of bias and discrimination with sexual and gender harassment in academic STEM has raised questions about the differences between discrimination and harassment. While on the same continuum, the differences between these forms of social violence are a matter of scale. Discrimination is prejudice and ill treatment that stems from stereotypes that operate at the level of culture. It shapes behavior and policies that lead to disparate outcomes and chilly climates (Carr et al. 2000).

The term "harassment" traditionally has meant to exhaust and fatigue. It comes from the French word *harer*, "to set a dog on" (Procter 1984). Gender harassment occurs at the level of individual and interpersonal interactions in academic workplaces and is intended to both dehumanize women and denigrate our capacity as knowers. Sexual harassment involves unwelcome sexual advances and coercion to engage in sexual activity. Such harassment erodes collegiality in sites of STEM knowledge production and unjustly exhausts and fatigues women in academic workplaces. Though I argue that we need to understand the differences between sexual and gender harassment, their effects on disadvantaged group members of science are, unfortunately, remarkably similar. For example, a study of women in male-dominated fields found that nine out of ten women who were harassed experienced no sexual advances but suffered adverse effects on their health and career similar to those who were sexually harassed (Leskinen, Cortina, and Kabat 2011).

In the following chapters, I aim to answer these questions by probing ideological, material, and cultural practices of high-tech workers, synthesizing scholarship in equity in STEM and feminist STS, and paying close attention to how women and their allies within STEM fields can collaborate to enact institutional transformation. Much important knowledge about the structural, organizational, and interpersonal barriers to women's success and advancement in STEM fields has been generated by female STEM practitioners (Bystydzienski and Bird 2006). However, advocates for gender equity in STEM make claims about culture, the exploration and verification of which will require greater collaboration and cooperation between them and feminist STS social scientists. On-the-ground emic perspectives are important because they privilege the experiences and unique positionalities of people who are participating in the epistemic and cultural practices of STEM fields. However, if institutional transformation is the end goal, then incorporating outsiders' perspectives on the cultures of STEM (e.g., those of social science researchers) will continue to be helpful to attend to silences, misinterpretations, and lacunae of knowledge that have yet to be uncovered. For example, my feminist analysis of cultural norms in computing reveals that the white male standpoint in STEM fields is so deeply embedded, not only in norms and workplace culture but also in the positivist tradition of Western science, that performances of masculinity are taken for granted. Women technical professionals must navigate these unspoken norms and values. As I discuss in chapter 5, women in computing find this navigation to be an exhausting exercise of filtering out their lived experiences so as not to disrupt how the dominant class defines the social identity behaviors of engineers, the problems worth solving, and the methods that have validity.

Equity in STEM scientists and feminist STS scholars alike are engaged in the struggle to transform exclusion in STEM. This is a political demand, and resources and ideological shifts are required to satisfy this demand. Feminism in science requires political engagement, like Nancy Hopkin's efforts at institutional transformation, and ideological work, like Wendy Faulkner's call for pluralism in the cultural identity of engineers in order to break the ideological bind between engineering identity and gender identity. For many readers, this work requires interrogating the different methodological approaches to feminist interventions. For some who are persisting in technoscience, better inclusion practices are sufficient to transform the tech industry. Conversely, within projects aimed at overhauling how the industry operates within other structures of power, like the state and racial capitalism, radical labor organizing is the only path forward. Together, feminist labor activism can coexist with those amplifying the lived experiences of pioneering women in STEM to disrupt the "arrogant perception" (Lugones 1989) that universalizes a singular identity of a computer scientist or engineer and a singular definition of competency to reproduce dominant class rule in STEM.

3 CONTRADICTIONS OF CARE: ALTRUISTIC ASPIRATIONS AND REPRODUCTIVE POLITICS IN COMPUTING

Talented girls and women are wondering: What are the social contributions of computer science and engineering? Some conclude it is a field detached from communal and civil engagement and lacking moral purpose. This can lead these high performers to choose to invest their talent in other fields. In other words, computing's contribution to humans and society is not clear, despite the fortune that computing bosses have spent promoting a myth that computers are a critical means "to renew participatory democracy" (Dean 2009, 36). Worse, the workplace culture in the technological fields often contradicts the munificent claims from Big Tech leaders that computers and algorithmic systems are best positioned to solve the world's most complex social ills. How can this claim be credible when computing departments and workplaces fail, year after year, to solve the participation and harassment problems in their own backyards?

In this chapter, I argue four points. First, fixating on *possible* benefits that computing bosses may offer society perpetuates a fantasy that distracts from the harms caused to women of color and other historically disenfranchised scientists in the computing workforce. Second, these harms are penalties meted out by dominant groups as payment for daring to transgress labor norms in the neoliberal economy, a market dependent on stereotypes and a scientific worldview that hews to Cartesian schisms between mind and body, the social and the technical. Third, this technocratic fantasy merges with positivist fervor in a moment of soaring inequities to produce a discrete form of patriarchy that, much like its antecedents, nonetheless relies on vast volumes of exploited, unremunerated labor. Finally, the way to untangle this knot of synergistic structures of domination is by paying attention to the altruism of my participants.

We know that altruistic aspirations play a role in the underrepresentation of women in computing (Carlone and Johnson 2007; Diekman et al. 2010; Cuny and Aspray 2001; Margolis, Fisher, and Miller 2000; Carrigan 2017). Many nonbinary and women tech workers who persist in these careers yearn to use their technical skills in service of social change in their workplaces, communities, and the world at large. In this chapter, I reimagine segregation and sexism in high-tech as a reproductive justice issue. I argue that nonbinary and women tech workers, regardless of race, sexuality, or parenthood status, must grapple with three intersecting phenomena: a culture of overwork; preconceived notions of gender that permeate computing culture; and finally, a contradiction of care between their own values and aspirations and those of their bosses. Big Tech talks a big game about its socially revolutionary impact, but my participants felt thwarted when trying to use their technical skills to serve others.

This contradiction of care between the public welfare aspirations of some technologists and their bosses is a promising site for collective action in Big Tech. I frame the oppositional consciousness of historically disenfranchised technologists as a contradiction of care, whereby some workers who yearn to contribute to the reproduction of society's collective well-being—*to further the public welfare*—confront Big Tech's bottom line objectives. This contradiction of care in computing workspaces takes place in the larger context of digital capitalism, which demands the individuation of workers and the privatization of social systems of support—*the infrastructures of public welfare*—so that people are expected to provide for themselves and any dependents via the patriarchal family (Brown 2019). Not only does Big Tech fail to live up to its widely publicized altruism, but it tries to conceal its social harms (Nafus 2018; Benjamin 2019; Noble 2018; Carrigan, Green, and Rahman-Davies 2021). These transgressions account not only for why the field of computing remains segregated, but they also reveal how the field contributes to right-wing economic politics that disenfranchises and impoverishes communities of color and women who are economically independent.

Mediating these contradictions of care can catalyze an oppositional consciousness that could transform individual tech workers into resistant and collective subjects (Hartsock 1998; Sandoval 2000). To do so, I propose that we take seriously the public welfare aspirations of technologists who are historically disenfranchised from high-tech and organize around them in order to hold computing merchants accountable to the public. Antiquated gender stereotypes in tech workspaces are a symptom of neoliberal politics driving computing corporations and orchestrating the redistribution of wealth upward, consolidating it into fewer hands and constraining access to networks of computing architecture to an elite few from majority groups. To understand how these forces operate at a global scale, we must first understand the particulars of the contradictions of care and reproductive politics in the workspaces of computer science and engineering. This demand for reproductive justice in digital capitalism needs amplification if workers worldwide hope to galvanize the political force needed to level the economic playing field and redistribute the fruits of the Age of Information more fairly.

YEARNING TO GIVE BACK

What is the benefit of all this? There's *no social impact*. I'm just helping to make [the corporation] money. Helping the customer is not enough, because it's all about the bottom line—only [the corporation] benefits. . . . I believe in the importance of giving back. It's a huge part of my story.

Olivia, an African American mid-career professional, left her job as a software engineer at a renowned Fortune 50 tech company because she "yearned to give back." This painful contradiction of care was a significant theme in many of my participants' stories. Olivia questioned how she was benefiting society and if the computing commodities she helped create were even benefiting customers. Because Olivia yearned to make social contributions but did not have the opportunity to do so as a software engineer in industry, she returned to university to earn a doctorate in human computer interaction (HCI), a subfield in computer science and engineering that integrates the social and technical aspects of computing. By switching from software engineering to HCI, Olivia persisted in the computing field while reconciling her work with her "altruistic identity," which Heidi Carlone and Angela Johnson (2007, 1199) define as women of color who use "science in direct service of humanity." Science in service of others is a form of collective care, a way to give back to others and find meaning in one's work.

Some people in this study felt frustrated in their attempts to combine their computer science identity with an altruistic identity because the field lacks a reputation for altruism. For example, Lynn, a white software developer at a high-tech corporation, said she is anxious that her occupation is not recognized as one that contributes to the social good.

LYNN: In the field of medicine you can say, "I'm working on a cure for cancer," or "I'm helping people," and people might not know the details, they might not know the science behind it, but they understand the goal.

COLEEN: Right, right. Which is . . . ?

LYNN: Some kind of social good, or leaving the world a better place . . .

Perhaps this desire for one's social contribution to be recognized is why a significant number of participants in this study saw the biomedical field as a viable avenue by which to contribute to the social good. Biomedicine in the US has "evolved out of tradition of service to suffering humanity" (Loustaunau and Sobo 1997, 126) and thus may be at an advantage for attracting people who yearn to use their skills in service of the higher good. For example, Sylvia, an African American doctoral student, wants to use computer technology to enhance public health infrastructures. She explains:

> Because that's kind of just who I am. But it's also my mentor. She always talked about [how] "you really need to do something that would affect everyone; you don't want to just . . . write it in a paper and then nothing happens. . . . You need to apply it, and you need to be helpful." That's why I've been working with the public health department.

Sylvia not only aspires to enhance public welfare; she also had the encouragement from a trusted female mentor who overcame the challenges of the "double bind" (Malcom 1976; Ong et al. 2011) to do the same. Sylvia's mentor gave heartfelt advice to apply her technical skills to a collective endeavor serving public welfare, perhaps as a means of investing in her student's persistence and success in computing (National Academies 2022; Carlone and Johnson 2007). Regina, a doctoral student from Taiwan, explained: "I want to go into biotech because I'm really interested in biology, so if I do a start-up, I think it will be related to nutrition. . . . I really like to see what people eat, how it changes their system, and how that turns into diseases." Becca, a white doctoral student, also wanted a technical career in health: "What I want to do is accessible health stuff. I feel like the technology there has more potential with people who are blind and low vision. . . . I want to be enabling people who have an impairment to have easier access to health."

CONTRADICTION OF CARE AND THE GLAMOUR OF THE SOCIAL GOOD

Becca's and Regina's altruistic aspirations are admirable, but will they be able to find such fulfillment? Paying attention to contradictions of care along fault lines of altruism highlighted a gap between the noblesse oblige touted by Big Tech bosses and how participants in this study described their work and outputs. One pattern I noticed was that when computing bosses exalted the social benefit of their commodities, all too often, they were referring to its *potential* social benefit, with no mention of risks or societal side effects. While aspiring to contribute to the well-being of society is indeed a lofty goal, computing leaders deliver promises instead of evidence that they serve the social good. In this section, I focus on current working conditions in computing—not digital merchants' best intentions dressed up by world-class flacks. I offer evidence as to why we should be skeptical of Big Tech's glamour of altruism and its claim that its leaders are destined to lead humanity forward.

For example, Microsoft Research produces an expensive booklet (some of its pages are three-dimensional) to advertise to computer science and engineering faculty the social benefits of the work they do: "We collaborate with leading researchers in medicine, education and earth and environmental sciences to transform society for the better through technology" (Mundie and Hey 2011, 3). The booklet is a promotional tool to convince professors that Microsoft Research's investigations have the potential to be useful for both "commodity computing and . . . the creation of knowledge services that are relevant to the research community" (17). For example, sensor nodes in the Amazon "could help scientists develop better solutions to climate issues" (21); biosensors embedded in contact lenses "could help monitor glucose levels in diabetic patients" (39); and "robots can be used to explore areas too dangerous or difficult for human teams to search" (41).

While it may be true that some computing commodities like those featured in Microsoft Research's PR packet have potential benefits to humans and society, the most profitable uses for these technologies take priority. Lynn, a white early-career software engineer, told me that she and one of her professors built an application for an eye-tracking device intended to help people with disabilities, but the application was eventually developed for marketing purposes in order "to track where people look on the screen for retrospective [marketing] analysis." Her collaboration with this professor was a success, and she was pleased that they published their findings. However, Lynn reflected that her colleagues seemed to like the idea or the *potential* of applications for people with disabilities much more than the actual implementation of such applications:

> I wanted to do something for people with disabilities, and I felt like I got all this positive experience in academia for it, and my perception of industry was [that it was] not going to care so much; it's not going to be a priority to serve people with disabilities, because it's expensive and probably not on their priority list. So then I went into academia, and I realized people in academia also don't care about the disabled as much as I might have thought. They liked the drawing program with the eyes because it was exciting and sexy, but when you start talking about, like, practical accessibility issues, people kind of turn off.

Shawna, a white, early-career transgender woman, had an experience similar to Lynn's, except her colleagues were more than indifferent—they were hostile. Shawna teamed up with an HCI professor to create applications for disabled computer users. In this collaboration, she not only faced resistance from her theory/algorithms adviser, but she also faced resistance from her peers:

SHAWNA: The lab itself was always a bit boisterous. . . . They just really were pushing the technology and focusing more on the computer part, as opposed to the human part. And I felt that whenever I brought up the human issues that they were ignored, mainly. In fact, I earned the moniker, "Accessibility Bitch."

COLEEN: Oh, my God! That is so offensive.

SHAWNA: Yeah, actually, I took it as a compliment.

COLEEN: Really, even with the "B" word?

SHAWNA: Hey, I subscribe to the magazine.

Shawna's and Lynn's views from inside the computing workplace invite skepticism about the viability of computing commodities' service to humanity. If these altruistic efforts and the people leading them are maligned and discredited in the workplace culture, how will such aspirations actually come to pass?

These contradictions of care—between the *potential* of computers to serve humanity and the actual work being performed in computing worksites today—need to reconciled in order to crack the Bro Code. The speculative promise of computer commodities' advancement of the social good does not stand up under scrutiny. Such promises cannot be kept under the current labor conditions in which computers are designed. For example, Microsoft Research recognizes its high performers with prestigious technical recognition awards. They claim that these awards recognize *"work that changes our world for the better"* (Microsoft 2013, A9). In 2013, an all-male, majority white Kinect skeletal tracking team received this widely publicized award for developing video game technology that tracks players' movements. How exactly do video games that track players' movements change the world? Apparently, by shifting the "paradigm for the entertainment industry . . . and selling 18 million units" that year (Microsoft 2013, A9). Microsoft continues to leverage this technology to read gamers' body language as they consume advertisement messages in order to promote more personalized choices for their consumptive habits. I am sure the company's stockholders are proud, but boosting sales for video games hardly qualifies as a service for humanity.

Google also uses fanciful rhetoric that connotes service and magnanimousness to promote its products. For example, at a Google I/O conference in 2014, a singular message thrummed throughout the three-day event: *ubiquitous computing will solve the problem of "disconnection."* The company said it will unify consumers' work and personal lives. David, a white male director of engineering, framed the company's wearable products as "revolutionary," their tracking of their wearers' behaviors and vitals as a "contextual stream," vowing to achieve the "seamless integration of users' personal and digital lives in an intrinsically human, delightful way." Much like Microsoft's award fanfare, Google's performance of altruism is misleading. The computer merchant is hawking data collection tools of human behavior that drive the corporation's operations and on which its profits depend (Zuboff 2019; Carrigan, Green, and Rahman-Davies 2021).

The gossamer-thin guise of "doing good" crafted by Big Tech's marketing teams works to blur the potential benefits of ubiquitous tech with evidence of impact. This wide gap between computing's promise and its actual impact on humans and society is driving the contradictions of care in

computing workspaces. Instead of fixating on *possible* benefits to humanity that computing commodities might offer in the future, the present is
at stake, fraught with actual detriments to society. Women of color and
other disenfranchised members of the field who yearn to combine their
technical identities with their altruistic ones and create meaningful impacts
with computers can illuminate what needs attention in the here and now—
actions key to cracking the Bro Code.

REPRODUCTION RENDERED INVISIBLE

Big Tech is not only failing to meet the collective reproductive aspirations of
its workers. It is also failing to support the work necessary for its workers to
care for themselves, their families, and their communities. The field's con-
servative reproductive politics are more evidence that computer technology
is not amply meeting human needs. In this section, I pivot from the politics of reproduction regarding public welfare in computing to examine the
contradiction of care in terms of reproductive labor, subsistence work that
reproduces the labor force, both on a day-to-day basis and generationally.

Jobs within computing organizations are extremely time-consuming
and designed for workers with little to no reproductive responsibilities. It
is a framework that assumes a particular gendered organization of social
reproduction (Valian 1999; Williams 2000; Acker 1990). This framework,
based on sexism rather than any biological imperative of women and men,
governs organizational behaviors and role assignments in prestigious fields
(Acker 2000). This cultural process is further exacerbated by broader heterosexist codes that assign women primary responsibility for labor in the home
and helps explain the persistent gender gap in computing fields (Watt and
Eccles 2008; Xie and Shauman 2003; Valian 1999; Schiebinger 1999).

It's no secret that long hours are required in computer science institutions. Carla, a white senior leader in industry, joked that in her spare time
she likes to overwork. Pei, an Asian American senior leader, confirmed
Carla's sentiment: "The work is endless. I work even on my days off." My
study's participants did not frame the work-life binary as a balancing act
but instead challenge us to reframe reproductive labor in terms of compromises and trade-offs. This lens makes space in the work/life debate for
inquiry into the politics governing reproduction, work, and leisure time in

the US. Furthermore, challenging these politics has the potential for broad-based coalition-building. Kelly, a white senior technical fellow in the corporate sector, admits to working a hundred hours a week for many years:

> I have no personal life. I am not an example of work-life balance. . . . You can't have it all. Women wreck their lives trying to be superwoman. I never wanted kids, never felt like I needed a husband to be complete. Over the years, I've seen that women who want family life must carry the burden of this cultural baggage.

Valerie, a foreign national from Russia and information technology (IT) leader who has worked on Wall Street for over 25 years, never wanted to work in a female-dominated job and never wanted to have kids. She compared high-tech work to doctors' long hours: "But at least doctors have shifts; in the tech world, you have no life. You are like a dog on a leash. The only people here with kids are men with wives. How do women in IT with kids do it?" She said many more women worked in computing in Russia when she was in her early-career stage, and the culture was collegial and less punishing than US computing culture. She attributed the culture of overwork to the overrepresentation of men in US computing.

To extend Valerie's question, how do high-tech companies account for the social reproduction of their laborers and their future workforce? The common stereotype of the individual computer scientist is someone who, in essence, eschews normal habits of social reproduction: bathing, eating well, and kinship. I call this cultural trope the *geek mystique*, and part of its beguiling heroism lies in the power to refuse the culturally devalued labors of care. This geek stereotype is also reflected in computing institutionally. Its culture of overwork signals the lack of regard that computing corporations and academic institutions have toward modes of reproduction in our society. Given the great influence computer technology has on our society, the effacement of social reproduction reflects and reproduces labor value within the US more broadly.

Kelly's and Valerie's experiences as senior computing professionals and child-free women bring attention to a critical failing of computing institutions—the diametrical opposition of social reproduction and technical production and the associated cost for both women and men in the high-tech sector, including the gig economy (Sharma 2018). Kelly's use of the phrase "the burden of this cultural baggage" is a negative reference to women's primary responsibilities for social and biological reproduction.

Valerie's description of the culture of overwork is no less grim and brings to mind David Floyd's (1992, 46–47) argument that technology entails a low valuation of women and care work because it is "embedded in and created out of society's dominant belief systems." Other scholars support this claim, documenting how computing reproduces structural racism and sexism (Noble 2018; Roberts 2019; Benjamin 2019; Hicks 2017). Adding the politics of reproductive labor to this conversation may help reorient conversations of labor exploitation in computing so that its workplace culture might be transformed to care for "the social and how the social is reproduced through care" (Sharma 2018).

SEGREGATION AS REPRODUCTIVE INJUSTICE

When technical women talk about gender in the context of work and gather together as women, they often talk about reproductive politics. The time- and energy-consuming unwaged labor to reproduce the labor force— or what Kelly, the white senior fellow in industry quoted above, called "the burden of cultural baggage"—is a site of struggle. Through a lens of reproduction, the cultural mechanisms that tolerate and support patriarchal politics in computing become clearer. In this section, I demonstrate how the means of reproduction influence participants' decisions and experiences in computing culture.

LEFT BEHIND AND INTEGRATED

In addition to the culture of overwork, computing bosses are famous for designing their commodities in terms of planned obsolescence, which can differentially affect mothers in computing. For example, Pei, the Asian American senior leader quoted earlier in this chapter, notes, "If you are in high-tech, you have to constantly learn new technologies. For example, an operating system can be obsolete in five years; a language is replaced by another in maybe seven years. It takes a lot of study time, which is challenging for a woman who has young kids." Illuminating the reproductive domains of planned obsolescence, Pei shows us how it operates to favor the young male worker who is well steeped in the latest technologies and systems organization (Cooley and Cooley 1980). Rajasree, a full professor with a large lab, put it more bluntly: "Motherhood means you are left behind."

For consumers, it is hard to keep up with every upgrade to your software products and the cost of machines that have a life span of a few years and a far shorter cultural value. From a labor perspective, it is an intensification of a computer scientist's work. In addition to the long hours and the requirement to always be improving, upgrading, or rendered obsolete, computing workers are, in many ways, virtually tethered to their workplace. Many participants remarked that a large part of the struggle around reproduction in high-tech centers on the increased workload by virtue of always being connected. Tony, a white male senior leader, claimed that he tried not to work on weekends. I asked, "What about email?" He replied wryly, "Well, that doesn't count." Despite Google's promise that the seamless integration of our personal and professional lives through digital commodities is revolutionary and delightful, always being accessible to your boss is a drag for anyone, regardless of gender. Heterosexual, cisgender men however, are rewarded culturally for being a breadwinner in ways that women are not. Often, they are sailing up the ranks with a "flow of family work" at their backs (Williams 2000, 5). Thus they are better positioned to withstand an intense culture of overwork and endless accessibility. Women who enter male-dominated computing fields must withstand intense expectations at work *and* social penalties for transgressing patriarchal role allocations in the labor force. Women of color are also targeted by a combination of racism and sexism and the consequences of being highly visible, which amplifies the harms of inhospitable workplace cultures.

THE LARRY SUMMERS HYPOTHESIS

One such social penalty (described extensively in chapter 2) is the Larry Summers Hypothesis. The viciously persistent myth that women are genetically designed to be bad at math and exceptional at wiping noses and cleaning toilets is so ingrained in the collective imagination of American society that even women who have overcome barriers to participating in computing have internalized this ideology that is critical to perpetuating occupational segregation in the US workforce. After I gave a talk on my research to a group of female electrical and computer science engineers, Kathy, a white mid-career professional at a Fortune 50 social media corporation, approached me to discuss the dearth of women at her company.

After describing her experience as the only woman on her team in a company where only five out of 800 managers were women, Kathy asked me, "But isn't it true that men's and women's brains work differently?" I asked her to explain what she meant, and she said, "Isn't there research that supports men are more logical and women more emotional and social?" Even though women have all but closed the math achievement gap, the stereotype that women are not good at abstract reasoning still persists (Barres 2006). In fact, when I told Karen, a white woman with an advanced degree, that studies on the math achievement gap showed that there was no such gap, she was skeptical.[1]

The Larry Summers Hypothesis is painful to women. Anita, a mid-career woman of color in computer engineering, shared her feelings about having her advanced spatial abilities dismissed because of her gender: "I hate being told that the people that scored at the very, very high end of the mathematics tests are almost all men. Well, it's like, 'Excuse me, I scored at the top end, too.' That hurts me."

Anita's emotions illuminate how the Larry Summers Hypothesis is a form of gender violence that makes advanced skills in mathematics incommensurable with women. Ideologies of science and gender are constructed to reinforce one another and exclude any threats to the feminine/masculine binary. For example, Tara, a white early-career professor, recalls:

> I was talking about applying to grad school with a faculty member . . . and he said, "Well, what are some of the things you're looking at [in graduate programs]?" I said, "Well, one of the things is how many women there are in the program." He said, "Oh, so how are we doing here?" I said, "We're doing really well at this school; we're almost at 30 percent." And one of the students popped up from the back of the room saying, "We must be making it *too easy*, then." And the professor just lets it stand.

The male student saw women's participation in computer education as a decrease in the rigor and quality of the department's pedagogy. The male professor failed to disabuse the male student of his prejudice targeting another student. The male student's logic also illuminates a structural level of violence at work here, one that strives to purge computing of undesirable elements, which, in this instance, correlates with femaleness. This is evidence that men pursuing computing careers benefit from a presumed competence that gives them unearned respect and an advantage in the world of computing, while women do not. When viewed through a multilayered framework of violence, these stories also illuminate the tightly woven ideological strands that uphold cultural assumptions regarding masculinity, scientific competency, and disciplinary prestige.

DOUBLE STANDARD

Put simply, women and nonbinary technologists are treated differently as cognitive laborers than their cisgender male peers. As Anita's experience with the Larry Summers Hypothesis shows, sexist ideology claims that men are better at math, ipso facto, they are entitled to dominate the ranks of computing and thus empowered to decide the future of humanity in homosocial congress. Tara again reflects on her experiences of bias in graduate school: "I wouldn't say that anybody went out and did anything on purpose—right? But certainly, there were things that I think happened that would not have happened had I been a guy." Tara uses the logic of unexamined bias theory, which stress that microaggressions can be perpetrated without perpetrators being aware of their actions. Reflecting on another level of sexism in her field, Carol, a white senior software engineer working in industry, shared one of her mentor's experiences:

> She was way older than me, and as far as I was concerned the system had eaten her up and spit her out. She wasn't married. You know, she didn't get the career advancement that she wanted, and I have no doubt would have got, if she had been a guy.

Carol's metaphor of her mentor's career experience is an example of the outcomes of symbolic violence in computing worksites, the way power operates to confer status, resources, and power to the superordinate members of groups (Bourdieu 1989). The vicious language that Carol uses to describe her mentor's experience as a computer scientist—not only devoured but also discarded—speaks to the brutality used to maintain the hierarchal status quo between genders in high-tech and to legitimate who matters in computing. A similar form of symbolic violence is also at play in the ways in which the pioneers of the computer science and engineering field have been black-boxed in the annals of the field's history because of their race and gender. The erasure of the contributions of women and technologists of color to the field in its nascent stages operates to legitimize who matters in US history.

Ben Barres, a white transgender man, found that passing as a cisgender man in the world of science protected him from sexism. He observed, "People treat me with much more respect: I can even complete a whole sentence without being interrupted by a man" (Barres 2006, 135). Shawna, a white early-career academic and transgender woman, confirms Barres' experience:

> But the really sort of interesting thing in all this is that I have had that perspective. You know, I was, like, coming from both sides. It's one of those [situations] where I'm like the classic resume studies . . . where they just changed the name. . . . And I can honestly say, "Yeah, guys aren't treated this way."

These stories all share a common theme of comparing the interpersonal and institutional experiences of women and men in computing careers. To persist in computing careers, women must bear the brunt of a range of gender violence, from being interrupted frequently to being energetically devoured and discarded. This violence denies women agency, competency, good health, prestige, and compensation in technical careers. Further, it robs their families and communities of generational wealth and reproduces the racial and gender ideologies that continue a legacy of exploitation in the US labor force.

GENDER IDEOLOGIES IN TECH WORK

During the Age of Reason and the advent of colonialism, philosophy and science divided the mind from the body at the same time the state divorced agrarian women and men from the land (Federici 2004). Together, these forces combined to subjugate and reify the natural world. In ancient times, Greek patriarchs exalted abstract reason and isolated themselves from nature, female power, and reproductive labor (Hartsock 1998). Today, gender politics in computing continue these legacies and enable men from dominant groups to participate in the life of the mind while externalizing their material needs to people who have been historically exploited. I argue that computer science and engineering is an example of the mind-body schism par excellence, evinced in its values regarding the technical and the social and an epistemological preference for the virtual over the material or social.

Women are often steered into performing "caretaking" tasks while men are steered into more technical work in the paid labor force. Tara's experience exemplifies this perfectly:

> My adviser at the time had two PhD students: myself and a guy. We were working on a big project and he said, "I'm going to put Jack in charge of these things, and I'm going to put you in charge of these things." I looked at him and I said, "So

basically you're putting Jack in charge of all the technical stuff, and you're putting me in charge of all the content." Yeah.

Even though Tara stuck up for herself and managed to prove her competence as a technical scholar, her adviser still undermined her by ignoring her technical skills and calling attention instead to her culinary talents. Tara again:

> A Turing Award winner came to visit my group, and my adviser was going around and he was saying things about each of the students. When it came to my turn, it was, "This is Tara, and she makes a great lasagna." And then, after stewing on it for a while, I said basically, you know, "I'm glad that you like the lasagna; I like to make it. But I really can't have this being the only thing that you're going to tell about me to other visitors." And he responds to this, "Fine, but aren't we being a bit oversensitive?"

His act of overlooking her technical talent and relegating her status to culturally appropriate labor roles is ignored, and he goes on to compound the problem with even more stereotypes about women's tender dispositions. Many other participants in this study reported being called oversensitive when confronting a male colleague about his sexism. These men's responses, reminiscent of victim-blaming techniques, serve to reinforce the bond between masculine identity and technical competency. Anne, a white senior leader in industry, succinctly describes how this hurts women: "Technical women must live with wrong assumptions that because they are women, they can't be as technical as men." To persist in computing, women must find ways to endure peers' and superiors' sexist assumptions regarding their talents and abilities and be prepared to be dismissed when resisting such sexism.

Stereotypes that cement technical competency with masculinity offer males preferential access to leadership positions in high-tech. The glass ceiling in tech has costs not just for individual women and their careers but also for the fight for women's equality in the US. Sheryl Sandberg, a white professional and the former chief operating officer of Facebook, in her keynote address at the 2011 Grace Hopper Celebration of Women in Computing conference, said:

> Technical jobs get paid a lot more, and they're where all the growth is. If we continue to have so few women go into and stay in technical careers, eventually the wage gap progress is going to go the other way. And we fought long and hard to get women as leaders; we don't have enough of them, but if technical skills

are increasingly important for leadership in every sector of the economy, if we don't have enough women in technology, we're not going to have enough future leaders.

In other words, the cultural tolerance in computing for mechanisms that put women at risk of attrition from the field affects women's ability to ascend to leadership roles in lots of different fields. At the time of this writing, news broke that the US Supreme Court overturned Roe v. Wade, the landmark reproductive rights law; this decision was penned in a fundamentalist fervor of moral outrage, no less. Segregation in a powerful field such as computing is symptomatic of the far-right politics of reproduction that now dominates US culture. The rarefied realms of leadership in intersecting structures of power bar a critical mass of technologists from groups historically disenfranchised from computer science. I emphasize "critical mass" here because token representation, like Sandberg's leadership at Facebook, does nothing to advance transformational change in institutions, whereas a critical mass of women's representation results in more fair distribution of role allocations in STEM workplaces (Carrigan, Quinn, and Riskin 2011). Sexist ideologies and policies in a field with an excess of global power intersect with other "configurations of inequality," like class and racial inequalities to constrain queer people, women of color, and white women's life-affirming activities and our choices regarding our bodies, labors, and futures (McCall 2001). These inequalities make us vulnerable to forces of immiseration and exploitation and reproduce systematic forms of injustice.

CARRYING THE CULTURAL BAGGAGE OF FAMILY

In the mid-1990s, Faith, a white cisgender academic, was kicked out of her computer engineering doctoral program when her adviser found out she was pregnant. Only after threatening legal action was she reinstated to her program. Not all women face such severe circumstances, but constraints regarding reproduction are acutely felt by many of my participants, especially in the early-career stage when they are planning their future.

Social reproduction may not be highly valued in computing, but it is a concern for women practitioners. I wonder if part of this anxiety relates to the knowledge that they lack a flow of family work to support their labor-intensive careers, coupled with worries about the cultural consequences of transgressing gender segregation in the workplace. Women in the training and early phases of a computing career trajectory expressed anxiety when they considered their futures and the potential conflict between remaining the best in their field and realizing their social reproduction aspirations:

CYNTHIA, a white undergraduate: I mean to be married and have both my kids by 33.

AVA, an Asian American undergraduate: Is that right? What if you don't have time? What if you're working up that ladder?

CYNTHIA: I will stop.

AVA: That's not for me. I'd like to [have children], but then at the same time, a lot of my motivation is to get a job—a good job, because I know I'll have to support my parents at a certain time, and you know, if at that time I don't have the money to support children and I need to focus on my career, then I will focus on my career.

Note how both women have social reproduction aspirations. For the white student, Cynthia, childrearing is more important than persisting in her career, whereas Ava, a woman of color, wants to prioritize her career as a means to achieve her reproductive aspiration of eldercare. The differences between these two undergraduate women may be related to race. In this exchange, we can see how care work is allocated across generations in the two women's families. Dominant white culture externalizes eldercare to institutions, whereas communities of color may have less reasons to trust these institutions. White women in this study discussed their family life primarily in terms of the nuclear family unit, whereas kinscripts for women of color included extended family and community ties and strong inclinations to provide for folks in their networks. The ideological and political coercion that assigns women primary care responsibility for unwaged labor in the home affects women differently; thus, organizing around reproductive labor in high-tech worksites must not be reduced to norms within white, Western nuclear family structures.

Shawna, a white transgender academic, expressed her frustration that white, normative family structures were prioritized by feminists in her department. She told me that an event to support women in computing focused exclusively on biological reproduction. She challenged the organizers of a lunch event for graduate students on work-life balance about why one of the few women professors in the department was not asked to speak. "[They did not] invite the one who had an adopted kid," she said. "This pissed me off. They said adopting kids is not the same as actually going through pregnancy

and maternity leave. Because, you know, the adoption process is so easy."
Shawna's anger at the marginalization of an adoptive parent from a group
discussion on reproduction highlights the fact that "discourses on rights and
needs are also stratified and organized in ways which are congruent with societal patterns of dominance and subordination" (Moore 1994, 100). Shawna
also argued that work-life balance conversations tend to privilege heterosexual white women and eclipse other violence that women in computing
careers must contend with, like transphobia, gender harassment, and racism.
In efforts to dismantle institutional sexism, we cannot privilege certain social
identities over others, or we risk reproducing racism and heteronormative
kinship.

Without exception, professionals with male partners in this study,
regardless of their status as parents, had chosen partners who were supportive of their careers. In order to persist in computing, these women rejected
role allocations that cleave to the "breadwinner" and "caretaker" binary.
For example, Diane, a senior European national and academic leader, discussed how she and her husband negotiated a move across country for
her career advancement: "He was not as driven by his career as me, and at
that time, we had two very young kids. So he quit his job and we moved
out west . . . He did part-time from home, and that was great because we
had young kids, and he was at home part-time working." Diane was not
alone in this experience. For example, Carol, a white senior leader in industry with two children, had a stay-at-home husband. Regina is a Taiwanese early-career professional, and when I asked if she and her partner were
going to move together for a job she had recently been offered, she said:
"He doesn't believe in long-distance relationships, so he will have to move
with me." Tara, the white early-career academic, reflected on negotiating
the job market with her husband, who also earned his PhD in computer
science: "My husband had said that he was willing to go wherever I thought
I needed to go, because he thought that I cared about my career more than
he does about his." These women's narratives show that the relations of
reproduction are central to women's participation in computing. Women
who persist in this nontraditional field must not only buck the status quo
of gender norms in the sphere of production (their computing worksites)
but also negotiate equity in the sphere of reproduction (their intimate
partnerships).

CONCLUSION

Too often, women are either not attracted to computing or leave the field because they perceive it as divorced from social concerns and helping people. Some argue that this lack of clarity on how computer science and engineering serve the social good is merely a public relations problem, but I disagree.[2] Women and girls see through the mythologizing propagated by expensive marketing. Women who persist in computing must work long hours while combating discrimination and harassment. They struggle with disillusionment when their altruism is fettered or, as we saw with Shawna, maligned. They must make strategic decisions in their personal lives about whether or not to partner and whether or not to have children. Those who choose to have male partners must successfully negotiate nontraditional role allocations in their homes in order to persist.

Gender segregation in the US workforce is a key strategy in coercing women into doing more than their fair share of reproductive labor. It externalizes and devalues care work in both the home and the digital economy, where caring, service work is taken up by "many women, people of color, and precarious workers" in order to survive (Sharma 2018). It is a process in which people's options are limited; it is the logics of oppression. The absence of paid parental leave and affordable childcare in the US encourages individuals to make inequitable compromises that reproduce traditional gender roles. Gender segregation is yet another form of structural violence that plays an influential role in whether women can exercise economic independence and reproductive autonomy.

Reproductive labor is more than childbearing and childrearing. It is an also an economic question about the role allocation of the care work done to ensure human subsistence. Making reproductive labor a matter of care in computer science knowledge production is an extension of work done by other feminist anthropologists who insist that reproduction is not to be ignored in political economic analyses (Ginsburg and Rapp 1995; Browner 2001). I see a correlation between the concentration of power and wealth in the hands of white men in high-tech and the heavy lifting that precarious workers do for reproductive labor in society. This role allocation is distributed unevenly across race, ethnicity, gender, and sexuality, and the intersection of multiple oppressions can leave fewer options for economic independence for women of color and lesbian, bisexual, and transgender women than white cisgender heterosexual people. The labor required to maintain and reproduce the labor force, both on a day-to-day basis and generationally, is assigned to women through cultural sexism and the legacies of colonialism, thus denying the majority of the population rewarding and lucrative career opportunities. These stereotypes not only block efforts to fairly distribute the rewards and benefits of computing technology but also distract attention from the larger problems of a culture of overwork demanded by computing bosses and their inability to manifest their promises to serve the social good.

This culture of overwork in the US labor force correlates with the defunding of social resources by forces of neoliberalism, which has intensified unpaid work in homes and communities—a burden that women disproportionately shoulder, filling in the gaps between the state and the market in order to maintain the well-being of their families and communities (Benería 1999; Katz 2001; Bakker and Gill 2003; Ehrenreich and Hoschchild 2004). For these reasons, among many, women of color organizing around reproductive justice do not separate reproduction from their economic lives (Silliman et al. 2004). Anti-racist activists insist that reproductive control means not only having access to legal abortion and contraception but also access to the economic means to bear and raise healthy, wanted children (Nelson 2003)—and, I would add, the choice to remain child-free.

Understanding women's experiences persisting in computer science and engineering is critical to broadening participation efforts because they are members of computing with a unique insight into US culture. They are outliers—at once the "coding elite" helping to fashion the infrastructure powering algorithmic societies (Burrell and Fourcade 2021). But they are also transgressors who contribute to a field with great sway, a field with a considerable amount of force to exercise over individuals, communities, and the multitudes of global society. Most importantly, women of color, nonbinary, and white women technologists who persist in computing have powerful, multidimensional viewpoints on our society and can therefore offer a unique perspective on cultural norms and values.

Paying attention to these workers' experiences illuminated a contradiction of care that is troubling. Some of computing's most disenfranchised workers care about matters that are different from their Big Tech bosses. In fact, a good number of technologists have goals in direct contradiction to their organizations' deepest-held values, which are a fusion of corporatism and technofetishism. Workers are targeted when they challenge the authority of digital bosses or the story that computational machines are magic and the salvation to the wicked problems that face life on this planet. Retaliations, such as Google boss Jeff Dean's firing of Drs. Timnit Gebru and Margaret Mitchell from their leadership roles at the company's AI ethics team for writing about the environmental and social threats posed by large language models, make it difficult for individual workers to successfully use their technical skills in service to the social good.

In this chapter, I have pivoted away from traditional topics around reproduction common in gender equity spaces—namely, motherhood. Instead, I have probed two other dimensions of reproduction that play a role in the stubborn segregation of computing: (1) the stereotypes that operate in computing workspaces to constrain women's talents to feminine-coded caring services and (2) the thwarting of tech workers' collective altruistic aspirations. Work-life balance and parenting, while important to moving the needle on inclusion in computing, cannot be the only demand we make on computer science and engineering institutions. We must also organize around collective altruistic aspirations in Big Tech. Feminist activism is both an attempt to reconcile a yearning to make social change within the individualistic norms that govern computing cultures and, concurrently, an attempt to reconcile the paradox of being part of a highly privileged class of workers and, as women, being ruled by men from dominant racial groups. Navigating the terrain of rupture, combined with aspirations for transformative action, may be the incendiary combination that ignites feminist consciousness—and one that can lead to collective action in pursuit not just of gender equity in computing but reproductive justice in broader cultural domains.

What would a world look like where all women were financially independent and free from the threat of poverty? What would meaningful work for all people look like, and what relationships and labor allocations would support the regeneration of human life and the fair distribution of wealth, opportunities, and resources? What role would computers play in this more just world? Based on the evidence that I presented in this chapter, I conclude that the ubiquity of computer technology in our culture has not helped our society make great strides toward either economic or reproductive justice. In fact, given the ubiquity of computing and the exclusion of women from leadership roles in a range of influential fields that required technical skills, Big Tech's regressive reproductive politics may be contributing to the rise of policies and laws restricting women's access privacy and reproductive health care. To remedy this, we must continue to consider reproductive justice within the context of a society that fetishizes computer technology, reveres its makers, and tolerates harms targeting those who question such relations of power. Transforming the value of social reproduction requires reimagining what, if anything, computing technology can offer those who do altruistic labor that cares for others and society. Broadening participation in computing requires centering the altruism of its more marginalized workers, which could very well transform societal values in the US and the technological tools we use to reflect and honor these values.

4 TECHNICALLY, "YOU'RE DIFFERENT, AND DIFFERENT ISN'T FREE"

Technological acumen is a form of social power in US society, which is thoroughly computerized, with the majority of the population frequently engaged in activities involving computers or computer-based technologies. Conversely, the computing workforce is highly segregated, comprised largely of members of dominant classes. This chapter focuses on the production and design of computing technology and the subjectivities of its creators. My concern is labor in computing and how women workers' embodied experiences doing this labor can elucidate the cultural mechanics of the Bro Code. Because I once worked in Big Tech but have since stepped out to become an anthropologist, I include my "insider" experiences in the field as data and then bring a structural analysis made possible from an outsider's perspective. I do so as a feminist, to occupy a similar plane of vulnerability as my research participants (Behar 1996; Forsythe and Hess 2001), and as an action-oriented anthropologist who seeks to underline the importance of collective action among tech workers (Anderson 2006).

The heart of my analysis beats with the cadence of feminist anthropology. Joining this rhythm are other forms of inquiries into gender and computing, specifically the history of computing, social psychology, and feminist science and technology studies (STS). Together, they break down how gender relations in the field were shaped by traditional roles, rules, and cultural stratifications governing US industry and the military (Hicks 2017; Misa 2010; Ensmenger 2010b). Stereotypical ideals of masculine identity and technical identity were fused to exclude women from computer engineering, and they thus shaped the practices and policies in the postwar days of computing. Over several generations of programmers, these practices calcified into a deeply entrenched, masculinist culture (Abbate 2012; Ashcraft and Ashcraft 2015; Misa 2010; Ensmenger 2010a, 2010b). Women technologists are marked as different, othered, and I will show how this othering comes at a cost.

In social psychology theories, unexamined bias is an oft-cited factor in the perpetuation of gender segregation in science and engineering (Smyth and Nosek 2015; Banaji and Greenwald 2013; Moss-Racusin et al. 2012; Steinpreis, Anders, and Ritzke 1999; Committee on Science, Engineering, and Public Policy 2007). The public perception that computing is detached from social engagement and lacking communal purpose also deters women from entering and persisting in the field (Cheryan et al. 2017; Cech 2013, 2014; Diekman et al. 2010, 2016). Feminist STS finds similar connections between altruism, computing, and women (Blanchard Kyte and Riegle-Crumb 2017; Litchfield and Javernick-Will 2015; Garibay 2015; Hacker 1981; Faulkner 2000a, 2000b; Cuny and Aspray 2001; Margolis and Fisher 2003). Furthermore, feminist STS scholarship illuminates how gender troubles in computing are reproduced by gender schemas, chilly climate, and the historical, interpersonal dimensions of sexism in science (Wylie 2012; Valian 1999; Sandler and Hall 1986; Harding 1991; Schiebinger 1999). Jobs within scientific organizations are designed for workers with little to no reproductive responsibilities, a framework that is gendered in US society (Williams 2000; Acker 1990). This organizational design correlates with the persistent gender gap in these fields, reinforcing women's primary responsibility for labor in the home (Watt and Eccles 2008; Xie and Shauman 2003; Valian 1999; Schiebinger 1999).

These theories of the history of computing, social psychology, and feminist STS offer an interpretative framework that elucidates why women are so grossly underrepresented in technical fields. But the social matrix generating labor norms in the US workforce—the values governing cultures within computer science and engineering educational and industrial sites and the normative processes by which computing technology becomes constructed as masculine (Lerman, Oldenziel, and Mohun 2003)—still needs greater explanation.

FEMINIST ANTHROPOLOGY OF REPRODUCTION

Besides babies, bias, and altruism, what are other causes of gendered labor segregation in computing? Feminists have established that men from dominant groups hold cultural power that allows them to define social relationships, economic values, and the meaning and purpose of science and technology (Rosaldo, Lamphere, and Bamberger 1974; Collins 2000; Lohan 2000). Feminists have also challenged claims of universality and objectivity in scientific knowledge production, leaving the norms of dominant groups open to scrutiny and challenge (Haraway 1988; Harding 1991). The contributions made by feminist anthropologists, especially the insistence that reproduction be made central in cultural and political economic analyses (Chapman 2003; Ginsburg and Rapp 1995; Martin 1992; Davis-Floyd 1992), are integral here. They enable a fresh perspective that shifts the spotlight of inquiry away from the marginalized and toward the practices, values, attitudes, and performances of dominant groups. Thus, feminist anthropological analysis extends reproduction beyond the bounds of the physical to consider instead its ideological function in sites of computing knowledge production.

With notable exceptions (Clancy et al. 2014; Carr et al. 2000), experiences of hostility and overt sexism in sites of computing knowledge production are underrepresented in academic discourse. While unexamined bias, childrearing, and incongruent career and altruistic aspirations are extremely important to understand in efforts to end labor segregation in engineering, we must recognize, investigate, and protest male violence against women and nonbinary people in the scientific disciplines. As a corrective to this dearth of scholarship, this chapter reveals and interrogates hostile environments and inequitable labor relations in computing. It explores the cultural beliefs, values, and labor practices common in computing knowledge production; offers evidence of gender and sexual harassment in domains of today's computing workplace; and documents the ways in which women respond to this violence.

ENCODING AND REPRODUCING TECHNOCRATIC RULE

I take seriously Robbie Davis-Floyd's claim that US society is a technocracy, where technological progress is equated with social advancements, and this reigning ideology is a source of power for the ruling class (Davis-Floyd 1992). Her work illustrates how a cascade of technical interventions in biomedical birthing practices is driven by a pervasive fear of natural processes and women's power. This fear similarly pervades computer science departments and workplaces. To support this claim, I adopt and expand on Davis-Floyd's conceptualization of technocracy beyond physical reproduction to include the processes and production of computing labor that regenerate historical patterns of labor segregation. In doing so, I am able to use her theoretical construct to explore gendered ideologies shaping technocracy in the US and the opportunities and constraints of women's power in the production of computing knowledge.

Davis-Floyd's (1992) concept of rites of passage is also useful in interpreting participants' stories of discrimination and exclusionary bonding rituals that solidify male hegemony. Hegemony operates through both authoritative rule and popular consent (Gramsci 1971). In other words, coercive powers structure institutional norms of exclusion and inclusion and, when married with everyday norms and "common sense" ideologies, reproduce the power of ruling groups (Gramsci 1971). Excavating and naming rites of passage in computing sites of knowledge production can provide a deeper understanding of the process by which computing labor is gendered and racialized.

According to Davis-Floyd (1992), rites of passage have four purposes:

1. To give humans a sense of control over their environment
2. To protect initiates during their transition from one social status to another and tap into their vital power
3. To cement core values of the culture
4. To celebrate these core values to ensure the reproduction of a belief system

I adopt this analytical tool, first, to better understand the social construction of computing workers who create and maintain computer systems in the US and, second, to interpret male bonding practices, which often involve hostile behaviors. Finally, I question valorizing the technical over the social. Reproducing the belief system that technical knowledge is superior to social knowledge is a highly gendered rite of passage, invigorating and regenerating the value system that makes the rule of technocrats possible. These ritualized rites of passage signify the social matrix that creates the cultural values in computing sites of knowledge production. The core values developed and reinforced by these rites relate to formal modes of thinking that stress control, efficiency, and compartmentalization of knowledge. Initiates who maintain and reproduce such core values are considered meritorious and deserving of their success. These compulsory logics influence not only computing sites of knowledge production and computing commodities but, more broadly, society.

What do the experiences of women who are valiantly trying to desegregate computing say about *core values* binding masculinity and technology and the cultural reproduction of these values into a powerfully *dominant belief system*? Further, how can the transitioning identity of the geek from a lowly social status to an elite one inform analysis of initiation into the field and cultural nexus of power relations? I argue that processes and value systems by which people become computing professionals reproduce labor segregation in high-tech fields and reflect a culture ruled by gendered, technocratic ideologies.

GEEK MYSTIQUE

Since the advent of the personal computer, the social standing of the geek has changed. Gone are the days when the computer practitioner was a pariah, though the fog of this stereotype still lingers, negatively affecting the field by turning off young women from exploring the computing industry (Cheryan et al. 2009). The lone male computer genius is, in today's mythical landscape, "a true American hero" (Misa 2010, 261). US society labors under this *geek mystique*, where white males have much material and symbolic power but still struggle with a stereotype of social awkwardness. The contradiction between the geek mystique, the power that computing practitioners hold due to expert skills in an elite, prestigious field, and the geek stereotype is critical to understanding the specific kind of social identity that reproduces male hegemony in computing. Computer knowledge producers reflect and reproduce a value system that prizes rigor and precision over collegiality, numbers over stories, and strict codes, including dress. These values privilege dominant group members' identities.

Who is the geek, and who does the geek stereotype claim to embody and empower? As described by five of my participants in remarkably consistent ways, the stereotypical geek is a person of male gender identity who works in the dark and prefers machines to people. Karen, a white mid-career professor, described the geek stereotype:

> What you see on TV is that brains don't matter and pretty girls can't be smart. The mass media portrayal of tech workers isn't any more nuanced: you sit in the dark, eating pizza and playing video games.

Becca, a white doctoral candidate, had a remarkably similar description of the geek stereotype: "[Computing has] a negative persona attached. It's radical. So, it's a guy in the basement eating pizza and [drinking] Mountain Dew." Colleen Lewis, Ruth Anderson, and Ken Yasuhara (2016) also found the geek stereotype to be characterized as a singularly focused, asocial male. The content and the consistency of the language used to describe the stereotypical image of a computer scientist may be evidence of Davis-Floyd's second rite of passage, whereby an initiate is separated from a preceding social state.

The geek stereotype symbolizes how "competent" computing professionals move from the social world to the virtual one and, in doing so, signal their choice to prioritize the virtual over the social world. Other social activity is discouraged, and a myopic focus on computers is expected. Tony, a white male mid-career professional, explains how this manifested in his initiation to the field:

> I remember really clearly my first class at Stanford [University] in computer science. There was this guy who was on the basketball team. For all I know, he was on a basketball scholarship. And I remember the professor saying to him, "You have to choose—computer science or sports. You cannot do both."

Tony's undergraduate computer science professor is imparting technical wisdom, and he expects disciple-like reverence in return. This is an example of a rite of passage in the computing classroom that encourages one right way of producing knowledge to the exclusion of developing other talents and inquiries. This pedagogical approach also mutes students' curiosity about the integrated computational elements of a program (Turkle and Papert 1990). It translates into labor market practices where devices and systems can be integrated into a worker's labor practice without knowledge of their internal workings. This labor practice, called "black boxing" by computing practitioners, mirrors how the inner workings of the computing field appear to the majority of digital consumers: opaque and veiled in mystery.

Not only is social activity frowned on in computing, so too is socially applied research. Shawna, a graduate student in computer science, described her struggle to gain support from her adviser Rick to use qualitative social science methods in her research:

> Rick talks a good game, but he's not supportive of education research. It's a softer science. Oh, "veneer of science," that's how he describes it.

Computer scientists' resistance to qualitative science reflects the second stage in rites of passage: protecting computing initiates from dangerous outsiders who threaten ritual conductors'—senior members of computing—unrestricted access to the power that their acolytes supply to their system. As in other male-dominated institutions—for example, christian religious sects that declare that there is only one path to "Truth," one legitimate way to participate in the organization.[1] To make invisible the social, material aspects of computer practices is to create a cultural mindset whereby technical artifacts and those who make and control them are superior to those concerned with social need and social reproduction (Cech 2013). Who do these kinds of social relations serve best?

The geek stereotype has recently shifted from soda choice and social awkwardness to a peremptory bravado reminiscent of the stereotype of the nouveau riche. While many computing practitioners today are quite wealthy, a few obscenely so, this cultural shift is not a story of rags to riches but rather one of outcast to ruler, where the geek once stereotyped as a misfit is now a highly influential figure. The geek mystique not only helps to illuminate the particulars of the workplace environment that women technical professionals must navigate in order to persist in their chosen field, but, more broadly, it suggests a new stage of technology evolution in which power wielded by the newly initiated signals a new pattern of social relations (Hakken and Andrews 1993). This new stage is characterized by a white male hegemony over ideas and artifacts that has reached such a widespread level of dissemination that some computing experts can feel a sense of hubristic control over the paradigms of reality perceived by the majority of people in the US. This hubris informs a specific kind of masculinity at work in high-tech environments, one vital to cracking the code of labor segregation in computing.

CEMENTING CORE VALUES

Male hegemony in computing is a sign of a much larger imbalance of power in US society. Racial stereotyping is also programmed into the Bro

Code. The geek mystique operates in computing as a racial code (Benjamin 2019). For example, Emmanuel, a cisgender male software engineer from Ghana, responded to my question about whether he wore his current attire, a sweatshirt with an expensive label, to his high-tech workplace. "Yeah, this is cool," he said, touching the fabric of his ensemble fondly. "Unless . . ." Then he gently and methodically pulled the hoodie over the back half of his head and looked at me askew. Without saying a word, Emmanuel invoked the memory of Trayvon Martin and drove home the devastating costs of wearing a hooded sweatshirt while Black in the US. In Emmanuel's performance, he showed how traditional garb of coding experts is racialized. The hooded figure, a symbol of the Bro Code in current computing lore and its attendant power in society, is available to whites only.

Like common grooming habits and sartorial standards in US culture, men from majority groups in computing exert power by maintaining cultural norms that maximize their comfort while women and other technologists of color experience heightened scrutiny and surveillance. For example, Emmanuel said there is an unspoken rule among his male peers of color not to be seen walking or congregating in groups larger than three; otherwise, they felt hostility and suspicion from their white peers.[2]

The internal processes by which computing workers are initiated into and disciplined by this labor force elucidate the shifting parameters of power in tech environments as perceived and experienced by workers marginalized by their social identities. For example, the stereotype of the geek as someone who adorns their walls with Star Trek posters and builds towering pyramids of Mountain Dew cans in their cubicles and labs has evolved to reflect the foothold of power that computing professionals have gained in US society. Unfortunately, the evolution of the geek is not following a linear progression to egalitarianism or to a "democratic technoscience" (Eglash 2002, 61). Instead, the geek stereotype continues to signal the power of the "pale male" (Lazowska 2002) and the power structures that prioritize their comforts.

In other words, the geek mystique in broader society enables workplaces cultures that tolerate or even encourage the belief that white men have a greater competency in scientific and technical knowledge production than their peers. This cementing of social identity and technical prowess is a core value of computing culture, bonded by a technical fetish that reigns the day. This core value not only shapes the quality of the workplace environment but also plays a role in how commodities made by computer scientists are confused with society's triumphant progression toward freedom and democratization (Dean 2009). Some male practitioners leverage this phenomenon in efforts to achieve elite, even mythical, status in US culture.

"CUZ YOU'RE A GIRL"

Feminist ethnographers have documented male students' peremptory attitudes toward others in computing, especially women (Faulkner 2007; Barker and Garvin-Doxas 2004). Early initiates in the training phase of a computing career quickly learn which gender identities are most valued, and some avowedly heterosexual white men leverage this existing hegemony to bolster their feelings of belonging and competency.

Sharon, an Asian American undergraduate student, told me of the hostility her female friend experienced from a male peer:

> My friend's classmate told her that she wouldn't do better than him in Physics 122 because she was a girl. And I was like, "Oh, no, he did not!" Well, she got a better grade than him—so. That's the sweetest revenge!

Evelyn also had an experience with a male peer who presumed he was more technically competent than she was:

> We were doing the group project . . . and one of the guys was like, "Oh, you're a girl. You don't know what you're doing. You can [make] the instructions pretty and all that stuff, but I'll take care of the computer." I'm like, "One, I know how to take care of a fan in a computer. Two, like—grrrr!" He thinks he's a geek god.

Both Sharon's and Evelyn's stories demonstrate that some male students feel the need to prove their competency by leveraging a sense of entitlement related to male identity. Sharon compares her peer's arrogance to a god complex, suggesting that his initiation into the computing field is a rite of passage similar to those who belong to orthodox belief systems predicated on an exclusivity of the faithful. The male peers of Sharon and Evelyn seek to belong in the technological community by dismissing and marginalizing their female peers.

Julie, a white early-career software developer in industry, also spoke about navigating sexist behavior in computing, this time on the part of a computer science and engineering professor:

> He was great . . . but he was the epitome of an egomaniac—I used to joke with some of my classmates that you would get a check minus if you're a girl who questioned what he said in class.

Julie's experience exemplifies women computer scientists' contradictory feelings toward and relationships with men in their field. In this instance, Julie seeks to work with a male professor who she respects, so she uses humor to negotiate his paternalistic attitude toward her. Both Sharon's and Julie's stories illuminate not only the sexism they faced but also the egotism exhibited by some men as well.

Doctoral student Shawna had a similar experience with a senior male computing professor. When she told him that she had decided to incorporate qualitative methods into her dissertation project—focused on helping disable computer users—he replied: "Well, you know, it's okay that you're doing, you know, lesser fields of computer science, because you're a woman." In response, she joked to me that she didn't take him too seriously because she had "more balls than him."

Becca, a white doctoral computer science student, experienced a similar conflict when her intimate partners dismissed her accomplishments because she is female:

BECCA: At my last internship after my freshman year . . . my boyfriend at the time was like, you know, the only reason you're getting this internship is 'cause you're a female.

COLEEN: Someone you cared about told you that?

BECCA: Oh, yeah.

COLEEN: Oh my, that must've been devastating. So, he said the only reason you got your internship was because you were a girl?

BECCA: Yep. That's not all . . . another ex-boyfriend I've had in this department, yeah, he was trying to explain to me how I was, like, of average intelligence and I'd have to work hard. He said he was more capable but didn't have as much work ethic or something like that. He told me that once. And then I started yelling and—basically what I got out of him—I was just drilling him 'cause I'm not afraid to drill somebody. And what he finally said was he was upset that I got so many more fellowships than he did.

Becca's former partners were threatened by her success and turned to sexist reasoning to bolster their sense of belonging in this competitive field. An illuminating exchange between Ava, an Asian American undergraduate student, and Cynthia, her white peer, demonstrates the complex gender relations in computing and how women's perceptions differ:

CYNTHIA: People don't like outright discriminate, or like [say], "Oh, you don't know what you're talking about; you're a girl." Like, I've never heard that or anything.

AVA: I have.

CYNTHIA: Like slightly seriously?

AVA: Very seriously.

Their exchange epitomizes two camps of women that I met during this research into male hegemony in computing fields: those who believe "outright" discrimination is alive and well and those who do not. Cynthia holds a leadership position in her engineering sorority and helps organize undergraduate women *as women* in engineering majors at a top research university. Based on this activism, and my two interviews with her, I believe that Cynthia knows that her field could be more welcoming to women, but she perceives her own and other women's paths in computing to be free of *overt* sexism. In this sense, she is different from some other female computer scientists who responded peevishly to questions regarding gender. For example, a female undergraduate student called the Grace Hopper Celebration of Women in Computing a "celebration of separatism," criticizing this women-only function as unnecessarily divisive and exclusionary.

My goal in the following section is to act as Ava did and offer stories documenting evidence of overt discrimination, including harassment. Others, like Cynthia, who want to fix the low numbers of women in computing, must recognize violence is at play in high-tech workplaces and in the halls of higher education institutions, whether or not their personal experiences confirm it. Taking this seriously and acting on it can inform and invigorate social movements to desegregate STEM and combat injustices that reproduce cultures of exclusion in these fields.

SEXUAL AND GENDER HARASSMENT

(January 2001): Tim D. was hired as a vice president and became my new manager. In Tim's first team meeting with his direct reports, he told a story about parading about our office building naked. He said a security guard asked him to put his clothes back on. Apparently, he was so tickled with this escapade that he returned to his office and called his 23-year-old female executive assistant at home at 9:00 p.m. to share it with her. I was disgusted and creeped out that he shared this story at our meeting as an "icebreaker."

Tim's antics—and others that followed—were the impetus for my attrition from Big Tech and the initiation of legal proceedings against my former employer, Colossus. The field memo above was taken from said legal proceedings. This naked parade of power was the most absurd thing I had witnessed, but not entirely out of character for an organization that actively cultivated and fostered male-bonding rites of passage to cement a stereotypical masculinity as a core value of the organization as it moved from being a start-up to a Wall Street darling.

I share my own story to support my argument that sexism and hostile environments in high-tech are reproduced not only through unexamined bias and microaggressions but also by sexual and gender harassment and the silencing of those who protest these injustices. Sexual and gender harassment were common in my research participants' lives, too. A male senior manager at Gryzzl (Cary 2015) groped a student participant repeatedly during her internship. A male student stalked a full professor, and when she brought this to her male chair's attention, he said she was "a bleeding heart liberal" who deserved what she got.

Julie, a white early-career user experience designer, connects this kind of sexism with hate:

> So there are the geeky kids who respect intelligence. Then [there are] the ones that have the ego problems that are threatened by women; it just doesn't end up going well. I mean, I can cater to it for a while, but I just lose. I mean, with women—like an ego-driven boss or manager—it's just a pain in the ass, but it feels like it's *really* a pain when it's a male having the ego issue being that you're female. Then you're dealing with hate issues—and sexist issues.

The emotions present in Julie's account tell us much about sexist male leadership in computing. The words "pain" and "hate" signal the level of violence imposed by male managers with "ego problems." To further support Julie's insights into male violence in computing, I share the details of an incident of harassment at a technology conference. Ada, an African American mid-career computer scientist, spoke out against sexism at a March 2013 PodCon conference and quickly became the target of hate. During a panel presentation, two men behind her made sexual innuendo jokes. Although flustered, she tried to ignore them. Then the conference featured a young girl learning to code. Ada says that this girl motivated her not to sit back and endure another instance of sexual harassment: "I realized I had to do something or she would never have the chance to learn and love programming because the ass clowns behind me would make it impossible for her to do so."

She tweeted a photo of the two offenders with the note: "Not cool." Ada was supported by the PodCon conference staff who spoke to the men and reminded them of PodCon's code of conduct. Her post went viral, and Ada was fired from her company "for dividing a community she was supposed to unite." In addition to losing her livelihood, she was the target of a barrage of racist and misogynist messages, including threats of rape, murder, and dismemberment. In this case, speaking out against sexism was deemed divisive, and a woman who broke the code of silence regarding sexism was threatened.

Like Ada, I was reprimanded at my high-tech workplace for calling out unexamined bias publicly in meetings. Both colleagues and superiors told me that these types of complaints were better handled one-on-one and in private. In private, I made repeated complaints of bias and both gender and sexual harassment to my boss and to human resources (HR) staff. I complained three times to HR about one repeat offender, a peer with whom I worked closely. My colleagues also made two complaints about him, and an anonymous female employee spammed our entire department about this man's incessant habit of sitting on the edge of a desk in front of women colleagues and scratching his testicles. The anonymous spammer insisted that he stop this form of sexual harassment. Not only was his behavior tolerated, but this former Navy officer was promoted to a senior leadership position by the department's vice president, also a former Navy officer.

CODES OF SILENCE
In her book *Lean In: Women, Work, and the Will to Lead* (2013, 12), Sheryl Sandberg asks technical women what they would do if they were not afraid; "I asked myself that a number of years ago," she wrote, "and I started getting on stages and talking about being a woman." It is telling that the woman whom *Forbes* magazine named the fifth most powerful women in the world in 2011 (Sandberg 2013) was afraid to speak about her gendered standpoint in cultures in computing. At the 2013 World Economic Forum's annual meeting in Davos, Switzerland, Sheryl recounted how her lawyer warned her not to speak out about discrimination in her field, to which she responded: "If someone wants to sue me because I'm talking about gender discrimination, go ahead" (Sandberg, quoted in Stewart and Wearden 2013, 2). In a more

just society, it would be the harassers and the institutions that tolerate them that would be worried about being sued, not the people targeted by harassment. Instead, in computing, men's treatment of women—undermining, objectifying, and harassing—is normal; it is simply the way things are, and women who speak out about this treatment risk punishment (Carrigan, Green, and Rahman-Davies 2021; National Academies 2018).

Still, it is important that women working in technology fields are finding the courage to share not only their experiences of sexism but also their experiences of a coercive pressure to remain silent. These testimonies break with cultural norms that marginalize women's voices and experiences as alien and unwelcome and expose these codes of silence. Still, as Ada's and Sheryl's experiences demonstrate, the potential consequences of transgressing normative codes in computing are steep. For example, Josephine, a white senior software developer whom I met at a computing conference, was mad about her company's "leadership problem." She backed up her feelings with numbers—only five senior managers out of 800 were women. After sharing this data point, she stopped herself, turned bright red, and said: "Hold on—I want to keep my job." Lawsuits, harassment, and unemployment are just some of the consequences women must consider before challenging male hegemony in computing.

Interpreting women's experiences in computing through the lens of Davis-Floyd's conceptualization of rites of passage in technocracy reveals several core values. First, women are not technically competent, and those who were "allowed" in the field are trespassing on male domain. Second, women are objects who exist for male gratification. Those who protest these normative values may face retribution, including lawsuits and unemployment.

RITUAL MATING: REPRODUCING THE BOND BETWEEN MASCULINITY AND TECHNOLOGY

The ideological marriage of masculinity and technical competency is maintained and reproduced by rites of passage related to organizational belief systems and power relations that favor the dominant class. Women's lived experiences and their emotions help to excavate the fundamental systems of belief undergirding computing: control, normative masculinity, precision, hysteria, hostility, hero posturing, and the superiority of the technical over the social. These beliefs, forged in the crucible of patriarchal power relations, form the social matrix of computing technology production. This social matrix is reproduced in ways best understood by Davis-Floyd's (1992) fourth intention of a rite of passage: celebrating the culture's belief system in order to reproduce it. Gendered and gendering labor processes serve to indoctrinate computing workers' to the core values in computing commodity production, including constant observation, intense evaluations of others, and the devaluation of sociality, with concerning implications for broader cultural domains in the US.

CONSCIOUS AND PERMANENT VISIBILITY

Just as consumers of digital technology sacrifice privacy for the convenience and pleasure of its tools (Solomonides and Levidow 1985; Zuboff 2019), so too do its producers. Some Big Tech corporations use proprietary open-source software to allow employees to oversee their peers' work. Lynn, a white early-career software engineering, defines this work style as "a cultural issue that does not appeal to women." It is not intended to exclude women, she said, but inadvertently has that effect because it is not an anonymous process and can make underrepresented group members feel that much more conspicuous within the organization. Thus, in addition to being tethered to one's mobile communication devices, computing professionals are accessible to their employers through competitive jockeying and peer oversight. Companies benefit from these practices because they foster a sense of urgency that gets work done more quickly. This scrutiny can stress even the most accomplished workers, like Lynn, who disdain the spotlight and would prefer to work without being constantly observed. Thus, in both the production and consumption of computing technology, actions are publicized and under constant observation.

HAZING CANDIDATES

Another rite of passage specific to initiation into the computing workforce is the public process of hiring interviews at technology corporations. Carol, a white senior software engineer, describes the interview process at her former job, saying: "We just drove the hell out of candidates." Her male colleagues, however, went easy on the female candidates and later doubted their competency. Carol vocally objected to her male colleagues' negative stereotypes about female candidates' competence but does not make a connection between this and the aggressive and grueling hiring process. Janice, a white senior leader in academia, *does* makes the connection between bias against women candidates and the structure of the interview process, stressing that the common practice of hazing job candidates needs to be transformed in order for gender parity in the computing workforce to be realized. Within the context of other labor practices common in computing, hazing candidates in the interview process makes more sense. It is the first of a series of rites of passage that convey repetitiously to initiates that excellence is defined not only by one's competency but also by one's ability to "hack" it: to endure and withstand derision and hostility in one's workplace.

RIGOR AND COMBATIVENESS

Many women who persist in computing take pleasure in particular aspects of their technical work, especially in the precision that coding requires. However, a dark side of this aspect emerged in this study, one that serves as another example of a rite of passage. The demand for control and precision in computing can lead to a combative climate that is differentially harmful to underrepresented groups. Diane, a senior academic who is white, told me, "[In] our field, because we're computer scientists, we're very precise, and I think we badger each other too much about precision. Like, if something isn't precise, you're going to be challenged, you know. And I think it's meant well, but I think it's wearying."

Other technical women reiterated Diane's sentiments, frequently citing the field's emphasis on "precision" and "rigor." Significantly, research participants viewed these values and practices negatively, describing them, for example, as "shoddy," "hypercritical," "nasty," "a bully mentality," "put-you-down BS," and "adversarial rudeness." Cultural norms on being precise and intensely accurate in order to ensure rigor creates "abrasive" communication practices and behavioral norms, thus eroding collegiality in sites of computer knowledge production. For example, Theresa, a white mid-career professional, described her experience:

> What I would see is, like, you know, we'd start these bug meetings every morning called "war team meetings." Literally, who yells loudest gets the floor. I would really feel good when I hear things like, "Damn, she's such a fucking steamroller." Absolutely! But then . . . on the way home, I would actually feel bad about my behavior at work, you know. I would cry a lot at work, because I also felt like I had no sense of self.

Another participant suggested that this combative behavior might trickle down from the top: "I have sat in the room with [one of the wealthiest people in the world] when he just goes, 'That's the stupidest thing I think I've ever heard. What are you trying to do, just destroy this company?'" When she told him that his behavior was inappropriate and to change the tone and tenor of his delivery, she was confronted with both the tears and anger of this powerful global leader. His employees who mimicked this behavior, like Theresa at "war team" meetings, reported feeling bad afterward. Tony, a white mid-career professional and former McTech employee, explained:

> I saw a lot of people be mean to each other and . . . people there would talk about how tough they were, but I saw so many people acting abrasive and tough and going back to their office and being upset about it. You know what I mean, like people are like; a lot of techies are actually very sensitive.

Tony asked us to consider the sensitive side of computing professionals. Theresa asked us to consider the divided consciousness that emerged while she negotiated a hostile workplace environment and her personal values. Both participants, I argue, exhibit signs of oppositional consciousness (Sandoval 2000), a rupture catalyzed by their attempt to reconcile their personal values with their organizational workplace culture. The sensitivity that Tony reminds us to consider happens away from public view. However, these private moments of reflection and reckoning uncovered in this ethnography offer possibilities for interventions that could help computing laborers integrate their personal values and their computing work. These moments represent computing workers' yearnings for a change in the core values espoused by their leaders. Women leaders are standing up to powerful men and refusing to tolerate their histrionics, suggesting that more senior women leaders could help change the entrenched combative cultural norms rife in computing workplaces. The impact that Big Tech bosses have on their workers' behaviors also suggests that educating senior executive leaders on the importance of collegiality may go a long way to improving organizational cultures in computing workplaces.

Cultures in professional high-tech settings are rigorous in the sense that they are harsh environments with extreme conditions, even for dominant groups members, let alone those already taxed by injustices in broader social domains. In other words, while hostile work environments are bad for all workers in the organization, these conditions have a differential impact on group members who are also targets of racism and sexism. For example, consider what it means to inhabit a woman's body when outnumbered in a male-dominated environment that rewards combativeness among colleagues. Now consider me, the only woman in a 600-square-foot conference room with three men. The vice president of information technology (IT), a 300-pound former Marine, screamed at us while pounding his hand on the table. All I could think was, "He's blocking the door. I can't get away." This frightening experience of fearing violence in my high-tech workplace has led me to pay close attention to fear in other women's narratives to better understand men's coercive power at work in computing and how this power operates in concert with the ideologies of technocracy to reproduce male hegemony in one of the world's most influential, lucrative fields.

PERFORMING THE AMERICAN HERO

A male executive from Transco shared another example of how some men perform power in computing. He described his experience of his supervising two groups—software engineers and hardware engineers. Before important product launches, the male-dominated hardware team would find a big bug a week before launch and want to hold up the time line. The storyteller refused them, so they would stay in the office all night and day, not shower or go home, eat pizza and drink soda, and "heroically" deliver on time. Afterward, the boss would give them all awards. One day, the female director of the software team said to her manager: "Do you notice my team goes home at five every day, including during launches, and we deliver no problem on our deadlines—no drama and no awards?" The male executive was stunned to reevaluate the situation in this light. He reflected, "The women-led, more diverse team made the work look effortless—on time, every time."

The male-led hardware engineer team periodically created crises in order to look like the "heroes." Janet Abbate (2012) argues that since the advent of computing in the 1950s, the field has constituted itself as being in "permanent crisis" (Abbate 2012, 73), and she claims the manufacturing of crisis was a challenge to disciplinary boundaries and gender identity. Similar dynamics were at play in the gender performances in the IT department at Transco. The male computer scientists, in this instance, performed a particular kind of heroism that included a willful denial of self-care and positive health practices. Were they trying to embody the now-elite status of the stereotypical geek while also performing the popularized discourse of the new "American hero" (Misa 2010), blazing cyber-trails in the digital landscape? My interviewee stressed the gendered nature of the performance and his own reverence of it. Why did he reward this behavior, even though his female-dominated software team produced steadily reliable, positive results? The Transco executive's story pulls back the curtain to reveal the patterns of behavior creating "heroic power" in computing culture, whereby heroes are celebrated for their feats and their behavior idealized for other members of the culture to emulate.

I was very familiar with these types of histrionics in my interactions with the software architects and engineers at my former job. The nontechnical members of our interdepartmental team—all men, save me—would often roll our eyes at our colleagues' theatrics and referred to them wryly as "the high priests of IT." Masculine ideals in computing and increasingly prestigious occupational identity combine to generate a mythical image of religious proportions. The "latter-day priesthood of nerds" (Misa 2010, 259) reflects a cultural aspiration of some technical workers, characterized by elite status, male separatism, and a not insignificant amount of dramaturgy.

EXPERIENCES OF BEING OTHERED

Senior women with whom I conducted life-history interviews frequently mentioned weariness or told stories of the exhaustion of their peers and mentees. Listening to their reflections on critical phases of their careers, I got the sense that the transition from advanced education to the professional world was particularly stressful. In other words, for women in computing, the early-career stage, the passage to professional life, is particularly perilous. Proving oneself and finding new networks of support after leaving others behind is difficult enough without the additional taxation of being a member of an underrepresented group in a field that prizes aggressive critiques.

Diane, the senior academic quoted earlier, explained:

It's not that people are bad, or people are negative, or people want to put you down—it's just the way we think, and the way we behave, and the way we're trained. And it's just wearying after a certain point, but it's especially wearying if you're a woman and you're not really ever getting any good validation, and criticism is all you're ever hearing. It's very wearying. I'm getting really tired of it.

Women's attrition from scientific fields in the early- to mid-career stages is often explained as the woeful overlapping of the tenure clock and the biological clock (Xie and Shauman 2003; Williams 2000). This is an incomplete conclusion. Regardless of whether a woman computer scientist wants to bear children, she must still confront dominant gender norms that reward women for some behaviors and punish them for others.

For example, Susan, a white senior computing professional, augments Diane's discussion of women's exhaustion, connecting it with epistemic violence:

> It seems that we still have to prove ourselves more than the men do, still have to show we're just as smart as everyone else in the room. For many of us, over time that effort simply gets exhausting, and we leave the profession.

Susan illuminates how women's capacity as knowers is doubted in computing, an injustice that seeks to denigrate women's intelligence and constrain them from articulating, and perhaps even consciously understanding, their experiences within male hegemonic modes of knowledge production (Fricker 2007).

Carol, the white senior software engineer quoted earlier, told me that epistemic violence works not only to disqualify women's scholastic, strategic, and creative contributions but also our lived experiences. Carol had been in computing for almost 30 years, having got her start by working for a fast-paced company much like the one depicted in Tracy Kidder's (1981) classic tale of bringing the personal computer to market. As Carol explained: "One of the biggest barriers [to equality] is having to be a guy. You're surrounded by guys. You want to fit in. You don't want them to see you as different because as soon as you're different, you don't belong." She worries that speaking from her standpoint as a woman and using her own "modalities" to describe things would violate gender norms proscribed in her workplace. To minimize being different, she not only adopts male-centered modalities of thinking, she also censors herself:

CAROL: I just found, after decades, that to be exhausting. I think it grew on me in ways that I didn't expect it to, you know. It's just little things, right. It's just like—there's just probably a thousand different little things that you would do different, like lunchtime conversation. All the things you can't say. You know, "Oh my God, I have cramps today." Or . . . "Goddamn, I forgot my earrings this morning." I mean [those things are] just irrelevant, but you're running this filter all the time. As long as you're running that filter, you're not just you but they are themselves—they are comfortable.

COLEEN: So, say you did bring up something that goes beyond "the filter." What would be the consequences?

CAROL: Uh, you get marked as being different. . . . You know, you're different—you're different. And different isn't free.

Carol suppresses her emotions at work and feels it necessary to hide elements of her personality related to her female identity. If Carol's "outsider within" (Collins 2004) perspective equates difference with oppression, then, paradoxically, being free means not being herself at work. This type of discomfort that some women feel when transgressing boundaries of gender and technology may be culturally designed to maintain male hegemony. Participants in this study reported how much they worked to "prove" their competency, rigorously performing their technocratic worth, despite their "othered" bodies. I was privileged to interview many powerful women who possessed self-confidence, a high regard for their competencies, and influence in their organizations. But these qualities came at a cost—an energetic cost. Much like Theresa (the "steamroller" quoted earlier), who felt she had lost her sense of self in her workplace, Carol relinquished a part of her authentic, embodied self and assumed a muted comportment to conform to masculine norm in her workplace. Over time this has taken a toll on her energetically. The experiences of participants in this study suggest a type of alienation unique to women and men of color in the computing workforce that could play a role in their high attrition from the field.

Sherry Turkle and Seymour Papert (1990) call for epistemic pluralism in computer science. Carol's experience asks us to demand more—ontological pluralism—the freedom to be fully human, fully oneself in the computing labor force. Carol feels exhausted from filtering out the elements of her being and behavior related to her body and gender performance. Her coerced behavior appears a manifestation of what Kenji Yoshino (2007) calls "covering," toning down a disfavored identity to fit the dominant norms of one's culture. In Carol's experience, the cultural norms at her company, whose products are used by billions of people, insist on gender performances that conform to stereotypical masculine characteristics. These relations of power reinforce the ideological bind between computing competency and a particular kind of racialized gender identity that oppresses through cultural norms and penalizes individuals expressing "othered" embodied experiences.

Assimilating into white male hegemonic practices, epistemologies, and behaviors does not necessarily mean that you pass, but it may mean that you successfully avoid "being singled out." For example, when male colleagues draw attention to a female coworker's gender, it can serve to maintain male hegemony and valorize maleness as a measure of prestige and competency. The often violent "other-ing" of femaleness in computing signals the "fragility" of male gender identity (Harding 1986) and the regeneration of sexist labor practices in a global industry that, paradoxically, prides itself on innovation.

CONCLUSION

Nancy Hartsock (1998, 107) argues that "women's lives make available a particular and privileged vantage point on male supremacy, a vantage point which can ground a powerful critique of the phallocratic institutions and ideologies." In our digital era, many people consume computing commodities, but very few create them or critique them. A significant majority of the creative few are male. Women computer scientists and engineers have a unique social identity, and their stories and experiences paint a concerning picture of the institutions that produce computing technology and the gendered labor conditions within them. Far from meritocracies, many computing organizations are instead ritualized sites of initiations for an elite class. I found patterns in my participants' experiences that elucidate values and behaviors unique to dominant group members in computer science and engineering fields.

The stories of women in computing and their underrepresented male peers illuminate the *geek mystique*, a cultural phenomenon whereby the geek has transformed from unpopular to powerful, thus incorporating the values, practices, norms, and symbolic identities of this unique stereotype of masculinity into everyday sites of computing knowledge production (Smith 1990). This cultural phenomenon is made possible in this digital era of technocracy. We live in a culture that worships technological artifacts, reveres its makers and often equates the two with human advancement. However, in the production of technology, the geek mystique rewards and empowers some people while denying and denigrating others. Despite the triumphant, even revolutionary rhetoric that heralds the innovative promise of computer technology, the power relations in computing classrooms and workplaces suggest regressive and oppressive behaviors rather than egalitarian, democratic ones.

Mapping the structural, epistemological, and interpersonal elements that constitute the geek mystique illuminates the ways that dominant class rule in computing is maintained and reproduced. In this chapter, gender dynamics made plain the means, method, and scope of male hegemony, which ranges from naked parades of power to dogmatic impositions of combative behaviors, precise rationality, and intense evaluative styles. Rites of passage characterized by precision, aggression, hysteria, and the eschewing of social activities and socially relevant research make clear the core values that form the social matrix of computing technology production. These core values—enforced and reinforced through these rites of passage—stress control, normative masculinity, hostility, and the superiority of the technical over the social. Initiates who maintain and reproduce such core values are considered meritorious and deserving of their success. These compulsory logics have implications for computing commodities, organizations, disciplinary norms, demographics, and, more broadly, society.

Despite popular claims to the contrary (see Ceci and Williams 2011), overt discrimination is alive and well in technology fields. Research participants' private moments of reflection and reckoning reveal a conflict between their personal values and their organizations' values. These contradictions make the violence of the dominant group's rule visible. Women in high-tech fields face marked differences and constraints, and how they navigate and evaluate their experiences of being in the minority informs strategies that can eradicate the barriers that prevent them from accessing powerful, lucrative positions. Furthermore, transforming computing culture from hostile and aggressive to welcoming and collegial has the potential not only to change who produces computing technology but also the core values of its production, with possible impacts on social applications.

5 WOMEN MAKING CULTURE: PROFILES OF PERSISTENCE IN COMPUTING

Kelly knew at the age of six that she wanted to be an engineer. She loved math and science, and this passion, along with the popular television show *Star Trek*, inspired her occupational aspirations. One day she told her neighbor that when she grew up, she wanted to be chief engineer on the starship *Enterprise*. The boy laughed at her. Twenty years later, their paths crossed again. Kelly recalled: "At 26, I had my doctorate in engineering, so when I met him again, it was my turn to laugh." Even at a young age, Kelly knew her mind and her emotions and remained undeterred by sexist derision of her career goals in technoscience.

Leith Mullings (1997) coined the term "transformative work" to refer to everyday work that women do to resist and transform constraints in their lives. Mullings developed this concept while doing fieldwork on Black women's reproductive strategies in the context of the politics of Central Harlem. This experience laid the groundwork for generating and sustaining broader social movements dedicated to justice. While often time-consuming, stressful, and exhausting, transformative work can be a source of satisfaction that comes from caring for community (Mullings 2005). Mullings's concept is a useful frame with which to valorize the labor (enacted both individually and collectively) required to negotiate and mediate social inequalities in computing organizations—labor that cares for and sustains marginalized communities under siege by interpersonal and institutional violence.

In this chapter, I blend Mullings's analytic frame of transformative work with Dorothy Smith's (1987, 1990) feminist approach to institutional ethnography to make sense of how women in computing persist and what their experiences can tell us about institutions ruled by the Bro Code. Smith pioneered "a method of inquiry that problematizes social relations at the local site of lived experience" (Walby and Anais 2015, 211). Women who navigate organizations ruled by managerial, organizational, and controlling processes that produce ideologies to legitimize domination become alienated from their own experiences (Smith 1987). These processes, as they are manifested in this study, are what I call the Bro Code. This chapter presents excerpts of stories from participants in this study who resist this alienation and persist in computing education and workforce. Three themes structure this chapter—emotions, sponsors, and strategies to persist—and each helps us to understand, respectively, the personal, interpersonal, and communal dimensions of the lives of technoscientists' who persist in computing despite intersectional constraints. I highlight participants' personal characteristics, aspirations, emotions, and support systems (both kin and professional) and the labor required to overcome cultural and interpersonal barriers to contribute to the computing profession and, by extension, US culture. The women in the present study dare to compete as equals of men in arenas where—as demonstrated in previous chapters—the Bro Code dominates. Their lived experiences can help inform the public on the inner workings of a highly secretive, powerful field and offer opportunities for collective organizing to contest the outsized power Big Tech wields in our world.

Of particular interest to me is to document what Smith (1990) calls "rupture," moments in women's lives where they feel the tension between their own consciousness and the reigning ideology and cultural norms of the Bro Code. As Hyejin Iris Chu (2011, 57) observes, "Women in engineering live on the boundary between two different worlds. One is the world of engineering ruled by men—invented by fathers and built along patriarchal rule, [while] the other is womanhood." Women transgressing this boundary must negotiate the dictates of two very different worlds. Stories gleaned from my research on these transgressors offer an interpretative framework through which we gain a broader understanding of how gender, race, class, and technology are constituted and how these factors interact to produce the Bro Code. Viewing the work that women do in computing as potentially transformative means more than just striving to desegregate computing and advance individuals' careers. It also requires unpacking critical elements in a technical career that limit or impede efforts to use one's talent in computing to advance social justice. Throughout this chapter, I want to celebrate the efforts and emotions of women who persist, despite formidable odds, and emphasize my participants' efforts to not only transform their own lives and workplaces but also to use their technical skills to transform our culture through social change.

In the chapter ahead, when I first introduce a research participant, I will provide their pseudonym, gender identity, race, career stage, subfield, and the type of institution they were navigating at the time they spoke with me. In subsequent references to these participants, I will note their pseudonyms, with their race and institution type in parentheses.

EMOTIONS AND CREATIVE COSTS

A significant majority of this study's participants expressed proficiency in math and science, and credited this talent for their participation in computing. For example, Julie, a cisgender, white early-career software developer in industry, said: "I got into engineering because I had strong math and science scores. I mean, consistently." Additionally, computer scientists and engineers can feel intense pleasure and exhilaration for their work (Hacker, Smith, and Turner 1990). When I asked Julie what she enjoyed most about programming, she became brightly animated: "I loved learning how to test and fix and try and find which switch is the one that's off—aha! It's cool." Participants particularly enjoyed analytical challenges. Alisha, a cisgender African American doctoral student, told me: "I enjoy the intricate nature of computers, the speed that you can do [work] with the computer, and now they're getting smaller and smaller, and you can do much more [than] you could do maybe five or ten years ago." Brandy, a cisgender Asian American doctoral student, said she liked combining logical and creative thinking in programming, and the problem-solving part especially motivated her career in computing research. Sylvia, a cisgender African American doctoral student, also discovered programming in college and described the experience in terms of love:

> When I went to university, I took a computer science class just to see how it would be. It was Intro to Visual Basic, and I was just in love with it, I loved programming, and we had to create our own program. I loved it, so then I just switched to computer science. . . . I just found it was so fun, and I fell in love with this creative thing that I did.

Diane, cisgender and white and a senior leader in academia, also fell in love with programming in college: "When I got to college and learned how to program, I loved it. I knew I was in the right field, right away. Yeah, so that was nice. I love to program. I really enjoy it." Carol, a cisgender white senior software engineer in industry, called herself "a tools gal. . . . I got really lucky. I found this process that pays obscene amounts of money, one I find deeply satisfying." These narratives reflect participants' passion for what they do and challenge the Larry Summers Hypothesis (discussed in chapters 2 and 3), which denigrates women as incapable of excelling in mathematically oriented fields. The present research debunks this perni-cious myth to show that mathematical acumen and passion for program-ming can motivate women's career aspirations and support their persistence in computing. Beyond protest of this cretinous dimension of the Bro Code, my attention to participants' emotions about their work highlights the parts of their job in which they feel engaged rather than estranged.

Though the Bro Code dictates that logic is superior to emotions, male technical workers also displayed passion in their work. During participant observation at a small civic-minded start-up, I observed a six-person team launch a new product. An authentication password was crashing the server. The team was in a flurry of activity. The team leader, an expressive, jovial fellow, opined: "[It's] Murphy's Law; right before a launch, something will go wrong!" As he returned furrow-browed to his computer, his colleague, Joe (cisgender white male), lit up and a satisfied grin crept across his face. I knew even before he announced it that he had fixed the problem. He was keenly emotive but shared his success casually, in an offhand manner. I learned later in an informal chat with his colleague, outside their workplace setting, that Joe is introverted and very stoic. I was lucky to witness Joe's emotions, the pleasure he derived from his programming skills, since he adheres to a Bro Code norm to hide emotions.

Tony, a cisgender white senior leader in industry, shared further insights into the emotions and pleasure derived from computing work, saying "some programmers are in love with the creativity of a creation. They think of themselves as makers, like, a maker of culture." It is understandable why computing professionals perceive themselves as makers of culture. People in the US live in a world mediated by their creations. High-tech laborers are culturally significant in the twenty-first century as bearers of technical knowledge and, as Tony stated, "makers of culture" (Oldenziel 1999). Tony then juxtaposed this love and pleasure with another dimension of the Bro Code: "There's a culture of workaholism. Culture of abrasiveness. Culture of, like, hierarchy, where people treat you like shit if they can—if they're higher than you. And I don't see why the work has to be that way." Combativeness and a culture of overwork are the price that workers in computing pay to do what they love and to reap financial reward. This conflict between one's intrinsic passion and talents and the culture of the Bro Code needs attention. It is these moments of contradiction that may signal rupture (Smith 1990) in a computing worker's consciousness, sparking recognition that the Bro Code denigrates creativity and the contributions of people with less power in a society stratified by race, class, gender, and sexuality. Perhaps then, this rupture might motivate women in computing to resist marginalization in this field, not (just) to assert their rights as women but to assert their right to pursue a career motivated by love and passion and to contribute to society as a maker of culture.

My data suggest that women who persist in computing are extremely driven to succeed. For example, Joe, a cisgender white undergraduate student, had this observation:

> Girls within the department tend to be at the top of the department. Like, if they're in there, they tend to be at the level of awesomeness. Yeah, and they're more involved with getting internships. They tend to take heavier class loads. They tend to focus more on their schoolwork. They're much more driven than men.

On the one hand, women's grit to succeed could be a way of finding a sense of belonging. On the other hand, within the context of the workaholic culture, the drive to exceed expectations in an already intense field could have negative consequences (e.g., poor health outcomes). Further, it could be a consequence of the internalization of what a number of senior women in this study, observed: "Women have to be twice as talented to be considered half as good."

BRAGGING

In previous chapters, we have explored some behaviors attendant to the Bro Code—namely, competitiveness, combativeness, hazing, and bullying. Janice, a cisgender white senior leader in academia, added another dimension to the Bro Code, which she calls "macho behavior":

> Macho behavior is the experience you have when you go into a class—it particularly happens in early computer science courses—[and] there are one or two

people in the class, almost always male, who have been working with computers since an early age. And they are just so excited to meet a computer scientist—a real one—that they can't stop talking about their skills. "Oh, I did this when I was 12."

Janice considers this macho behavior a form of bragging and one of the most significant barriers to women's persistence in computer science undergraduate education because it intimidates those who did not have the social resources to tinker with computers during childhood. It is one way that men from dominant groups in computing enact the *geek mystique* (a concept I explored in chapter 4), a performance of power and confidence predicated on cultural codes governing masculinity and computing technology. Becca, a cisgender, white PhD student, described how this type of behavior turned her off from computing. Of her undergraduate experience, she said:

> I love math. Computer science was to me, like, the most evil thing, and I never wanted to do it. What happened was there were a lot of people that were more technically inclined than me, I guess. I had the math background, but a lot of them had the computing background, and it was really daunting that other people were just kinda, like, whipping through these assignments. These guys would tell me: "You just do this . . ." and I'm like, "Huh? I've never heard the terms before." I just felt really left behind.

Becca's experience in introductory computing was intimidating. Her male peers, early adopters of computing, did not explain terms but, instead, acted as if the next steps for assignments were obvious. This lack of support signaled that she did not belong, which affected her emotionally and colored her perception of the computing field as "evil."

IMPOSTOR SYNDROME

Tara, a cisgender white academic, described her experience with this particular form of macho behavior, which was similar to Becca's:

> I took computer science [in high school] because I thought it might be interesting, and I hated it. And the reason that I hated it is because I thought that I wasn't any good at it. And the reason that I thought that I wasn't any good at it was because there was sort of a guy who was across the way from me, and I mean, he knew exactly what he was doing with the coding. You know, he could code it all instantly. And it took me a really long time, and I really felt bad at it. But, in fact, I was not [bad at it] because we took these exams—the class was affiliated with a local university, and we took their exams—and I was the only person in the class to get any sort of "A" on the exams, but I didn't feel like I knew what I was doing.

Janice (white academic leader) had a name for the feelings Tara expressed—the impostor syndrome—which she described as "the feeling you have that everyone else but you thinks you're really successful. I suffer from this big time. And yet deep in your heart, you just don't think you're that successful, and you just feel like you're going through the motions . . . you feel like a failure." Janice stressed that the impostor syndrome can persist even when one is getting external validation of success, like Tara was when she found out she was the best in her high school class at college-level computer science exams.

In contrast, Theresa, a cisgender, white mid-career academic who identified as feminist, expressed a strong dislike of the impostor syndrome concept. Theresa felt the concept kept the focus on individual women's struggles and dangerously framed the Bro Code as an internal barrier to overcome rather than as a symptom of a cultural problem in computing. In other words, the impostor syndrome reflects a personal cost of navigating a hostile culture, an internalization of a culture that signals that women are less talented and less competent than male peers. Internalizing these Bro Code values means one can begin to feel as if they are true. "One day," Theresa remarked, "I will have the balls to do an anti-impostor syndrome workshop at Grace Hopper [Celebration of Women in Computing conference]." She felt the conference needed to foster more structural critiques of sexism rather than further burden women with the charge to fix themselves to assimilate into their technical classrooms and workplaces.

Theresa's critique of the impostor syndrome prompted me to examine who among my participants discussed this topic. In this study, only white women said they feared they were merely simulating the role of a competent computer scientist. Though several women of color were candid with me about the pain that white supremacist patriarchy caused for them, none mentioned or displayed the self-doubt characteristic of the impostor syndrome. White women who identified as feminists, like Theresa, also appeared to have robust skills for coping with hostility and the ability to analyze individual experiences within the context of structural constraints.

For example, Sylvia, a cisgender African American doctoral student, shared how she overcame her self-doubt as an undergraduate: "I had this one class that was really difficult, which made me think, 'Why did I commit to computer science?' But then I found that everyone was having the same problem with the class—then I didn't feel too crazy." Realizing she was not the only one struggling was a moment of consciousness-raising for Sylvia that inoculated her from discouragement. Diane, a white senior leader in academia, experienced a similar consciousness-raising moment. When she was unhappy in her first tenure-track job, her friend helped her to examine the situation and shift her criticism away from herself and onto her institutional environment. "It took me a while to figure out that it was the hostile environment, and it wasn't me or the job itself," Diane reflected. The danger of the braggart form of the Bro Code is it can isolate minoritized group members and foster self-doubt and isolation, which threatens women's persistence in the field.

Shawna, a transgender, white early-career academic, adds another layer to this aspect of the Bro Code. She described how some male professors in computing exacerbate feelings of isolation and incompetency in their women students:

SHAWNA: I had some official mentees; we had set up a first-year mentoring program, and my mentee was really having difficulties working with her adviser . . . and she was having some difficulties in some classes. There was one day, in particular, where I had five female grad students come by my office [to] talk about how they were the only one who had done really, really poorly in this class.

COLEEN: Oh, they all thought they were the only one, too.

SHAWNA: The instructor had pretty much taken care to suggest that it was only their problem; [he] did not mention that it was common. [By] the third one, I'm like going, "Wait a minute, you do know that there are other people in class who didn't do as well as you." They had no idea!

Note how Shawna framed the male instructor's role in this experience. He did not assure women that they were not the only ones struggling with the complexity of course material. Further, he went out of his way, Shawna believed, to make them feel alone in their struggle. I was not surprised when Shawna told me that this instructor was an adherent of the Larry Summers Hypothesis. Shawna thus designed her mentoring strategies around counteracting this pattern in the Bro Code to help her students build self-efficacy, which means having positive feelings toward the tasks you do, their value, and your ability to successfully complete them. It plays a significant role in women's persistence in engineering (Marra et al. 2009).

Women of color in the present study often expressed high self-efficacy. For example, Olivia, a cisgender African American doctoral student who left her Big Tech job mid-career to pursue social computing, took great pride in her accomplishments and found overcoming barriers rewarding. When I asked her what other women can learn from her example, she declared: "Hey—I can do anything—kids should see that!" Regina, a cisgender Taiwanese doctoral student, stated: "I do want the image of computer geeks to be overthrown. This is why I like being [an athletic] performer. I'm like, 'Hey, I can kick your ass physically, and I can also sit in front of a Mac.'" White women expressed more self-doubt and lower self-efficacy as compared to women with other racial and ethnic group experiences. This could be due to my whiteness affecting what participants were willing to trust me with. It could also mean that white women, as compared to, say, Regina or Olivia, are more susceptible to stereotypes about proper gender roles because of particular enactments of patriarchal relations within white communities in the US. In contrast, participants of color in this study were highly adept at showcasing their ability to act as agents of their own destiny (Browner 2001; Maternowska 2006).

I was especially impressed with the self-assuredness expressed by Alisha (African American doctoral student) and her ability to self-advocate:

> Coming from my background . . . even to get into this program, [I knew] it wasn't easy. I knew I wanted to get into this program but I had to, you know, talk to the adviser [and] let him know, "Hey, I'm a hard worker. I can get in there and do the work." But my background is so much different from a lot of students that come here. Some of the classes they've taken I may have not taken. But, I got in and worked hard, and I did a very good job.

Alisha had to bridge gaps in academic preparedness and move from a predominantly African American community to a computer science and engineering program with only one other African American student. Then, she gave herself credit for navigating these circumstances with aplomb. When I pressed Alisha on what motivated her to overcome challenges such as successfully networking with her predominately white and Asian American peers, even when she felt out of place, she stated firmly: "You just have to." Later in our conversation, she recalled a period when her motivation to finish her dissertation research lagged; ultimately, what spurred her to continue on was "the accountability factor, because I have people counting on me." She persisted because she wanted to make her family proud and be a role model for younger folks in her community. This finding supports my prior research in which students who have overcome structural obstacles in the pursuit of educational achievements are motivated not only by individual personal gains but also by commitments to family and community members (Carrigan et al. 2019). This "accountability factor" signals that for those who have faced social disadvantage, persistence in computing is an investment in a collective identity and community.

SPONSORS: TALK BACK AND PASS IT ON

Women in this study relied on more than their internal resources to persist in computing. My data revealed a consistent pattern whereby the positive influence of others' support and encouragement was crucial to participants' success. All participants were sure to tell me about the people who have inspired them, supported their careers, and helped them navigate hidden rules, avoid pitfalls, improve skills (both technical and social), minimize stress, and advocate for advancement. These "sponsors" had a significant impact on my participants' aspirations, networks of access, and strategies for persistence. A sponsor differs from a mentor in that their support is highly visible, as they use their authority to actively advocate for those they sponsor. Sponsors take mentorship to another level: they not only give advice to their mentees, but they actively support them, go out of their way to help them avoid pitfalls, and invest in their mentees in a holistic sense. "Where a mentor might help you envision your next position, a sponsor will lever that position for you . . . a sponsor believes in you more than you believe in yourself" (Hewlett 2010, 5).

SAME-GENDER SPONSORS

Evidence suggests that women faculty in computer science and engineering have a positive impact on women's persistence in the training stages of computing careers (Diekman et al. 2010). My research supports these findings. For example, Whitney, a cisgender Latina graduate student, told me how she is inspired by women faculty in computing: "It feels really great to take classes with female professors. It makes me feel proud and I want to be as accomplished as them." Becca (white PhD student) spoke highly and frequently of her sponsor: "Both she and I label her as my academic mom. . . . She just basically opened all these doors for me. . . . She's a blessing, seriously." Alisha (African American doctoral student) described how her sponsor outlined a long-term career path for her:

> There is a very influential person from my career environment. She is the deputy director of the laboratory that I work in. My research center has seven labs. The lab that I worked in is the Information Technology Lab, and she was the one that kind of got me along this path, [saying] "Hey, you need to get your master's; you need to get your PhD," [and] putting me in different leadership development courses, leadership development programs. So, I give her a lot of credit for the place that I'm in right now.

Sylvia (African American PhD student) also described the importance of her sponsor in her career choices:

> Dr. Keller [name changed] was amazing because she is the one who got me into Minority Access in Research Careers. She would tell me I should apply to this program and I didn't—I just didn't—and so she called my dad and told him I would be amazing for the program. So, oh my gosh, I applied, I got in, and even now she still encourages me.

Carol (white senior leader in industry) described how her sponsor's support inspired her to do the same for other women:

> [My sponsor] was just completely awesome, and I was this young woman in her purview, and she scooped me up. Now, whenever there's a young woman in my field of vision, I scoop her up. It is just that culture matters, and if you care about culture, then it behooves you to pass it on. . . . I have my ideas of what culture should look like . . . probably more now that I'm more senior and definitely old enough, as the saying goes, to wear purple. I really don't give a rat's ass what you think. . . . I know what culture should feel like. I know how we could treat each other.

Carol invoked culture here and how women passing on the mentoring they received early in their career can help to transform computing culture currently ruled by the Bro Code. Carol's sponsor, a legend in the history of US computer technology, gave Carol concrete, practical advice about her male peers that not only released Carol from an ongoing burden but also gives us further insight into another aspect of the Bro Code:

> It's like, these guys, they're always talking about [how] they're working on this really important thing and this other guy's working on this seriously important thing. I asked my mentor, How do they know that this stuff is so important? She said, *"They're making it up"* [author's emphasis]. And it was so helpful; it's like this huge load off my shoulders. . . . It was such a boost of confidence [for] me . . . to know the stuff that you think is bullshit, you might be right.

In chapters 1 and 4, I discussed at length this kind of mythification—an entrenched, speculative belief system that reproduces the chasm between what Big Tech leaders say they are contributing and their actual impact on society. Myth-making plays out both globally and locally. Examining it locally, in computing organizations and from the perspective of people who work from their margins, some men in tech cultivate a geek mystique by bragging about their prior experience with computers and speculating about how their technical outputs are of monumental import. In graduate school in the 1980s, Carol's male peers convinced her that their aspirations were true facts. Their triumphalism may have sprung from material, ideological, and cultural forces that undergird the power of Big Tech on a global scale. This aspirational, cocky form of the Bro Code mirrors the global PR campaigns of their billionaire bosses—men who look like them and whose divine mystique trickles down to these bros by virtue of their birthright. Carol's sponsor helped break the spell of the geek mystique early in her career, a critique that encouraged Carol's persistence and her transformative work in computing to help other women succeed, too.

Same-gender sponsors can also make crucial interventions that increase persistence in computing. Shawna (white early-career academic) described how a female full professor kept her from dropping out of her graduate program:

> [The toxic relationship] with my adviser just kept getting worse and worse . . . and eventually it led to a point where I was on the verge of a mental breakdown. . . . I had given up. Rebecca [name changed] came into my office one day and said, "I'll help you find a new adviser." Honestly, I am saying that moment was the whole reason why I stuck it out in grad school. I actually called her out with a special acknowledgment at the end of my defense, because I can honestly say I would not be here without her.

Shawna's sponsor, Rebecca, gave her options other than sticking it out with a male adviser who was causing her serious harm. Beyond providing individual support to Shawna, Rebecca also worked communally to spearhead organizational networks of support for graduate students in computer science and engineering:

SHAWNA: I will say that [my school has] improved the safety nets quite a bit, and that's all Rebecca's work.

COLEEN: Can you be more specific? What safety nets?

SHAWNA: So, basically what Rebecca does is, you have a review of progress every year. Before no one really paid attention to it. Now, both our graduate adviser and Rebecca go through each of those reviews of progress and identify potential at-risk students.

COLEEN: Oh, wow!

SHAWNA: So then they reach out to those students; in particular, Rebecca reaches out.

Rebecca was performing care work in a solo capacity, a role not formalized as a department policy or procedure and yet one Shawna credits with her persistence in getting a doctorate in computing. Shawna valorized this labor performed outside the Bro Code, and we would be wise to consider at what cost to Rebecca this labor came. Same-gender sponsors are indeed critical to desegregating computing, but senior women should not shoulder this responsibility individually. They deserve institutional support, including resources, recognition, and recompense.

CROSS-GENDER SPONSORS

Given the low numbers of women in computing and especially in senior leadership positions, women graduate students often rely on men to advise their thesis and doctoral projects. Unlike Shawna's hostile adviser described above, some men excel at cross-gender sponsorship. For example, Wendy, a cisgender white leader in industry, spoke fondly of her male mentor:

> In my case, I had a male Engineering Fellow who was very supportive of women engineers and worked hard to make sure we had opportunities. He understood the importance of the technologies I worked on and asked challenging questions. I also had a woman VP who was quite skilled at working the system and sometimes felt pressured to give up her own technical career. She knew where the roadblocks were. Both listened well [and] offered great advice and a shoulder to lean on when things were not going too well.

Diane (white academic leader) also stressed the supportiveness of her male graduate adviser and connected his support to her persistence in computing, despite the high rate of attrition among her female peers:

> Well, I was lucky. I had a great adviser. He was incredibly supportive—I mean, there were women dropping out around me, and I don't think I had the awareness to really understand, as well as I do now, the dynamics of why. So it wasn't

good for everyone, is what I'm trying to say, and maybe I didn't appreciate how good I had it at the time.

After Olivia (African American PhD student) finished her master's in computing, she decided she "was done with school." After seven years of working in industry, however, she grew tired of working only to expand the corporation's bottom line. She returned to school to get her PhD in part because of the impact of one of her professors:

> Dr. Dave had great classes. He brought industry to classes; most of the other professors were dull. Dr. Dave made computing part of the real world and made me want to teach. He inspired me to become a professor.

Though men dominate the senior ranks of computing, glowing reports of their sponsorship of women were few in the present study. The stories I have shared tell us how impactful this essential skill of mentoring is to broadening participation in this influential field. Skill in mentoring and sponsoring early-career practitioners is not innate to people of certain genders and race/ethnicities; rather, it is a skill that should be encouraged and rewarded in senior practitioners. Unfortunately, it is not. This transformative care work is still, at present, valued and enacted outside the Bro Code.

ALLIES

Men in computing need to join efforts to desegregate the field and destabilize the imposed dominance of the Bro Code. The best way to foster support for diversity in STEM from dominant group members is to create, recognize, encourage, and recruit allies. An ally is someone who advocates for minoritized group members but does not share their social identity. Male allies are needed at all stages of computing careers—from peers in the educational stages through senior levels of leadership.

Men can be effective allies to women in computer science and engineering, especially men who are underrepresented in other identity aspects, have a female partner who works in computing, share equally in domestic responsibilities, or have a daughter (NCWIT 2013). Julie (white early-career software developer) gave me examples of this kind of support:

> With my current coworkers, they are a lot more socially adept [than past colleagues]—they're not hard-core academics; they've studied more, like, art and design, but they're kind of still dudes' dudes . . . they played sports, and they like to party a lot, but they're all married and have daughters, which is something

that's really cute. It is cute. And I think it makes men a little bit cooler to work with when they have a daughter and they're close to their wife. It makes a huge difference—or if they have sisters that they really like.

Joy and Kara, two cisgender Asian American undergraduate students, explained in a group interview what it is like to have male allies who "are cool to work with."

JOY: Just because I also have guys who are in my group, I feel like they're just—they're just gentlemen.

COLEEN: Okay. So, then, you feel respected?

JOY: I do. I mean, a couple of people, they're definitely a little more self-absorbed, and they don't like to interact as much with me. But, I mean, I want to say, like, maybe five out of the seven people in my group, they've treated me pretty well. Maybe I've just been lucky and I've been sort of just working with . . . stand-up guys, but I don't know. They're always just kind of, you know, like, "Oh, it's a woman. Let's be nice to her." It probably does help that I'm usually the one who knows what I'm doing, too.

And, for a similar perspective, there is this comment:

KARA: The only professor who I think kind of noticed females for a second was an ally, 'cause he sent out emails to a few of us [women] saying, "Hey, I just want to let you know, congratulations on doing really well in my class." And he's just sort of a sweet guy.

During my participant observation at a small civic-minded start-up, I observed Agnes, a cisgender, white early-career professional, interact with three male coworkers who displayed ally behavior:

AGNES: Thanks for holding my hand, Ken. I feel safe here with all you smart people. I learned two new shortcuts.

AARON: Now you are around other tech people all day. You'll learn lots of shortcuts instead of languishing in isolation!

TONY: Yea—and thanks for fixing my mistake, Agnes—you get an eagle-eye badge!

Rather than showing off, Aaron made a point of making Agnes feel a part of the team, and Tony credited her with helping him. These are two examples of ways that men can practice welcoming disenfranchised practitioners in high-tech.

These narratives share a common theme: women in computing appreciate being welcomed, respected, and valued by their male peers. Males in computing leadership positions have the opportunity to make institutional contributions to inclusivity. For example, Jason, a male senior leader in industry who is cisgender and white, described his hiring policy at his start-up. With the goal of hiring more women, he requires hiring managers to interview women for engineering jobs even if "on paper" they do not appear as strong. He noted that evaluation of candidates privileges a small slice of technical skills to the devaluation of other skills needed for the job. In the interviews, the women often impressed the search committee and were hired. Jason's analysis of gender politics was nuanced and astute, especially his anecdotes about how some male computing professionals not only self-promote but also manufacture drama for attention and accolades. In my eyes, Jason cemented his status as an ally when he implicated his own behavior in his critique, demonstrating the self-reflection and humility required for men to become part of the solution to cracking the Bro Code.

KIN

Kin—in the sense of both one's first family and one's chosen family—also played a role in this study in women's interest and persistence in the computing field. Alisha (African American doctoral student) remarked: "My father has been a great influence in my life, and he told me a long time ago, if I could understand science and math that I could basically do or be whatever I wanted to do—whatever I wanted to be in life. So, I took that to heart." Olivia (African American doctoral student) was also inspired to become a computer engineer by a family member:

> My uncle is an electrical engineer, a genius, and he introduced me to a new side of things. He would explain things in two or three different ways [and] tell me another way to approach the problem until I got it. I admired that he could teach me all these different ways, and in school there was only one way explained and I felt lost. My uncle opened these doors for me . . . that was the engineer in him. I wanted to be like my uncle. I have friends that get stuck all the time, and I can teach them what my uncle taught me. He said: "Don't let anyone call you stupid." He often said: "We can do it."

Parents and close family members are not the only people who inspire women to invest in a computing career. In the course of this study, I found that male partners also encourage women to take up computing as a career and persist. In fact, every woman in this study who was in the mid-career or senior stage of her career and partnered with a man had an agreement in which her career took priority over his. Helen, a cisgender Asian American graduate adviser in academia, first clued me into the influence of partners on women in computing. She keeps in touch with women long after they leave the program. She talked about her students, both present and former, in terms of genealogy and likened them to her "grandchildren . . . a family tree." From her position in this lineage, she observed that the majority of straight women who persist in computing have steady male partners who support their careers.

Tara (white early-career academic) told me that her male partner suggested she take computing classes. She said: "He definitely helped me a lot, especially in the early classes." Carol (white senior software engineer in industry) also described the role a male partner played in her becoming interested in technology:

> It was the very early eighties, and there was a very big recession. I got laid off, and I tried so hard to find another job in that field and there was just nothing, nothing. And one day I was home doing nothing, and my boyfriend at the time who worked at Data Inc. [company changed] . . . he had a book, a manual that he had brought home on microcode. . . . I picked up his manual because I was bored and read it, and when I was done I tossed it over the side of the chair and said, "Well, that's trivial." And my boyfriend at the time said, "Are you serious?" And I said, "Well, yes." And he said, "Well, if that looks really easy to you, then you should consider doing this" because there were not a lot of people who had degrees in computer science at that time.

Thirty years later, Carol still credits her ex-partner with helping her find a lucrative job that she loves. When I asked Jessica, a cisgender Asian Canadian undergraduate student, if she had a mentor, she thought it about for a minute and said: "My partner is in tech also and helps me regularly . . . perhaps he would come closest as a mentor."

Janice (white senior leader) told me about being recruited for an executive position in academia and how her daughter Fiona and husband Phil supported not only her autonomy in decision-making but also her nonrational approach to this life-changing choice:

JANICE: I kept on trying to drop out of the search 'cause I really was not interested in moving. And [the search committee] kept on saying, "Just come to meet [us] 'cause we want to calibrate other candidates against you." And then, "Just come and do the on-campus interviews," et cetera. So, they make me the offer and I say, "I'm not coming if I have to make the decision quickly. . . ." And by this time, Phil, my husband, was probably more in favor of going than staying because he found the school we were at really quite arrogant. It really is quite arrogant. . . . So, we're having lunch in the airport. And my daughter Fiona says, "Mom, I know what you're going to decide." And I said, "So, tell me." She says, "No, I'm not willing to take that kind of responsibility for your life." I said, "Fine. Tell Dad I'm going to go off and find a ladies' room. But as soon as I make the decision, I want to be able to check with you [to find out] if you knew or not." So, anyway, she told him. And then the next day at 3:00 p.m. is the phone call when I have to make a decision. And I'm sitting looking out, you know, [at] a gray, drizzly day. I'm looking out at the water, and I'm painting. And, all of the sudden, literally, the clouds part, and a shaft of light hits the water, and it's a quarter to three. And I went over to Phil and I said, "Phil, could I choose to go to [the new university] just 'cause it's this magical thing that we're going to miss if we don't go . . . even if I don't have any rational reason to choose to go?" And he said, "Sure."

COLEEN: For magical reasons, he supported you?

JANICE: Yeah, . . . then I ask Phil what Fiona said I was gonna do. And he says, "Oh, she knew you were going to move. She's watched you for the last three weeks, and you were trying really hard to find a reason to go. But she knew you'd figure out some reason or other to go."

COLEEN: She knows you well.

JANICE: Yeah, she does.

Janice's "kinscript" is a testament to how women's intimate relationships influence their computing career trajectories. It is a positive example of the concept of "rupture" (Smith 1990), a moment in the technical woman's life when the tension between her own consciousness and the reigning ideology of rationality in computing are in conflict. Janice had reached an ascendant position of leadership in a field that values formal hyperrationality. With the support of her family, she made decisions using a more creative, nonrational process. Janice's story of her career path and decision-making process speaks to a yearning to follow one's heart that loved ones can best empathize with and support.

LEAVING HOME

In order to advance their careers, other participants had to make difficult choices related to place. An important element of pursuing a computing career trajectory is the willingness to move away from home for a degree program or job opportunity. The theme of transitioning from one place to another frequently came up in my interviews. Race also emerged as an important factor in this theme. Participants from historically underrepresented racial/ethnic backgrounds described their transitions away from their homes and away from their kin with varying degrees of pain and discomfort. Alisha (African American doctoral student) described her experience moving away from home to attend an out-of-state school:

ALISHA: So, coming from the environment that I come from, I guess it's home, because I'm from Louisiana [state changed], so I already knew a lot of people in my work environment before I even got there, just on a personal level, just knowing them because I'm from Louisiana. And coming [to Pennsylvania and] not really knowing anyone, um, really, I'm the minority either way you look at it. The first time I came here, I . . . felt like an outsider. . . . As the semester progressed, and even in that second semester, I got more comfortable. I met more students, and the second time around, since I'm back this semester, it's like I've made a few friends and I feel more comfortable in this environment.

COLEEN: So why did you return to Louisiana?

ALISHA: I just really love home. . . . I like to travel, but I really love the South. So, when that opportunity came to return home, I jumped on it.

Sylvia (African American doctoral student) also noted the shock of homogeneity that greeted her at a predominately white institution:

SYLVIA: I went to Wisconsin [state changed] for school, and I'm African American. There's not [many] African Americans there. So, I went from seeing, you know, everyone like me, to like, aw! I'm just seeing everyone of [a] different culture!

COLEEN: That must have been a big shock, too!

SYLVIA: It was! At first you start feeling self-conscious about yourself, wondering "Huh? Everyone else looks the same way." Everyone started looking the same way, and I was just self-conscious, like, there's something wrong with me. I think time helped me work through that.

Olivia (African American doctoral student) also took some time to acclimate to her new community:

> After graduation, I decided to go into industry. I was a little burned out on academia. [My company] was awesome. I moved to Seattle from the South. [Seattle is] a predominately white area—at first, it was tough to socialize outside work. But I started to get close to people.

These stories of transitioning from one's community to a solo member of one's race and ethnicity in predominately white communities testify to the price of pursuing a computing career as a woman of color (Malcom 1976). When considering the social impact of computer technology, the disciplinary norm requiring practitioners to move does not allow women, and particularly women of color, to practice their skills in their chosen communities. Furthermore, there is additional evidence of rites of passage operating within computing. Rites of passage, a phenomenon discussed at length in chapter 4, are formal practices that codify core values in a high-tech culture to ensure the reproduction of the underlying belief system foundational to the Bro Code. In the case of leaving home as a rite of passage in the field of computing, it divorces workers from their communities and social fabrics more generally while privileging the global, the virtual, and the ideals of the hypermobile ruling class.

STRATEGIES FOR PERSISTENCE

In the sections above, I reported the personal characteristics and interpersonal relationships that are crucial to women participants' successes and advancements in computing. In this section, I share persistence strategies that women learned "on the job," not because they are foolproof or even desirable courses of action, but because they can shed light on the social dynamics in computing cultures that marginalized workers must navigate to persist.

THICK SKIN AND DARK HAIR
Once, at conference in Silicon Valley hosted by a Big Tech corporation, Kate, a cisgender, white early-career academic, told me over lunch that she had a student who asked how to handle sexism in labs. Because I am a social scientist who studies this form of injustice, she asked for my advice.

The following field note demonstrates the conflict that I felt about my exchange with Kate:

> Kate asked me, "What do I tell her? It doesn't get better and to complain is dangerous." I told her to legally document every incident of sexism, no matter how subtle, by sending an email to yourself. I said, "Don't be afraid to get litigious; documentation over time is the best offense." However, later that night at dinner with Linda, a senior academic woman, I asked what her advice to this assistant professor would have been. She said the only way to persist in academic computer science and engineering is to toughen your skin and learn productive ways to vent.

In considering my field note, it is important to reiterate that I did not persist in Big Tech, whereas Linda has persisted in the field for over 30 years. Getting litigious on one's own, like I did, may not be the best strategy for someone who wants to remain in the field for the long term, because it will likely make one a target of retaliation, which affects one's ability to remain in the high-tech labor force. Kate's observation—"to complain is dangerous"—is chilling. Those who are targets of violence are then ostracized. For example, in my experience, protesting sexism hurt my career, and I gained a reputation for being "oversensitive," an agitator and not a team player. Timnit Gebru, an Black woman senior leader in industry, was fired from Google for several reasons, one being her critique of Google's diversity and inclusion practices. Gebru said: "Your life starts getting worse when you start advocating for underrepresented people" (Metz 2021). Emi Nietfeld, a former Google employee who is white, reported the sexual harassment she experienced at the company and was then targeted by exclusionary practices, even by coworkers she cared for and trusted (Nietfeld 2021).

After our dinner conversation, I wondered what Linda meant by "vent." I thought of group interviews where women discussed sexual and gender harassment and bias with levity and even humor. I remembered Diane's smile when she discussed her female colleagues who helped her get through graduate school. I thought about the impressive extracurricular activities in which many of my participants engaged—poetry, race car driving, acrobatics, marathon running, sculpture, and volunteering with underserved children. These could be framed as creative ways to "vent" and thereby relieve the strains of working in an intense field dominated by the Bro Code. These are all examples of both collective and individual forms of venting that women practice to persist as disenfranchised members of computing.

Elena, a cisgender, white senior academic, agreed that there is a certain amount of tolerance required in persisting. She said:

> In addition to the knowledge and skills required by their profession, I think that women in technical fields should have a bit of thick skin, to not be impacted by how different they may look in meetings, to ignore comments, sometimes intentional and sometimes accidental, about their not belonging, and to gently interrupt to take their turn in discussions.

Elena's "turn the other cheek" advice worried me at first because it encourages passivity in the face of violence. However, I concede that women on the front lines of desegregating computing must employ a range of strategies to order to persist. Many women in the educational phase of a computing career have taken this advice to heart. Corrine, a cisgender, white early-career professional, identifies as "a social person" and was one of three women in her undergraduate computing classes of 60 students. Early in her undergraduate career, she dyed her blonde hair black and continues to do so five years later: "Being known as both talkative *and* blonde isn't what I need." Joy (Asian American undergraduate) also drove home the importance of having a "tough skin," and she connected to the concept to hair color:

JOY: I guess if you're going into any of the STEM majors, you kind of have to have a tough skin.

COLEEN: Yeah. And how do you develop tough skin?

JOY: Kind of have to be manly, if you will. I don't want to say "manly." I feel like we're just adopting—male characteristics.

COLEEN: Which are?

JOY: Not like the—not stereotypical, like, girly-girl stuff. Limit the blonde moments.

By dyeing her blonde hair black, Corrine appears to be hewing closely to this Bro Code dictate. Blonde hair within the cultural domain of US society can denote sexual availability and a lack of intelligence (Urla and Swedlund 1995), both of which can be dangerous to marginalized community members struggling to prove their competence. Persistence may require, at times, acquiescing to the Bro Code, tolerating the hostility of peers and bosses, and navigating stereotypes about women.

BREAKING THE RULES

Conforming is not always the best strategy of persistence, though. Sometimes breaking the rules worked too. Sylvia (African American doctoral student) explains:

SYLVIA: You can do other things besides what they teach you. Like, for me, even though as an undergrad we would go in the classroom and [the professors would] be like, "Okay, create this project," and then they would give you this really boring thing, but what you can do [is] go to the professor and be like, "Can I do something else?"

COLEEN: Oh, good for you! And what did they say? What was their reaction?

SYLVIA: They used to always be like, "Sure, you can do whatever project you want."

Janice (white senior leader in academia) described how she and her colleagues were able to significantly increase the number of women in her department:

JANICE: We changed the intro course to [computer science], both in terms [of] the way it was taught and how the material was framed. The contents of the material provided more choice. So, for instance, we knew that women liked to have a sense of control over what they were doing. Actually, men do, too. And so instead of getting only one homework assignment, you can pick either of two problems to work on. Of course, they have exactly the same content in them. But one of them is a biology problem and one of them is a robot [problem], for example.

COLEEN: Oh, I see. So, they can choose the context, and the content remains the same?

JANICE: Exactly.

COLEEN: And it's the same problem-solving.

JANICE: Yes.

Like Sylvia, Janice demonstrates that when women are given more choice and agency in regard to the problems they solve, they are more likely to persist in computing. This suggests that the content of the problem being solved matters to women in computing.

Independence of mind also benefited Tara (white early-career academic) in persisting in computing:

TARA: The reason that I did not drop out is because I realized early on that one of the really important things in my graduate career was that you can't expect your supervisor to be everything. . . . You need to figure out where you are going to get various [networks of support] from. . . . I spent a lot of time figuring out what I wanted to do and where that diverged from what my adviser wanted me to do—what I should do anyway.

COLEEN: So, sometimes you pursued your own path against the advice of your adviser?

TARA: Yeah. . . . My adviser at one point literally said that he thought that getting a PhD should be one student sitting alone in a cubicle doing their work, and I firmly rejected that notion.

COLEEN: Oh, geez, that is the stereotype of the lone geek.

TARA: Right. So, you know, I said no, and I went out and I found support there. I rallied the other students, and we went out and had breakfast every other week at IHOP because that's how it worked out for us.

Tara rejected not only her adviser's advice but also a dimension of the Bro Code—the "lone genius" myth of scientific knowledge production—which, I suspect, is her adviser's idea of the best way to earn a PhD in computing and a relic from the Enlightenment era, long left behind in post–World War II scientific industry in the US. Tara broke this lone genius stereotype haunting the Bro Code by taking a collective, cooperative approach to her education, which proved critical to her persistence.

PUTTING OUR MINDS TOGETHER: COLLECTIVE ORGANIZING

The power of women's collective organizing was evident in my data. For example, there was great levity in my group interviews with women computer science and engineering undergraduates; struggle was shared and received with humor and, in these interviews, women expressed a confidence born of belonging. Diane (white senior academic) moved to the US from Europe for a graduate program in computing with four other women from her undergraduate program. They all lived together, studied together, persisted together, and graduated together in five years. Diane's self-efficacy was especially high when she talked about her and her cohorts' skills and successes: "We just felt like we were in charge of the rest of the class!" Much like the transformative work performed by the women in Mullings's (1997) study of reproductive labor in Harlem, women in the training, early, and mid stages of a computing career depend on their female cohorts to survive the Bro Code. Beatriz, a cisgender and Latina early-career academic, suggested that computing organizations provide funding to bring women together:

> There should be more money for mentoring—women mentoring other women. I'll tell you, [it can be] something simple. One thing that made a difference, even at Carnegie Mellon [university name changed], . . . was funding for lunch for female graduate students once a week. That made the difference, because we had to eat. And if there's a place where it's just women . . . where there's no men, you know, and you can just gripe and support each other, it turns out we all had the same problems.

These lunches not only provided "productive ways to vent," to use the words of Linda, the senior academic quoted above, but also facilitated moments of consciousness-raising that Sylvia, the graduate student quoted above, had when she realized others were struggling in her classes, too. Breaking with the loner expectations of the Bro Code and communing with other disenfranchised members of computing inoculated people in this study from resignation and attrition. Beatriz deftly framed these opportunities as institutional responsibilities that require monetary investment.

Until computing leaders institutionalize structures of support for historically disenfranchised members, women continue to find and create ad hoc solutions. For example, Anita Borg, a pioneer in computing, started a women's group in the women's bathroom at a conference on operating systems in 1987 in order to gather scattered, isolated women into a community with a collective identity (Abbate 2012). Cynthia, a cisgender white undergraduate, joined a sorority for women in engineering majors because she was the only one of her existing friends who was "science-minded" and felt welcomed by other science-minded women:

> What's great about the engineering sorority is you have that camaraderie where you meet once a week, and you just need to, like, bitch about some teacher or some class. . . . Everyone else knows what you went through; they all were, like, "Yeah, I totally understand. You know, it sucks now, but just wait a little bit, you're going to be fine." They'll give you hints, teachers to avoid, or hints on homework—they'll give you homework help. If you're struggling, we have what we call a scholarship chair—you go to her and [say], "Hey, I'm in this class. I am sucking at it right now. Is there anyone who can help me?" And then she goes and talks to people who took that class, or who are in the class right now. They're like, "Hey, so-and-so's struggling. Do you think you can like help her out?" And

we set up study sessions. And we have an old scholarship binder where whenever we feel like donating, we just donate our old homework or practice exams for future generations to go through and be able to benefit.

I asked Cynthia whether her woman-centered network of support functioned much like the "old boys' club" in terms of succession planning:

COLEEN: There's a legacy that you're putting in place for succession, for more women engineers to come behind you.

CYNTHIA: Yeah.

COLEEN: So, do you think that helps other women persist as well in engineering?

CYNTHIA: I think it really does. Kind of just knowing that you have a group of girls that you'll go have fun with. We try to take classes together. A lot of our newer pledge classes have been . . . bigger groups. . . . I was with a group of three. [Now] we've had up to, like, 11 girls in one pledge class recently. They become really, really close with each other, and really good friends, and so they all plan their schedules around each other. . . . They just all *put their minds together*. And it just fosters this more *collaborative* thinking, where everyone gets to the right answer faster, rather than all of them separately struggling.. [author's emphasis]

I stress the last part of Cynthia's comment to bring attention to the cognitive effects of women cooperating in computing, which augment the social support these women-centered collaborations provide. These values were also the impetus for the formation of the Latinas in Computing group, formed in 2006 at the Grace Hopper Celebration hosted by the Anita Borg Institute. African American women in computing also see the benefit of organizing together in the fight against the Bro Code. A program aimed at understanding the intersectional experiences of Black women in computing, sponsored by the National Science Foundation, found that "collectively creating an action plan for and by black women in computing . . . was beneficial for organizing a movement around black women in computing to fight against not being seen or heard" (Burge, Thomas, and Yamaguchi 2017). Women of color in computing have to contend not only with the misogynistic dimensions of the Bro Code but also the white supremacy and white privilege encoded into the field's culture. Fostering ways to collectively organize around race and racism—both in the computing discipline as a whole and in individual worksites—is critical to subverting the

Bro Code and the hegemony of white masculinity in the practice, production, and application of computer technology. These forms of organizing not only allow opportunities to vent and compare notes on the experiences of being marginalized in the tech workplace and foment consciousness-raising, they also help facilitate moments of respite from the imposition of the Bro Code. For example, early in her career, Carol (white senior leader in industry) took part in a group for women in systems, hardware, and design engineering fields. She credits this group mentorship with her career persistence because she had "a place where I was me—where I didn't have to be anyone else. I was with my homies, and this had a profound effect on my life."

CONCLUSION

In this chapter, we have examined—at individual, interpersonal, and institutional levels—women's lived experiences persisting as computer scientists and engineers. Despite facing barriers to inclusion, like their male colleagues' cocky assurance about their technical prowess and lack of institutionalized support to combat racialized sexism in the field, participants in this study persisted in their careers through the strength of their own passion and grit and through networks of mutual aid from other women, male kin and allies, and importantly, their sponsors. Their experiences can help elucidate what changes might transform the practices, demographics, and applications of computer technology. In chapter 6, I reflect on these experiences to suggest further actions that may nurture such transformative changes.

The majority of participants in the present study expressed aspirations to contribute to society—they want to leave the world a better place. I found a strong correlation between participants' social justice aspirations, their persistence in computing, and their personal commitments to supporting other women. However, technical fields have historically devalued and even denigrated social and humanistic knowledge and continue to do so today (Riley 2014). Further, they also thwart the social aspirations of practitioners in the field (Cech 2014; Litchfield and Javernochf-Will 2015), all while waging a relentless public relations campaign extolling the social revolutionary effects of computers (Carrigan, Green, and Rahman-Davies 2021; Dean 2002). This contrast between the exaltation of computing's social contributions and its actual outcomes is why there is a clash between my participants' yearning to use their computing skills for social good and the prevailing cultural values within the field. The resulting rupture that some technical women experienced offers the opportunity to amplify existing efforts to organize against the threats Big Tech pose to the world. Not only do the participants in the present study have insider knowledge about the cybernetic infrastructure that undergirds the global economy, they know all too intimately the harms and injustice perpetuated by the Bro Code.

To make sense of my participants' persistence and ruptures, I framed them in terms of transformative work—Leith Mullings's concept of the everyday work done to resist oppression that can be the impetus for larger social movements. The transformative work that some cisgender and transgender women and nonbinary people do every day in order to persist in computing can serve as a blueprint for cracking the Bro Code. When people who are far outnumbered in their organizations find ways to connect with one another, this communion can interrupt not only the process of internalizing one's toxic environment but also the myth-making power of technocracy. Computing workers who navigate their marginalized positions in their field by pursuing their aspiration for social justice "open up the possibility of common ground where differences [of class, race, and gender] might meet and engage one another" (hooks 1990, 13). Capitalizing on the shared yearning of some computing workers to contribute to the communal good may be a way to bridge computing's much-touted benevolentness and its actual outputs and impacts.

To do so will require further efforts at organizing and building coalitions. The informal and formal networks of support documented in this chapter occurred in academic sites and professional societies. Tech workers are also organizing. For example, in 2018, more than 20,000 Google employees across the globe staged a walkout against sexual harassment and systemic racism in the company (Wakabayashi et al. 2018; D'Ignazio and Klein 2020). Organizing against militarization, racism, and sexism in academic and professional societies has been increasing, and, as I discuss in chapter 6, further coalition-building with labor activism in Big Tech may prove beneficial.

6 TRANSFORMING THE COMPUTING WORKFORCE AND THE SOCIAL ARCHITECTURE OF ITS LABOR VALUE

Cracking the Bro Code, with an intersectional theory of care grounded in women's lived experiences in computing, aims to help transform the cultural norms and moral codes that constitute high-tech worlds. Gender and racial discrimination within computing worksites correlate with the unethical and sometimes unlawful activities of powerful institutions whose profound influence on the globe's population amplifies their transgressions to crisis proportions. In its current form, computer science makes human society vulnerable to surveillance, unemployment, weaponry, climate disasters, objectification, and instrumentalized rationality that undermines civil liberties and civic engagement. Also, Big Tech is anti-tax, and its success in avoiding civic responsibilities is decimating the states and communities in which Big Tech operates. Here, let me echo Maria Klawe's directive to President Barack Obama—it is urgent that we focus on injustices in the computer science and engineering workplace specifically. Despite the successes of #MeToo, the growing public criticism of Big Tech, and the promises made by its leaders to do better, its failings pose a serious and far-reaching threat to society.

Throughout this book, I have argued that solving problems generated from a matrix of gender, race, technology, and labor requires cracking what I call the Bro Code. It is not my intention to spotlight the white, masculinized liberal subject in order to reinscribe his power. Rather, I invoke the frame to study what values break institutional commitments to equity and justice in US society and how we are increasingly enculturated to tolerate such transgressions.

TECH LABOR ON THE CRITICAL EDGE OF CARE

Because of the generosity of mentors in technoscience, I have had the opportunity to be a part of the social movement to broaden participation in engineering and computing. This afforded me access to many sites in which I could do "deep hang" in technoscience culture. Further, my mentors in anthropology have shared with me the tools to lend critical insights into Big Tech's cultural failings that result in harms and social ruptures ripe for collective organizing.

By design, the majority of my participants are folks whom I call "tech persisters"—people who, despite facing steep barriers to access, opportunities, and respect in computing, continue to lend their labor and talents to the field. Many of them are change agents who challenge rather than serve the maldistribution of resources and regard in these worksites, often in collective efforts aimed at ending gender and racial segregation in science, engineering, and technology. They are the experts who have made my research possible, and I care about the role they are playing in challenging and resisting abuses of power in computing. Tech persisters are resilient. They navigate a culture trying to weed them out, often through harassment. I want you, esteemed reader, to care about the harms of incivility in computing workplaces and support those persisting in this labor force. Tech persisters take risks to tell their stories and organize, even in small ways. But is this enough to transform how the computing industry operates globally and correct its asymmetries of opportunities, power, prestige, and resources?

In the years following the completion of the formal interviews that comprise a substantial part of the data informing this book, more and more brilliant minds are defecting from tech and calling attention to its injustices from the vantage point of lands beyond Silicon Valley. Borrowing a term from Brian Barth (2019), I see people who leave tech and then agitate against its wrongdoings as "tech defectors." Tech defectors trouble tech from the outside—as members of independent nonprofit research organizations, social sciences departments, and labor union organizations. The relationship between tech persisters and tech defectors in the fight to desegregate one of the most powerful, wealthy fields in the world needs greater care and attention.

Those who participate in gender equity in science, technology, engineering, and mathematics (STEM) organizations have led a discursive shift in

US politics that has strengthened the verve and rigor of public critique of Big Tech bosses. Many of the tech persisters in this study had individual moments of rupture, when they recognized the ideologies of the Bro Code shaping their everyday experiences. This rupture often sparked mutual solidarities with other women and nonbinary technologists. For example, in February 2017, Susan Fowler's blog post about sexual harassment at Uber went viral (Fowler 2017). She had the courage to raise her voice and share her lived experiences of gender violence in Big Tech. Fowler's visibility in the public sphere as a whistleblower catalyzed a snowball effect for other people to come forward—people whose talents and well-being have been squandered in computing.

When you see a tech persister take such risks, you know that they are standing on the shoulders of other brave folks. Fowler says she got the courage to tell her story because, in formative moments of collective consciousness-raising with women and nonbinary peers, she realized many others had experienced sexually harassment at Uber and that the company was covering up its male employees' violence. A critical mass of consciousness-raising like this example culminated in a rupture at the level of the body politic in the US, weakening Big Tech's ability to enforce a hegemonic rule by tapping into cultural mythologies, tech fetishism, and the geek mystique (Ames 2019).

Many interlocutors in this study had experienced similar moments of consciousness-raising and were thus spurred to collectivize against racism and sexism in more formal channels.[1] Formal organizations give validity to word-of-mouth campaigns. Further, this validation of a woman's word can inoculate the testifier against the gaslighting techniques of troglodytes. These agencies have played a meaningful role in archiving and disseminating scientific evidence and lived experiences of gender violence in science and engineering; thereby, they remind us that it is not in our heads and that, in fact, racialized sexism is woven into the very fabric of tech organizations' cultural values. Further, as I described in the introduction of this book, leaders in these communities can influence policy at the upper echelons of government like Klawe did during President Obama's administration.

While tech persisters organizing from within the field of computing helped to dim Big Tech's "charismatic" shine in broader public discourse (Ames 2019), further efforts are needed to strengthen coalitions with tech defectors and eliminate impediments to collectivity formation and solidarity in the world of computing knowledge production. Failing this, equity advocacy in STEM may manifest greater fairness within workplace culture but will struggle to achieve justice.

Bourgeois politics undergirding technoscience are the "elephant" in the labs and boardrooms of computer science. This elephant is one "freighted with a legacy of having been built, in the first place, to shore up the positions of elite and powerful entities" (Dunbar-Hester 2020, 242). The social movement to broaden participation in science and technology, much like other progressive organizing efforts in information technology and communication fields, is in danger of being co-opted and commodified, thus reifying the very structures of power change that agents hope to undermine (Dunbar-Hester 2020; McInerney 2014). In other words, less harm and incivility in computing workplaces and greater representation of women and nonbinary coders will not alone solve socioeconomic imbalances of power wrought by computing technology.

In order to envision and enact social justice and a future for humanity beyond the dictates of Big Tech, I suggest forging formal and lasting coalitions between tech persisters and tech defectors in the quest to transform computing. The former have ample, streamlined organizational structures and wide networks; the latter have independent organization and a radical vision for the possibilities beyond the authoritative imposition of the tech commodity fetish and the logics of racial capitalism. While I have documented violence in high-tech workplaces, more research is needed to connect this violence to other forms of violence—for example, militarism, white supremacy, neocolonialism, tax evasion, surveillance, rapacious profit motive, wealth hoarding, and the amplifications of genocide and fascism around the globe. The good news is that labor organizing is already occurring in academic arenas of computing and industry. For example, Big Tech workers are protesting harassment and discrimination at their jobs (Wakabayashi et al. 2018; Schiffer 2021) and the racist and militaristic ends toward which Big Tech's products are being used (Singer 2019; Schneider and Sydell 2019).

Of course, the binary between tech persisters and tech defectors is merely a heuristic that I have taken up to think with, to spur conversation about what it will take to have egalitarian distribution of resources, opportunities, and regards when it comes to the production of computing knowledge. Much like the boundaries between academic computing and industrial computer science, the boundaries between tech defectors and tech persisters are porous.

For example, though I defected from the computing industry, the Bro Code is still a constraint that affects me professionally in both my ethnographic research and interdisciplinary collaborations with technoscientists.

The people you have met in this book have shared their stories from inside the bundle of relationships that comprise Big Tech classrooms and workplaces. Their stories can add to growing agitation against the violence perpetuated by Big Tech and the collective resistance to its undemocratic impacts on society. All of the worlds I traveled in this study demand recognition. This has been my aspiration, one I have not been able to do in this book evenly. Even when the worlds that tech persisters and tech defectors inhabit overlap, more work needs to be done to catalog their different goals and, more importantly, differences in their "epistemic cultures" (Rosner 2018a, 124–125).

To conclude this book, I will enact a politics of care that honors the lived experiences of those who work within computing while also mapping a path forward for more investigations into the social architecture of labor involved in creating and making computing technology. In the remaining sections, I suggest how the knowledge from this book can help to, first, build solidarity in the world in which computers are made and, second, envision and enact the world needed in order to realize a "type of democratic participation that a just society would require" (Dunbar-Hester 2020, 231).

BRO CODE ENFORCERS

In an effort to greater personalize harms in computing worksites, I offer five characters amalgamated from the narratives that emerged from this research. I recommend that women and nonbinary computer scientists look out for the following types of gatekeepers. Based on my own experience and the sentiments of feminist legal scholar Joan Williams (2000), I recommend that if you come across any or all of these characters, you send yourself an email documenting your experience, in case one day legal channels become necessary to your well-being and career.

THE LADDER KICKER
The Ladder Kicker is a woman in computing who purports not to see gender and emulates the norms and values of dominant group members, to the disadvantage of other women in the organizations. Elizabeth Parks-Stamm,

Madeline Heilman, and Krystle Hearns (2008) found that both men and women in male-dominated organizations penalize successful women. I found that women do so as a means to preserve their own perception of competency. More specifically, the Ladder Kicker understands that power relations in her organization can remain stable while allowing the token participation of women in its ranks and leadership. She therefore seeks professional advancement by, at best, ignoring female colleagues and, at worse, thwarting their advancement in the organization. Thwarting takes the form of either ignoring and diminishing the accomplishments and talent of other women, weaponizing tears when race relations are on the table, or showing preferential treatment to men when hiring, evaluating, and firing. In regard to firing employees, Ladder Kickers perceive their male peers as bathed in a halo of presumed competence and future success. Ladder Kickers help reserve power for men and raise the bar of evaluation for women peers. Unfortunately, they are often rewarded for kicking the ladder out from behind them as they rise. Their antitheses are women who lift other women as they climb, mentoring other women to persist and become leaders (Cech and Blair-Loy 2010).

THE OBSTRUCTIONIST

Diane, a foreign national senior leader in academia, described her mid-career phase this way: "It was just very difficult; everything I did there were barriers. It wasn't only that people were overtly hostile in moments, but it was also barriers; it was just, like, every time you want to do something . . . it was just difficult." Diane's experience reminds me of Tara's metaphor (described in chapter 4) for persisting in computing. She said she felt like she was beating her head over and over against a wall.[2] The Obstructionist cements that wall. The Obstructionist uses precision questioning technique—a method of questioning that borders on interrogation—to let women and other members of disenfranchised groups know they are doing or might do something wrong. The Obstructionist laments that they cannot work with you because your ideas hold little value. Janice, senior leader in academic computing, characterizes the Obstructionist as someone at the board meeting who is ready to tell you that your contributions are "little pieces of shit rolled into a ball." Women in computing will often encounter the Obstructionist in the mid-career stage of a technical occupation, as Diane explains. Sexism in the early-career stages morphs into a more confrontational style once women make their way to the tables where decisions are made. Variations of the Obstructionist include pretending to be an "advocate" while trying to stymy inclusive progress with precision questioning techniques framed as truth-seeking.

At the heart of the Obstructionist's defensiveness toward the voices of feminists and people of color is a commitment to what Alison Wylie (2012, 65) called "conventional ideals of objectivity." The Obstructionist truly believes that gender and race do not influence the pursuit or outcomes of science (objectivity) and that those who occupy the elite echelons of computing knowledge production are best and the brightest, not the blessed and the privileged (meritocracy) (Margolis 2008). My research and experience as a change agent in STEM supports Wylie's insight. For example, Renee, a white professional working as part of a diversity and innovation team in Big Tech, told me that, in my research, I have to find a way to answer the question that most preoccupies Steve Ballmer, a white cisgender male who was once chief executive officer at Microsoft: "Why diversify? Apple is innovative and it's not diverse."[3] Now, Ballmer is retired, and I am still fielding versions of his question from other senior technical men: "Why should I *care* about broadening participation in computing?" Like Renee, they believe my job as a feminist is to convince them to care about harassment and segregation. Like Dick (the man who mistook me as a wife at a strictly professional function), they cannot see my role in science as anything other than providing morally coded goods to men—as a nursemaid tasked with awakening their moral consciousness. Obstructionists camp out in science and technology Studies (STS), too, and encumber thinking about science as a common good. We who seek justice and meaning instead of generalizability as a matter of fact can be called normative and corrosive. We belong in the streets, not the ivory tower. The Obstructionist blends objectivity and meritocracy to try to discredit feminism and block widespread uptake of the movement to transform orthodox politics in technoscience.

THE CREEP

BECCA, THE WHITE PHD STUDENT: Some men are very, very cocky.

COLEEN: I've noticed that with computing. Some guys are really, really cocky. I went to interview some guy. We went out to lunch and he's like, "This is a great date. You know this is a date, right?" And I was like, "What the . . . ?"

BECCA: Wait, did that seriously happen?

COLEEN: It seriously happened. And I was like, "Are you kidding me?" I was shocked—so when you talk about cocky. . . .

BECCA: That does not surprise me at all.

COLEEN: So, tell me why it doesn't surprise you.

BECCA: I think [it is] the sexualization of females. . . . When I came to grad school, I was a target. I'm not even kidding. I had advances, like, full-on sexual advances by three guys. They didn't care when I said I had a boyfriend. They kept asking me out.

Stephanie Shirley, one of the first woman in England to start her own software company in the 1960s, described the sexist dynamics of computing in similar terms: "You were someone to be laughed at, flirted with, somebody whose bottom you could pinch" (Abbate 2012, 139). Sixty years later, the Creep is still alive and well in computing, sexualizing, and preying on women and nonbinary people early in their careers and, too often, protected by their institutions. For example, when sexual harassment allegations piled up for University of Michigan computer science professor Walter Laseck, the Information School severed its affiliation with him, but it was business as usual in his computer science and engineering department (Molina and Sussman 2021).

My own favorite story of the Creep will always be Tim, my "naked in the office" boss at Colossus (recounted in chapter 4), whom the executive leadership thought was qualified enough to serve as a vice president. Of course, Tim's unsettling behavior—getting naked in the office, calling his 23-year-old administrative assistant at home at 9:00 p.m. to tell her about it, and opening our first team meeting with this story—makes much more sense considering that Joe Buppo, Colossus's chief operating officer at the time, was widely referred to by women employees as "King Leer."

THE TROGLODYTE

The days of overt discrimination are not over, and the Troglodyte is living proof. In fact, reactionary politics are alive and thriving in Silicon Valley, and the Troglodyte is their spokesperson. Women with advanced degrees from the most prestigious computer science and engineering departments in the US academy told me how misogynistic the cultures were. In sum, not only were women faculty a rarity, but faculty members were very vocal about saying that women should not be computer scientists.

The Troglodyte appeared several times in chapter 4. Shawna recounted a story of a tenured professor in computer science who said it was okay that she was switching to a "lesser" subfield of computing because she was a woman, and Julie connected Troglodyte behavior to the "hate issues" some men have toward their women students and peers. Meredith Whittaker framed James Damore, a former Google employee who circulated a sexist manifesto at the company, as a quintessential Troglodyte (Whittaker and Taylor 2020). She notes that Damore's highly orchestrated distribution of a screed against his women colleagues (pivoting on *that* musty old chestnut—you guessed it—the Larry Summers Hypothesis) exposed the extent of far-right-wing extremism at Google and how it made transgender technical workers especially vulnerable.

THE HIGH PRIEST OF TECH

The High Priest is one who lords their technical skills over others. Like the priests from my childhood parish and my Catholic college, they feel called to their work. This sense of calling makes them vulnerable to illusions of grandeur and pedantic communication styles. The High Priest often uses acronyms to demonstrate an insider's privileged knowledge and embraces the meritocratic philosophy that manifests in a belief that those who are around the table are the ones who deserve to be there. High Priests are found in classrooms, bragging about their long history of tinkering with computers to impress professors and intimidate classmates. They are also the "geek ruling class" (Hakken 2003, 5) in high-tech corporations and academic institutions who perpetuate microaggressions against their peers to intimidate them in the name of maintaining the mystical prestige of their ascendant profession.

SEIZING THE MEANS OF COMPUTING PRODUCTION

In chapter 2, I argued that institutional transformation in technoscience will only be possible with the inclusion of outsiders' perspectives on its culture because their expert knowledge on power pairs formidably with the lived experiences of tech persisters. I extend this logic to claim that tech defectors and cultural scholars have unique assets in the fight for justice in computing production and outputs—namely, greater freedom and cognitive resources with which to critique the economic structure around which all computing firms are designed and operate: capitalism.

The US economy is predicated on the subjugated labor of people who have been and continue to be barred from leadership in structures of power based on their gender, race, or sexuality. The social movements to rectify long-standing violence and prejudice in US society, such as the American Indian Movement, the Black Power Movement, the Women's Liberation Movement, and Gay Liberation, have been under assault since the early 1980s. At this pivotal juncture in history, Ronald Reagen, a B-list actor, became the figurehead for a far-right activist movement in the US, whereby capital demanded the redistribution of wealth, recognition, representation, and political agency to the historically enfranchised. At this same time, in 1984), the advent of the personal computer positioned computing bosses to help lead this corporate takeover of public institutions (Dean 2009). Computers help to promote the cultural acceptance of neoliberal austerity policies that externalize social reproduction from the state to individual households. This economic regime externalizes many of its costs to women and communities of color, skimming astronomical profits from the spheres of reproduction and the exploitation of women's labor in both the home and the workplace. The voices that I center in this book are remarkable in that they are able to persist in sites that produce such immiseration and precarity. They persist despite the fact that their values and aspirations are in conflict with those of their bosses, the algorithmic lords of capitalist accumulation.

Earlier in this chapter, I suggested that sexual and gender harassment in high-tech could be more effectively resisted and prosecuted by amplifying coalition-building efforts across organizations led by both tech persisters and tech defectors. We need to pair these efforts with more labor organizing around the architecture of digital capitalism—its material, ideological, and cultural dimensions—all of which need sustained interrogation. Thus, I recommend we pay careful attention to tech workers' collective reproductive aspirations to use technical skills and expertise to serve public welfare as an important means by which to build solidarity across identities, organizations, and fields of study. These aspirations are the key to reimagining how to seize power over computing knowledge and its production and applications, "particularly that which could aid effective political action and constrain or eliminate predation by elites" (Táíwò 2020).

Tech workers who are women of color, and queer practitioners as well, are especially primed for labor organizing by a particular rupture—their elite status in the algorithmic workforce contradicts the alienation and harassment they experience along *multiple axes of identity* in said workforce. Further, as I have sought to demonstrate in this book, their shared aspirations to serve the social good positions them in direct opposition to their bosses who lean into the tenets of neoliberal regimes to erode social systems of support and bolster state control over the body politic. For example, Google's first union, the Alphabet Workers Union, wrote in a *New York Times* op-ed, "Our bosses have collaborated with repressive governments around the world. They have developed artificial intelligence technology for use by the Department of Defense and profited from ads by a hate group. They have failed to make the changes necessary to meaningfully address our retention issues with people of color" (Koul and Shaw 2021).

Unfortunately, computing bosses have long been members of the military-industrial complex in the US. Computer science and engineering, like other engineering fields, grew out of military initiatives paid for by US taxpayers, using public funds (Abbate 2012; Ensmenger 2010b). Kelly, the white senior technical fellow in the corporate sector, explains: "Growing up during the Cold War, science and engineering was well-funded by the military—probably 80 percent of all engineering was military funded." Without public funding from military initiatives, Big Tech and their bosses' wealth would not exist. Microsoft has been under fire from its employees for continuing to collude with the US military (Schneider and Sydell 2019). The Advanced Research Projects Agency Network (ARPANET), the original platform for the Internet, was a Department of Defense project (Abbate 1999). Siri, Apple's voice-activated command software, originated in Pentagon research on artificial intelligence and machine learning (Lohr 2012). Computing advances are often spawned from research funded by the military, with implications for the type of masculinities operating in computing organizational cultures and the purposes of computers in society (Rosser 2013).

Theresa, the white mid-career professional working in industry, shared how militarization in her workplace affected her: "I'd be in the bathroom crying 'cause I'm living against my values, and then being, like, 'Well, what the fuck is wrong with me? I need to toughen up. I need to, you know, just like the military, I got to get out there and do my job.'" Theresa was one of the majority of my participants who aspired to use her technical skills in service of social justice. Theresa's emotional conflict however, deepens our understanding of the contradictions of care discussed in chapter 3. First, Big Tech is not changing the world for the better, nor is it idling in neutral. It directly contributes to global warfare, has privatized tools that were created with public money, and pays tens of millions of dollars to lobbyists every year to deny the public oversight over corporate activities. Second, the combative culture left Theresa emotionally bruised, encouraging her to not just mute but to betray her own intrinsic values. The context of Big Tech's historical and cultural ties to the military also further explains why, as discussed in chapter 4, so many of this study's participants felt so battle weary.

Siri was sired in the crucible of war. This can help explain its patriarchal impacts on civil society. Amanda Marcotte (2011) declared that "Siri is sexist" because it offers users a plethora of options for escort services and erectile dysfunction medication but could not return queries on women's reproductive health services like birth control and abortion. Marcotte (2011, 3) concluded that Apple, "the tech company that is the standard-bearer for . . . innovative technology, can't be bothered to care about the concerns of half the human race." First women's access to health care, agency, and autonomy were disappeared from digital platforms, and now, in the last decade, bodily bans to reproduction freedoms are proliferating in state and federal policies.

Apple created a sexist artifact not only because women were missing from the design and implementation phases of production but also because the tool was designed for the purpose of control. Its initial association with the military—its original sin—taints its outcomes. This sexist artifact is an example of how computer technology is meant to serve existing power structures, centralize control, and limit what can be epistemically accessed and collectively conceived and acted on. The sites in which these artifacts are created reflect the paradigms underlying dominant worldviews, and getting more women at the design table is just part of the problem. The historical legacies of computing must be reconciled with who currently benefits the most from its commodities and who is being harmed.

With the cooperation of Big Tech, the administrations of George W. Bush, Barack Obama, and Donald Trump have demanded warrantless searches of US citizens in the name of national security. Resisting these kinds of violations of civil rights by going public often results in retaliation by the state and computing bosses (Au-Yeung 2021; Contreras 2021). This makes Emily Martin's (1992) suggestion that we imagine using technology to constrain elites' power much harder to implement because the risks are so high. To bring into starker relief the power of controlling technology and the possible outcomes if this power were collectivized, I ask you to imagine: What if workers and the public seize ownership and control of Big Tech institutions? What if individual citizens' freedoms and privacies were preserved? What if Big Tech's policies, practices, demographics, and artifacts were open to public review and revisions? What if the government was accountable to its people, and people's privacy was protected by a judicious balance of power?

My participants' aspirations for justice in computing worksites and outputs demonstrate how workers with specialized insight into computing commodities can make critical contributions to social justice causes outside their work, in broader public domains, like the preservation of civil liberties.

I do not conclude here with a deus ex machina but offer some strategies gleaned from my research and lived experiences. My recommendations are also inspired by the Level Playing Field Institute (2011),[4] AI Now Institute (2019),[5] and the National Academies report *Transforming the Trajectories for Women of Color in Tech* (2022).[6] I suggest that we demand of Big Tech these eight transformational changes:

1. Believe people who report identity-based harassment, protect them from retaliation, and get rid of nondisclosure agreements that silence survivors (Vassallo et al. 2016). In addition, fire predators.

2. Pay your fair share of taxes. Close tax havens, and give up your offshore accounts.

3. Divest from Wall Street, and refuse to cooperate with the National Security Agency, the Central Intelligence Agency, and all other US military operatives.

4. Stop union-busting. Fire lobbyists. Think of the millions of dollars you will save annually! Do not interfere with workers' efforts to collectively organize, and bargain fairly through unions.

5. Make reparations. Your tax-dodging has crippled local economies, so it is time to invest in social reproduction, including affordable housing, education,

land conservation, roads and bridges, and other social services—especially in underserved communities.

6. Cast a wide net in calls for positions in departments, panels, and leadership positions. White cisgender men with degrees from Ivy League computer science and engineering departments are not the only folks with talent and vision.

7. Create pathways to leadership for women of color. Tie advances in this area to managers' performance reviews. Spend 1 percent to 3 percent of gross profits on inclusion efforts and worker benefits. Be transparent about your demographics—both real and aspirational. Express zero tolerance for identity-based harassment, sexism, racism, and homophobia. Proactively train all employees, and *senior leaders especially*, in best practices for fostering inclusivity every two years.

8. Limit salary disparities between entry-level positions and executives.

Transforming computing will require greater transparency and public oversight to hold academic departments and companies accountable for their influence and impact on the world. These eight recommendations address the broader social domains in which computing is practiced and revered. Activism aimed at social change by technologists, and particularly activism in coalition with other workers, can foster new paradigms for the design and use of computer technology.

CONCLUSION

I have traced the intersectional roots of power that constitute the Bro Code, which enables cisgender, avowedly heterosexual men from dominant racial groups to have an outsized influence on workplace cultures of computing. Since computing firms dominate global commercial markets, selling underregulated commodities that much of the world depends on, it becomes crucial to examine the conditions under which these commodities were made. If we can transform these inequities inside computing worksites, then perhaps the world-changing power of digital commodities and algorithmic systems could be further destabilized and refashioned in order to better serve billions of people around the globe.

Denying women of color, white women, and nonbinary people the opportunity to develop and perfect the skills required for leadership in this century is part of a larger fundamentalist effort to roll back decades of progress toward a more just, egalitarian society. In fact, the Bro Code first was invented to exclude the aforementioned groups from the halls of learning and computer laboratories. Silicon Valley's current ethos of scaling up fast with little concern for social responsibility has its roots in the 1960s, when broad social movements for racial, economic, gender justice had significant influence over how engineers came to define themselves and the work (Wisnioski 2012). Now, given the field's wealth, reach, and power, it serves as a key ingredient in the solvent for erasing from public consciousness the ideas of collective responsibilities in civic society. In addition, it softens resistance to neoliberal austerity measures that transfer the responsibility for social reproduction from the state to the nuclear family, disproportionately affecting women.

The high-tech ruling class and the institutions they helm have been able to broadcast the Bro Code so widely, and with little opposition, because they are worshipped in the US. Part of their beguiling heroism, what I call the geek mystique, lies in the power to refuse the culturally devalued labors of care. The Bro Code mobilizes this disvalue in computing institutionally. For example, its culture of overwork and the exaltation of technical dimensions of computing work over social ones signal the lack of regard that computing corporations and academic institutions have toward modes of reproduction in our society. Given the great influence of computer technology, the effacement of social reproduction reflects and reproduces labor value within the US more broadly, with significant implications for gender and race relations.

Promoting proprietary computational machines as a revolutionary social project is thus a fantasy, one that we cannot afford (Dean 2009). For example, Oxfam, a global organization fighting poverty, has sounded the alarm that we are living in the time of greatest income inequality in human history, with the world's 10 wealthiest men now owning more wealth than the bottom 40 percent of humanity (Ruiz-Grossman 2022). Computing bosses top this list. Their leadership not only fails to contribute to the reproduction of the social collective but also operates in tandem with government officials and bankers to erode the social commons (Whittaker and Taylor 2020; Coleman 2013; Hakken 2003). As recent organizing activities by tech workers evince, lasting solidarities and durable coalitions across workers and communities are what scare this reigning bourgeoise class the most.

By placing reproduction at the center of my analysis, I found that participants' reproductive aspirations exceed the bounds of the biological. Organizing around the social good and the right for computing workers to use their skills and expertise in service of public welfare is the best way to contain the threats posed by Big Tech. Feminist discourse needs to shift beyond balancing work and family to acknowledge workers' painful choice between job security and social aspirations. Let's imagine the institutional transformations that would come about if these highly trained workers were to use their "mystical" geek powers in the service of the higher good. Perhaps this collective action can transform not only computing culture, from exclusive to inclusive, but also the applications of computer technology, from tools of social control to tools of social liberation.

ACKNOWLEDGMENTS

I wish to thank the people who made this book possible. Rachel Chapman has had a profound and lasting impact on my life of the mind. This book would not have been possible without her. Rachel inspired me to use anthropological tools to critique and transform unjust systems of power. Her intellectual breadth is matched only by her powerful, passionate commitment to activist scholarship—a commitment sustained by a love of knowledge and justice. Eve Riskin has also been a tremendous source of support and inspiration for me, without which I could not have completed this book. Her abundant generosity knows no limits. She encourages me to speak my mind and follow the ideas about which I am most passionate. Best of all, she has my back and connects me with the resources I need to be successful in my endeavors. Eve's professional network is vast, and she helped me recruit research participants. Joyce Yen has offered me many opportunities to grow intellectually and professionally. She went above and beyond to help me manifest my vision for this project, always believing in me and always being there to lend her support. Joyce's deep and broad interdisciplinary knowledge as well as her uncanny ability to directly address the heart of the matter has influenced every stage of this book.

Thank you to Teresa Mares, who inspires me with her intellectual prowess and unflappable professionalism that I strive to emulate. Following her example keeps me grounded, calm, focused, and most of all, ambitious. Her friendship was critical to the completion of this book. Devon Peña and Nancy Hartsock taught me all I know about the labor theories undergirding this book. Alison Wylie's mentorship and her work in anthropology, feminist standpoint, and science and technology studies inspired me to extend knowledge in these areas, too. My collaboration with Liesl Folks during the later stages of writing provided much inspiration for how to effectively combat sexism in science and engineering and provide support for women and nonbinary scholars navigating cultures of incivility. I am deeply indebted to her for her mentorship, generosity, brilliance, and wicked sense of humor, which makes fighting the good fight fun. Christine Grant and Margaret Eisenhart were also generous in their mentorship, and I am a better scholar because of them. A number of conversations over the last several years have shaped my thinking about equity, technology, and society, including my exchanges with Alice Pawley, Donna Riley, Wenda Bauchspies, Alison Godwin, Sapna Cheryan, Daniela Rosner, John Parker, Rashaunda Henderson, Colleen Lewis, Mary Gray, Julie Ivy, James Moore, Paige Smith, Anna Harris, Cyrus Mody, Joeri Bruyninckx, and Claire Horner-Devine.

I would also like to thank the editorial team at the MIT Press. Katie Heike, Winnie Poster, Suraiya Jetha, and Gita Devi Manaktala provided rich feedback and unwavering support. Three anonymous reviewers made brilliant recommendations that vastly improved this book. Thank you! I would also like to acknowledge Kristin Sanders and Melissa Cornish, who proofread numerous drafts of the manuscript and provided intelligent suggestions and invaluable development edits.

At Cal Poly, San Luis Obispo, several entities have been invaluable to my research, including my home department, Social Sciences (especially the generous mentorship of Stacey Rucas, Joan Meyers, Greg Bohr, and Terry Jones); the Science, Technology, and Society Program; the Center for Health Research (thanks to Alison Ventura and Suzanne Phelan); and the College of Liberal Arts Dean's Office (thanks to Doug Epperson and Kathryn Rummell for their support). Thank you to my student collaborators, including Michelle Bardini, Noah Krigel, Luci Simpson, Alana Salas-Yoshii, Abibat Rahman-Davies, Ell Hundertmark, Gabriel Medina-Kim, Erin McDaniel, Jivitesh Kamboj, and Miguel Del Real. Special thanks to Sophie Klitgaard and Madison Green, whose talent and commitment in the final stages of manuscript preparation were critical to its quality and completion.

I am also grateful to have strengthened the arguments in this book through talks. In particular, I wish to thank the School of Engineering Education at Purdue University; the Maastricht University Science, Technology, and Society Studies department; and the School of Engineering and Applied Sciences at the University of Virginia.

Thank you to my San Luis Obispo comrades who make California home for me. My thinking in the later stages of this work has been profoundly inspired them. Thank you Jen Lewis, whose command of cultural theory is breathtaking. Ryan Hatch shared critical frames from aesthetic theory that enhanced my methodological analyses. I am also grateful to Michael Huggins, Martin Battle, Krista Kauffmann, Charmaine Farber, Brian Pompeii, Nancy Arrington, Robb Moss, Aleks Wydzga, Martine Lappé, and Matt Harsh for their friendship and affectionate support. A special word of gratitude is due to Jenny Denbow, one of the finest feminist scholars in the world, who read and commented on several chapters. Thank you for your friendship and sharing your dazzling intelligence and vision with me.

I am also indebted to Caitlin Wylie and Patrick Grzanka for their smarts and savvy. Being in cahoots with them brings me much joy, and their advice on academic publishing in particular contributed to the completion of this manuscript. Cara Margherio's radical sensibilities and vision for combating racism and sexism in engineering inspired me, especially in the book's labor analyses.

I wish to thank my chosen kin in Seattle. Emily Haley was instrumental to this book in its early stages. Not only did she proofread drafts, she also cheered me on, cheered me up, encouraged me, and fed me well and often. Sam Yum has also been an incredible source of support on this journey. After long days and evenings of writing, he was there to lend a supportive ear. He also proofread a chapter, providing great advice and edits. I also could not have manifested this book in its final form without the love and support of Jo Saltmarsh and Matt Lerner. I am also grateful for the love, humor, and encouragement of Alicia Goodwin, Victoria Coleman, Dana Gold, Toby Keys, Erica Gordon, and Brian Mee, who all cared for me extravagantly during difficult moments and celebrated every small win with me.

Growing up, my parents, Janice Carrigan and Kevin Carrigan, gave me a wealth of educational opportunities and unlimited books from Notes & Quotes, our family bookstore. Their confidence in my capabilities has always been unflagging. Their support, love, and encouragement were invaluable. My brother Kevin Carrigan also championed this work. In difficult moments, his lighthearted advice and sense of humor never failed to uplift me.

This work was supported by a National Science Foundation Engineering Education and Centers Grant 1751314 and an American Association for University Women fellowship.

APPENDIX: SELECT ORGANIZATIONS COLLECTIVIZING FOR EQUITY AND JUSTICE IN COMPUTING

★ AI Now Institute: https://ainowinstitute.org
★ American Association for the Advancement of Science: https://www.aaas
  .org
★ American Association of University Women: https://www.aauw.org
★ American Society Engineering Education: https://www.asee.org
★ Anita Borg Institute: https://anitab.org
★ #AppleToo: https://appletoo.us/letter/
★ Association for Women in Science: https://awis.org
★ Black ComputHer: https://blackcomputeher.org
★ Black in AI: https://blackinai.github.io/#/
★ Black Women in STEM Summit: https://www.bwistem.com
★ Collective Action in Tech: https://collectiveaction.tech
★ Computer Research Association Widening Participation: https://cra.org
  /cra-wp/
★ Coworker Solidarity Fund: https://coworkerfund.org
★ Data & Society: https://datasociety.net
★ Data for Black Lives: https://d4bl.org
★ Design Justice Network: https://designjustice.org
★ Distributed AI Research Institute: https://www.dair-institute.org
★ Foxglove: https://www.foxglove.org.uk/tag/tech-workers
★ Google Walkout for Real Change: https://googlewalkout.medium.com

- ★ IEEE (Institute of Electrical and Electronics Engineers) Women in Engineering: https://wie.ieee.org
- ★ LATTICE (Launching Academics on the Tenure-Track: An Intentional Community in Engineering): https://advance.washington.edu/about/national/lattice
- ★ Lesbians Who Tech: https://lesbianswhotech.org/about
- ★ #MeTooSTEM: https://metoostem.com
- ★ Michelle R. Clayman Institute for Gender Research: https://gender.stanford.edu
- ★ Microsoft Research: https://www.microsoft.com/en-us/research
- ★ National Academies of Sciences, Technology, Engineering, and Medicine: https://www.nationalacademies.org
- ★ National Center for Women & Information Technology (NCWIT): https://ncwit.org
- ★ National Science Foundation ADVANCE: https://beta.nsf.gov/funding/opportunities/advance-organizational-change-gender-equity-stem
- ★ Society of Women Engineers (SWE): https://swe.org
- ★ STEM Women of Color Conclave: https://www.conclave-swoc.net/about
- ★ TechEquity Collaborative: https://techequitycollaborative.org
- ★ Tech Workers Coalition: https://techworkerscoalition.org
- ★ The Worker Agency: https://www.theworkeragency.com
- ★ Women in Engineering ProActive Network (WEPAN): https://www.wepan.org

NOTES

1. On how racism is embedded in platforms, see Buolamwini and Gebru 2018; Benjamin 2019; Noble 2018; Simonite 2018. For the ways in which transphobia is also coded into digital platforms, see Keyes 2018; Spiel et al. 2019. Finally, for more on how sexual harassment and other violations of consent become part of the algorithmic business model, see Carrigan, Green, and Rahman-Davis 2021.

2. For more perspectives on how the concept of "magic" operates as an emic term in computer science communities, see Rosner 2018b; Benjamin 2019; Sadowski 2020; Carrigan, Green, and Rahman-Davies 2021; Thomas, Nafus, and Sherman 2018.

3. Others have developed theories on technocracy (e.g., Broussard 2018; Sadowski 2020; Dean 2002; Davis-Floyd 1992), and I am indebted to their work in theorizing the Bro Code. Through this book, I will use the term technocracy with a theoretical sensitivity to Robbie Davis-Floyd's frame because the spirit of her work regarding the sociotechnical politics of birth in the US pivots on feminist theories of reproduction and therefore fruitfully applies to my approach in analyzing the digital economy.

4. I use Scott Frickel and Neil Gross's analytic frame for scientific and intellectual movements that describe "a collective effort to pursue research programs or projects for thought in the face of resistance from others in the scientific and intellectual community . . . for scientific and intellectual change" (Frickel and Gross 2005, 206).

CHAPTER 2

1. I use the term "underrepresented group members" to include women of all ethnicities as well as African American, Latino, and Native American men.

2. My inclusion criteria for delineating between gender equity and sexual harassment literature is whether the authors identity the deeper, more pervasive problems

that emerged out of remedial efforts to interrupt bias in STEM as harassment or not. This is not to say that research describing and theorizing exclusionary practices in technical fields could not qualify as gender and sexual harassment research (e.g., Margolis and Fisher 2003). Nor am I saying that gender equity scholarship is not produced by feminists.

CHAPTER 3

1. Steven Pinker (2005), in a book supporting "the Larry Summers Hypothesis," makes the case that women lack the innate capability for abstract reasoning. The basis for this claim is studies that purportedly demonstrate that there are a higher proportion of men at the high end of the scale of math, logic, and spatial tests. To buttress his hypothesis, Pinker relies on outdated and disproven data from 1985 on the gendered math achievement gap. He ignored data gathered since 1985 that shows the math achievement gap is nearly bridged (Barres 2006). The quality of Pinker's contributions to gender theory is also being questioned by scholars who have brought attention to his ties to convicted human trafficker Jeffrey Epstein (Flaherty 2019) and his dubious claims about rape and feminism (Manne 2020).

2. For a more in-depth discussion of this point, see Carrigan 2017.

CHAPTER 4

1. Following Mary Daly's example, "I have no need to capitalize christianity. This is obviously a matter not only of taste but of evaluation" (Daly 1990, 26).

2. The field note that opens the book's prologue depicted men who roamed the workplace campus in packs and women alone (and visibly distraught). What I failed to observe was the absence of men of color in groups. Thanks to Emmanuel, I see it now and better understand the racial dimensions of the worksite.

CHAPTER 6

1. For a nonexhaustive list of such formal organization, please see the appendix.

2. Tara's metaphor is reminiscent of Sara Ahmed's (2012) metaphor of diversity work being a brick wall.

3. To Big Tech bosses, workforce fairness and diversity are meaningless unless they increase "innovation" and profit. Jennifer Siebel Newsom and Jean Kilbourne (2017) captured this sentiment perfectly when they imagined these leaders' rationale for doing little to combat harassment and segregation in technical fields: "We've made billions of dollars while paying women less and with barely any women on our corporate boards, right? No one can deny that we've been leading the world in

innovation . . . while often *ignoring* women completely." The pursuit of diversity is as much a cipher in computing as is innovation—hype trumps reality. Terms like "innovation" and "revolution" are geek mystique speak for clickbait, human behavior data capture, and nudging people to buy more gadgets more often.

4. The Level Playing Field Institute (2011) produced an excellent report on how women and people of color in the IT workforce are forced into the margins. They make four recommendations for improving participation by underrepresented group members:

1. Develop a homegrown pool of diverse talent.
2. Address hidden biases and barriers within workplaces that disadvantage underrepresented groups.
3. Conduct research to both uncover hidden biases within the sector, and examine efforts taken by companies to increase diversity.
4. Get the word out within your company, networks, and communities.

The first recommendation is excellent. Two senior-level participants in this study learned programming on the job, and both lamented how the trend of companies growing their talent has faded. As discussed at length in chapter 2, unexamined bias is an important factor in labor segregation in computer science and engineering. However, on its own, bias decoupled from interventions combating racism and sexual harassment is inadequate.

5. Eight years after the Level Playing Field recommendations, the AI Now Institute (West, Whittaker, and Crawford 2019) also suggested ways that Big Tech could desegregate its workforce and retain women and practitioners of color:

1. Publish compensation levels, including bonuses and equity, across all roles and job categories, broken down by race and gender.
2. End pay and opportunity inequality, and set pay and benefit equity goals that include contract workers, temps, and vendors.
3. Publish harassment and discrimination transparency reports, including the number of claims over time, the types of claims submitted, and actions taken.
4. Change hiring practices to maximize diversity; include targeted recruitment beyond elite universities; ensure more equitable focus on underrepresented groups; and create more pathways for contractors, temps, and vendors to become full-time employees.

6. The National Academies (2022, 147–149) states the following:

1. To enhance the accuracy of data reporting, tech companies should disaggregate employment data by tech and non-tech positions, job titles, gender, and race/ethnicity—with particular attention to the intersection of race/ethnicity and gender—and make those data publicly available. Reports should include information about trends in recruitment, retention, and advancement of women of color.

2. Companies and organizations working within the tech sector should create pathways for women of color into leadership positions and create positions for diversity, equity, and inclusion professionals that are part of executive leadership.

3. Tech companies, with the assistance of a neutral central organization, should initiate an ongoing cross-sector coalition with each other as well as other stakeholders such as academic institutions—especially minority-serving institutions (e.g., historically Black colleges or universities, Hispanic-serving institutions, and tribal colleges and universities)—and professional societies. This collective would allow member organizations and institutions to connect with each other with the goal of supporting current and future women of color in tech and promoting effective recruitment, retention, and advancement strategies for women of color in tech across all entities.

4. Tech companies should expand employment options that promote work-life balance such as remote work, flexible work hours, parental and other family leave, and career counseling as a strategy to improve retention and advancement and expand recruitment of women of color.

REFERENCES

Abbate, Janet. 1999. *Inventing the Internet.* Inside Technology. Cambridge, MA: MIT Press.

Abbate, Janet. 2012. *Recoding Gender: Women's Changing Participation in Computing.* History of Computing. Cambridge, MA: MIT Press.

Abu-Lughod, L. 1990. "Can There Be a Feminist Ethnography?" *Women & Performance: A Journal of Feminist Theory* 5 (1): 7–27. https://doi.org/10.1080/07407709008571138.

Acker, Joan. 1990. "Hierarchies, Jobs, Bodies: A Theory of Gendered Organizations." *Gender and Society* 4 (2): 139–158.

Acker, Joan. 2000. "Gendered Contradictions in Organizational Equity Projects." *Organization* 7 (4): 625–632.

Adam, Alison. 1998. *Artificial Knowing: Gender and the Thinking Machine.* Florence, KY: Routledge.

Adams, Glenn, Donna M. Garcia, Valerie Purdie-Vaughns, and Claude M. Steele. 2006. "The Detrimental Effects of a Suggestion of Sexism in An Instruction Situation." *Journal of Experimental Social Psychology* 42 (5): 602–615.

Ahmed, Sara. 2012. *On Being Included: Racism and Diversity In Institutional Life.* Durham, NC: Duke University Press.

Alfrey, Lauren, and France Winddance Twine. 2017. "Gender-Fluid Geek Girls: Negotiating Inequality Regimes in the Tech Industry." *Gender and Society* 31 (1): 28–50. https://doi.org/https://doi.org/10.1177/0891243216680590.

Ames, Morgan. 2019. *The Charisma Machine: The Life, Death, and Legacy of One Laptop per Child.* Cambridge, MA: MIT Press.

Amrute, Sareeta. 2016. *Encoding Race, Encoding Class: Indian IT Workers in Berlin.* Durham, NC: Duke University Press.

Anderson, Leon. 2006. "Analytic Autoethnography." *Journal of Contemporary Ethnography* 35 (4): 373–395.

Ashcraft, Catherine, Wendy DuBow, Elizabeth Eger, Sarah Blithe, and Brian Sevie. 2013. *Male Advocates and Allies: Promoting Gender Diversity in Technology Workplaces.* Boulder, CO: NCWIT. http://www.ncwit.org/maleadvocateindustry.

Ashcraft, Catherine, Brad McLain, and Elizabeth Eger. 2016. *Women in Tech: The Facts.* Boulder, CO: NCWIT. https://wpassets.ncwit.org/wp-content/uploads/2021 /05/13193304/ncwit_women-in-it_2016-full-report_final-web06012016.pdf.

Ashcraft, Karen L., and Catherine Ashcraft. 2015. "Breaking the 'Glass Slipper': What Diversity Interventions Can Learn from the Historical Evolution of Occupational Identity in ICT and Commercial Aviation." In *Connecting Women,* edited by Valérie Schafer and Benjamin G. Thierry, 174. New York: Springer.

Au-Yeung, Angel. 2021. "Technology Employees Warn: Companies Should Expect More Uprising in 2022." *Forbes,* December 29, 2021. https://www.forbes.com/sites /angelauyeung/2021/12/29/technology-employees-warn-companies-should-expect -more-uprisings-in-2022/?sh=4dfd3f7c7154.

Awad, Never, Matt Krentz, Andrea Gallego, and Beth Viner. 2022. "The Pandemic's Lasting and Surprising Effects on Women in Tech." *Boston Consulting Group,* August 11, 2022. https://www.bcg.com/publications/2022/how-the-pandemic-continues-to-affect -female-leaders-in-tech.

Bakker, Isabella, and Stephen Gill. 2003. *Power, Production and Social Reproduction: Human In/security in the Global Political Economy.* New York: Palgrave Macmillan.

Banaji, Mahzarin, and Anthony Greenwald. 2013. *The Blindspot: Hidden Biases of Good People.* New York: Delacorte Press.

Barker, Lecia, and Kathy Garvin-Doxas. 2002. "Defensive Climate in the Computer Science Classroom." 33rd SIGCSE Technical Symposium on Computer Science Education, February 27–March 3, 2002, Cincinnati, Kentucky..

Barker, Lecia, and Kathy Garvin-Doxas. 2004. "Making Visible the Behaviors that Influence Learning Environment: A Qualitative Exploration of Computer Science Classrooms." *Computer Science Education* 14 (2): 119–145.

Barker, Lecia, Kathy Garvin-Doxas, and Eric Roberts. 2005. "What Can Computer Science Learn from a Fine Arts Approach to Teaching?" 36th SIGCSE Technical Symposium on Computer Science Education, February 23–27, 2005, St. Louis, Missouri.

Barnett, Rosalind C., and Caryl Rivers. 2004. "Men Are from Earth, and So Are Women. It's Faulty Research That Sets Them Apart." *Chronicle of Higher Education* 51 (2): B11–B13.

Barocas, Solon, Kate Crawford, Aaron Shapiro, and Hanna Wallach. 2017. "The Problem with Bias: Allocative versus Representational Harms in Machine Learning." Ninth Annual Conference of the Special Interest Group for Computing, Information, and Society, October 19, 2017, Philadelphia.

Barres, Ben. 2006. "Does Gender Matter?" *Nature* 442 (7099): 133–136.

Barth, Brian. 2019. "Big Tech's Big Defector." *The New Yorker,* November 25, 2019. https://www.newyorker.com/magazine/2019/12/02/big-techs-big-defector.

Barth, Joan M., Rosanna E. Guadagno, Lindsay Rice, Cassie A. Eno, and Jessy A. Minney. 2015. "Untangling Life Goals and Occupational Stereotypes in Men's and Women's Career Interest." *Sex Roles* 73 (11–12): 502–518. https://doi.org/10.1007 /s11199-015-0537-2.

Bauchspies, Wenda K., and Maria Puig de la Bellacasa. 2009. "Feminist Science and Technology Studies: A Patchwork of Moving Subjectivities. An Interview with Geoffrey Bowker, Sandra Harding, Anne Marie Mol, Susan Leigh Star and Banu Subramaniam." *Subjectivity* 28:334–344. https://doi.org/https://doi.org/10.1057/sub.2009.21.

Bauer, Henry H. 1990. "Barriers against Interdisciplinarity: Implications for Studies of Science, Technology, and Society (STS)." *Science, Technology, & Human Values* 15 (1): 105–119.

Behar, Ruth. 1996. *The Vulnerable Observer: Anthropology That Breaks Your Heart.* Boston: Beacon Press.

Bender, Emily, Timnit Gebru, Angelina McMillian-Major, and Shmitchell. Shmargaret. 2021. "On the Dangers of Stochastic Parrots: Can Language Models Be Too Big?" *Proceedings of the 2021 ACM Conference on Fairness, Accountability, and Transparency* (March): 610–623.

Benería, Lourdes. 1999. "The Enduring Debate over Unpaid Labour." *International Labor Review* 138 (3): 287–309.

Benjamin, Ruha. 2019. *Race after Technology: Abolitionist Tools for the New Jim Code.* Cambridge: Polity.

Benokraitis, Nijole V. 1998. "Working in the Ivory Basement: Subtle Sex Discrimination in Higher Education." In *Career Strategies for Women in Academe: Arming Athena*, edited by Lynn Collins, Joan Chrisler, and Kathryn Quina, 3–36. Thousand Oaks, CA: Sage.

Berdahl, Jennifer L., and Celia Moore. 2006. "Workplace Harassment: Double Jeopardy for Minority Women." *Journal of Applied Psychology* 91 (2): 426–436. https://doi .org/10.1037/0021-9010.91.2.426.

Blanchard Kyte, Sarah, and Catherine Riegle-Crumb. 2017. "Perceptions of the Social Relevance of Science: Exploring the Implications for Gendered Patterns in Expectations of Majoring in STEM Fields." Special issue *Gender and STEM: Understanding Segregation in Science, Technology, Engineering and Mathematics: Social Sciences* 6 (1): 1–17. https://doi.org/doi:10.3390/socsci6010019.

Blickenstaff, Jacob Clark. 2005. "Women and Science Careers: Leaky Pipeline or Gender Filter." *Gender and Education* 17 (4): 369–386.

Boice, Robert. 1993. "Early Turning Points in Professional Careers of Women and Minorities." In *Building a Diverse Faculty*, edited by Joanne Gainen and Robert Boice, 71–79. New York: Jossey-Bass.

Bonilla-Silva, Eduardo, and Tyrone Forman. 2000. "'I Am Not a Racist but . . .': Mapping White College Students Racial Ideology in the USA." *Discourse & Society* 11 (1): 50–85.

Bourdieu, Pierre. 1989. *Language and Symbolic Power*. Boston: Harvard University Press.

Bourdieu, Pierre. 2003. *Firing Back: Against the Tyranny of the Market 2*. New York: New Press.

Bowleg, Lisa. 2019. "Epilogue." In *Intersectionality: Foundations and Frontiers*, edited by Patrick R. Grzanka, 413–420. Oxfordshire: Routledge.

Bray, Francesca. 2007. "Gender and Technology." *Annual Review of Anthropology* 36:37–53.

Broussard, Meredith. 2018. *Artificial Unintelligence: How Computers Misunderstand the World*. Cambridge, MA: MIT Press.

Brown, Wendy. 2019. *In the Ruins of Neoliberalism: The Rise of Antidemocratic Politics in the West*. New York: Columbia University Press.

Browne, Irene, and Joya Misra. 2003. "The Intersection of Gender and Race in the Labor Market." *Annual Review of Sociology* 29:487–513.

Browner, Carole H. 2001. "Situating Women's Reproductive Activities." *American Anthropologist* 102 (4): 773–788.

Buchanan, NiCole T., and Louis Fitzgerald. 2008. "Effects of Racial and Sexual Harassment on Work and the Psychological Well-Being of African American Women." *Journal of Occupational Health Psychology* 13 (2): 137–151. https://doi.org /10.1037/1076-8998.13.2.137.

Buchanan, NiCole T., Isis H. Settles, and Regina Day Langhout. 2007. "Black Women's Coping Styles, Psychological Well-Being, and Work-Related Outcomes following Sexual Harassment." *Black Women, Gender + Families* 1 (2): 100–120.

Buolamwini, Joy, and Timnit Gebru. 2018. "Gender Shades: Intersectional Accuracy Disparities in Commercial Gender Classification." First Conference on Fairness, Accountability and Transparency. *Proceedings of Machine Learning Research* 81:1–15.

Burack, Cynthia, and Suzanne Franks. 2004. "Telling Stories about Engineering: Group Dynamics and Resistance to Diversity." *National Women's Studies Association* 16 (1): 79–95.

Burge, Jamika D., Jakita O. Thomas, and Royko Yamaguchi. 2017. "Computing and Intersectionality: The Social and Behavioral Structures at Play for Black Women in the Computing Sciences." Final workshop report, Howard University.

Burrell, Jenna, and Marion Fourcade. 2021. "The Society of Algorithms." *Annual Review of Sociology* 47:213–237.

Bystydzienski, Jill M., and Sharon R. Bird. 2006. *Removing Barriers: Women in Academic Science, Technology, Engineering, and Mathematics*. Bloomington: Indiana University Press.

Cain-Miller, Claire. 2010. "Out of the Loop in Silicon Valley." *New York Times*, April 17, 2010. http://www.nytimes.com/2010/04/18/technology/18women.html.

Campbell, Nancy D. 2009. "Reconstructing Science and Technology Studies: Views from Feminist Standpoint Theory." *Frontiers* 30 (1): 1–29.

Carlone, Heidi, and Angela Johnson. 2007. "Understanding the Science Experiences of Successful Women of Color: Science Identity as an Analytic Lens." *Journal of Research in Science Teaching* 44 (8): 1187–1218.

Carr, Phyllis L., Arlene S. Ash, Robert H. Friedman, Laura Szalacha, Rosalind C. Barnett, Anita Palepu, and Mark M. Moskowitz. 2000. "Faculty Perceptions of Gender Discrimination and Sexual Harassment in Academic Medicine." *Annals of Internal Medicine* 132 (11): 889–896. https://doi.org/10.7326/0003-4819-132-11-200006060 -00007.

Carrell, Scott E., Marianne E. Page, and James E. West. 2010. "Sex and Science: How Professor Gender Perpetuates the Gender Gap." *Quarterly Journal of Economics* 125 (3): 1101–1144.

Carrigan, Coleen. 2017. "Yearning to Give Back: Searching for Social Purpose in Computer Science and Engineering." *Frontiers in Psychology* 8:6. https://doi.org/10 .3389/fpsyg.2017.01178.

Carrigan, Coleen. 2018. "'Different Isn't Free': Gender @ Work in a Digital World." *Ethnography* 19 (3): 336–359. https://doi.org/https://doi.org/10.1177/1466138117728737.

Carrigan, Coleen, and Michelle Bardini. 2021. "Majorism: Neoliberalism in Student Culture." *Anthropology & Education Quarterly* 52 (1): 42–62.

Carrigan, Coleen, Madison Witters Green, and Abibat Rahman-Davies. 2021. "'The Revolution Will Not Be Supervised': Consent and Open Secrets in Data Science." *Big Data & Society* 8 (2): 1–13.

Carrigan, Coleen, Jarman Hauser, E. A. Riskin, Priti Mody-Pan, Jim Borgford-Parnell, Dawn Wiggin, Scott Winter, Scott Pinkham, and Sonya Cunningham. 2019. "Active Agents and Fictive Kin: Learning from Pell-Eligible Engineering Students' Class Standpoint." *Journal of Women and Minorities in Science and Engineering* 25 (2). https://doi.org/10.1615/JWomenMinorScienEng.2019025657.

Carrigan, Coleen, Noah Krigel, Mira Brown, and Michelle Bardini. 2021. "Articulating a Succinct Description: An Applied Methods for Catalyzing Cultural Change." *Human Organization* 80 (2): 128–139.

Carrigan, Coleen, Kate Quinn, and Eve Riskin. 2011. "The Gendered Division of Labor among STEM Faculty and the Effects of Critical Mass." *Journal of Diversity in Higher Education* 4 (3): 131–146.

Cary, Donick. 2015. *Parks and Recreation*. Season 7, episode 5, "Gryzzlbox," edited by Amy Poehler. Aired January 27, 2015. National Broadcasting Company.

Cech, Erin A. 2005. "Understanding the Gender Schema of Female Engineering Students: A Balanced Sex-Type and an Ideal of Autonomy." *Proceedings of the 2005 Women in Engineering ProActive Network/National Association of Multicultural Engineering Program Advocates Joint Conference.*

Cech, Erin A. 2013. "Ideological Wage Inequalities? The Technical/Social Dualism and the Gender Wage Gap in Engineering." *Social Forces* 91 (4): 1147–1182. https:// doi.org/10.1093/sf/sot024.

Cech, Erin A. 2014. "Culture of Disengagement in Engineering Education?" *Science, Technology, & Human Values* 39 (1): 42–72. https://doi.org/10.1177/016224 3913504305.

Cech, Erin A., and Mary Blair-Loy. 2010. "Perceived Glass Ceilings? Meritocratic versus Structural Explanations of Gender Inequality Among Women in Science and Technology." *Social Problems* 57 (3): 371–397.

Cech, Erin A., Mary Blair-Loy, and Laura E Rogers. 2018. "Recognizing Chilliness: How Schemas of Inequality Shape Views of Culture and Climate in Work Environments." *American Journal of Cultural Sociology* 6 (1): 125–160.

Cech, Erin A., and Tom Waidzunas. 2011. "Navigating the Heteronormativity of Engineering: The Experiences of Lesbian, Gay and Bisexual Students." *Engineering Studies* 3 (1): 1–24.

Ceci, Stephan J., and Wendy M. Williams. 2011. "Understanding Current Causes of Women's Underrepresentation in Science." *Proceedings of the National Academy of Sciences*108 (8): 3157–3162. https://www.pnas.org/doi/pdf/10.1073/pnas.1014871108.

Chachra, Debbie. 2012. "How Not to Think Like an Engineer." *ASEE Prism* 21 (6): 24.

Chang, Emily. 2018. *Brotopia: Breaking Up the Boy's Club of Silicon Valley.* New York: Penguin.

Chapman, Rachel R. 2003. "Endangering Safe Motherhood in Mozambique: Prenatal Care as Pregnancy Risk." *Social Science and Medicine* 57 (2): 355–374.

Cheryan, Sapna, Victoria C. Plaut, Paul G. Davies, and Claude M. Steele. 2009. "Ambient Belonging: How Stereotypical Cues Impact Gender Participation in Computer Science." *Journal of Personality and Social Psychology* 97 (6): 1045–1060.

Cheryan, Sapna, Sianna A. Ziegler, Amanda K. Montoya, and Lily Jiang. 2017. "Why Are Some STEM Fields More Gender Balanced than Others?" *Psychological Bulletin* 143 (1): 1–35. http://dx.doi.org/10.1037/bul0000052.

Cho, Sumi, Kimberlé Williams Crenshaw, and Leslie McCall. 2013. "Toward a Field of Intersectionality Studies: Theory, Applications, and Praxis." *Signs: Journal of Women in Culture and Society* 38 (4): 785–810. https://doi.org/10.1086/669608.

Chowdhury, Fahmida, Karlene Hoo, and Bozenna Pasik-Duncan. 2007. "Innovative Strategies for Retention of Women Engineers in Academia: Conversation with Successful Role Models." In *Gender and Engineering: Strategies and Possibilities*, edited by Ingelore Welpe, Barbara Reschka, and June Larkin, 137–154. Frankfurt: Peter Lang.

Chu, Hyejin Iris. 2011. "Masculine Engineering, Feminine Engineer: Women's Perception of Engineering and Engineering Identity." In *Gender and Engineering: Strategies and Possibilities*, edited by Ingelore Welpe, Barbara Reschka, and June Larkin, 54–61. Frankfurt: Peter Lang.

Clancy, Kathryn B. H., Katharine M. N. Lee, Erica M. Rodgers, and Christina Richey. 2017. "Double Jeopardy in Astronomy and Planetary Science: Women of Color Face Greater Risks of Gendered and Racial Harassment." *Journal of Geophysical Research: Planets* 122 (7): 1610–1623. https://doi.org/https://doi.org/10.1002/2017JE005256.

Clancy, Kathryn B. H., Robin G. Nelson, Juilenne N. Rutherford, and Katie Hinde. 2014. "Survey of Academic Field Experiences (SAFE): Trainees Report Harassment and Assault." *PLoS ONE* 9 (7). https://doi.org/https://doi.org/10.1371/journal.pone .0102172.

Cohen, Laurie, and Janet Swim. 1995. "The Differential Impact of Gender Ratios on Women and Men: Tokenism, Self-Confidence, and Expectations." *Personality and Social Psychology Bulletin* 21 (9): 876–884.

Coleman, E. Gabriella. 2013. *Coding Freedom: The Ethics and Aesthetics of Hacking.* Princeton, NJ: Princeton University Press.

Collins, Patricia Hill. 2000. *Black Feminist Thought: Knowledge, Consciousness, and the Politics of Empowerment.* 10th anniversary ed. New York: Routledge.

Collins, Patricia Hill. 2004. "Learning from the Outside Within: The Sociological Significance of Black Feminist Thought." In *The Feminist Standpoint Theory Reader: Intellectual and Political Controversies*, edited by Sandra G. Harding, New York: Routledge.

Collins, Patricia Hill. 2015. "Intersectionality's Definitional Dilemmas." *Annual Review of Sociology* 41 (1–20). https://doi.org/10.1146/annurev-soc-073014-112142.

Committee on Equal Opportunities in Science and Engineering [COSEMPUP]. 1998. *Biennial Report to United States Congress.* Washington, DC: National Academies of Sciences, Engineering, and Medicine.. http://www.nsf.gov/pubs/2000/ceose991/ceose 991.html#TOP.

Committee on Equal Opportunities in Science and Engineering [COSEMPUP]. 2006. *Biennial Report to United States Congress.* Washington, DC: National Academies of Sciences, Engineering, and Medicine..

Committee on Science, Engineering and Public Policy (Committee on Maximizing the Potential of Women in Academic Science and Engineering). 2007. *Beyond Bias and Barriers: Fulfilling the Potential of Women in Academic Science and Engineering.* Washington, DC: National Academies Press.

Contreras, Brian. 2021. "Tech Workers Are No Longer Afraid to Go Public. Here's How They Found Their Voices." *Los Angeles Times*, October 27, 2021. https://www .latimes.com/business/story/2021-10-27/protests-at-facebook-and-netflix-show-big -tech-workers-see-leaks-as-best-leverage.

Cooley, Mike, and Shirley Cooley. 1980. *Architect or Bee?: The Human/Technology Relationship.* Slough, UK: Langley Technical Services.

Corbett, Christianne, and Catherine Hill. 2015. *Solving the Equation: The Variables for Women's Success in Engineering and Computing.* Washington, DC: American Association of University Women. https://www.aauw.org/app/uploads/2020/03/Solving -the-Equation-report-nsa.pdf.

Correll, Shelley, Stephen Benard, and In Paik. 2007. "Getting a Job: Is There a Motherhood Penalty?" *American Journal of Sociology* 112 (5): 1297–1338.

Costanza-Chock, Sasha. 2020. *Design Justice: Community-Led Practices to Build the Worlds We Need.* Cambridge, MA: MIT Press.

Crenshaw, Kimberle Williams. 1991. "Mapping the Margins: Intersectionality, Identity Politics and Violence against Women of Color." *Standford Law Review* 43 (6): 1241–1299. https://doi.org/https://doi.org/10.2307/1229039.

Cuny, Janice, and William Aspray. 2001. "Recruitment and Retention of Women Graduate Students in Computer Science and Engineering." Committee on the Status of Women in Computing Research, Computer Research Association, Washington DC.

Urwin, Matthew. 2023. "Women in Tech Statistics Show the Industry Has a Long Way to Go." *BuiltIn*, April 23, 2023. Accessed June 14, 2023. https://builtin.com /women-tech/women-in-tech-workplace-statistics.

Daly, Mary. 1990. *Gyn/Ecology: The Metaethics of Radical Feminism.* 2nd ed. Boston: Beacon Press.

Daly, Mary, and Jane Caputi. 1987. *Websters' First New Intergalactic Wickedary of the English Language.* Boston: Beacon Press.

Daub, Adrian. 2021. "How Sexism Is Coded into the Tech Industry." *The Nation,* April 26, 2021. https://www.thenation.com/article/society/gender-silicon-valley/.

Davis, Dána-Ain, and Christa Craven. 2016. *Feminist Ethnography: Thinking Through Methodologies, Challenges, and Possibilities.* Washington, DC: Rowman & Littlefield.

Davis-Floyd, Robbie E. 1992. *Birth as an American Rite of Passage.* Comparative Studies of Health Systems and Medical Care. Berkeley: University of California Press.

Dean, Jodi. 2002. *Publicity's Secret: How Technoculture Capitalizes on Democracy.* Ithaca, NY: Cornell University Press.

Dean, Jodi. 2009. *Democracy and Other Neoliberal Fantasies: Communicative Capitalism and Left Politics.* Durham, NC: Duke University Press.

Denzin, Norman K., Yvonna S. Lincoln, and Linda Tuhiwai Smith. 2008. *Handbook of Critical and Indigenous Methodologies.* Thousand Oaks, CA: Sage.

Diekman, Amanda B., Mia Steinberg, Elizabeth R. Brown, Aimee L. Belanger, and Emily K. Clark. 2016. "A Goal Congruity Model of Role Entry, Engagement, and Exit Understanding Communal Goal Processes in STEM Gender Gaps." *Personality and Social Psychology Review* 21 (2): 142–175. https://journals.sagepub.com/doi/pdf /10.1177/1088868316642141.

Diekman, Amanda B., Elizabeth Brown, Amanda Johnston, and Emily Clark. 2010. "Seeking Congruity between Goals and Roles: A New Look at Why Women Opt Out of Science, Technology, Engineering, and Mathematics Careers." *Psychological Science* 21 (8): 1051–1057.

D'Ignazio, Catherine, and Lauren F. Klein. 2020. *Data Feminism.* Cambridge, MA: MIT Press.

Domingo, Carmen R., Nancy Counts Gerber, Diane Harris, Laura Mamo, Sally G. Pasion, R. David Rebanal, and Sue V. Rosser. 2020. "More Service or More Advancement: Institutional Barriers to Academic Success for Women and Women of Color Faculty at a Large Public Comprehensive Minority-Serving State University." *Journal of Diversity in Higher Education* 15 (3): 365–379. https://doi.org/https://doi.org/10.1037/dhe0000292.

Dubal, Veena. 2020. "Death of the Entrepreneur." In *This Machine Kills*, produced by Jereme Brown. Podcast, 1:26:22.

DuBow, Wendy, and J. J. Gonzalez. 2020. *NCWIT Scorecard: The Status of Women in Technology.* Boulder, CO: NCWIT. https://www.ncwit.org/sites/default/files/resources/ncwit_scorecard_data_highlights_10082020.pdf.

Dunbar-Hester, Christina. 2020. *Hacking Diversity: The Politics of Inclusion in Open Technology Cultures. Princeton Studies in Culture and Technology.* Princeton, NJ: Princeton University Press.

Edsall, Thomas. 2012. "The Reproduction of Privilege." *New York Times*, March 12, 2012. http://campaignstops.blogs.nytimes.com/2012/03/12/the-reproduction-of-privilege/.

Eglash, Ron. 2002. "Race, Sex, and Nerds: From Black Geeks to Asian American Hipsters." *Social Text* 20 (2): 49–64.

Ehrenreich, Barbara, and Arlie Russell Hoschchild, eds. 2004. *Global Woman: Nannies, Maids, and Sex Workers in the New Economy.* Oakland, CA: Owl Books.

Ensmenger, Nathan. 2010a. "Making Programming Masculine." In *Gender Codes: Why Women Are Leaving Computing*, edited by Thomas J. Misa, 115–142. New York: John Wiley and Sons.

Ensmenger, Nathan. 2010b. *The Computer Boys Take Over: Computers, Programmers, and the Politics of Technical Expertise.* History of Computing. Cambridge, MA: MIT Press.

Eppes, Tom, Ivana Mialnoviv, and Jennifer Snaborn. 2010. "Faculty Gender Balance: Best Practices for Undergraduate Institutions." *Gender, Science and Technology* 2 (3): 453–463.

Espinosa, Lorelle. 2011. "Pipelines and Pathways: Women of Color in Undergraduate STEM Majors and the College Experiences That Contribute to Persistence." *Harvard Educational Review* 81 (2): 209–240.

Essed, Philomena. 2001. "Towards a Methodology to Identify Converging Forms of Everyday Discrimination." United Nations Commission on the Status of Women, New York City. http://www.un.org/womenwatch/daw/csw/essed45.htm.

Etzkowitz, Henry. 2008. "The Coming Gender Revolution in Science." In *The Handbook of Science and Technology Studies*, edited by Edward J. Hackett, Stefan Fuchs, Namrata Gupta, Carol Kemelgor, and Marina Ranga, 403–427. Cambridge, MA: MIT Press.

Etzkowitz, Henry, Carol Kemelgor, and Brian Uzzi. 2000. *Athena Unbound: The Advancement of Women in Science and Technology.* Cambridge: Cambridge University Press.

Faulkner, Wendy. 2000a. "Dualism, Hierarchies and Gender in Engineering." *Social Studies of Science* 30 (5): 759–792.

Faulkner, Wendy. 2000b. "The Power and the Pleasure? A Research Agenda for 'Making Gender Stick' to Engineers." *Science, Technology, & Human Values* 25 (1): 87–119.

Faulkner, Wendy. 2001. "The Technology Question in Feminism: A View from Feminist Technology Studies." *Women Studies International Forum* 24 (1): 79–95.

Faulkner, Wendy. 2007. "'Nuts and Bolts and People' Gender-Troubled Engineer Identities." *Social Studies of Science* 37 (3): 331–356.

Federici, Sylvia. 2004. *Caliban and the Witch: Women, the Body and Primitive Accumulation.* New York: Autonomedia.

Fine, Cordelia. 2010. *Delusions of Gender: How Our Minds, Society, and Neurosexism Create Difference.* 1st ed. New York: W. W. Norton.

Flaherty, Colleen. 2019. "Pinker, Epstein, Soldier, Spy." *Inside Higher Ed*, July 16, 2019. https://www.insidehighered.com/news/2019/07/17/steven-pinkers-aid-jeffrey -epsteins-legal-defense-renews-criticism-increasingly.

Forsythe, Diana E., and David J. Hess. 2001. *Studying Those Who Study Us: An Anthropologist in the World of Artificial Intelligence.* Writing Science. Palo Alto, CA: Stanford University Press.

Fouad, Nadya A., Wen-Hsin Chang, Min Wan, and Romila Singh. 2017. "Women's Reasons for Leaving the Engineering Field." *Frontiers in Psychology* 8. https://doi.org /10.3389/fpsyg.2017.00875.

Fowler, Susan. 2017. "Reflecting on One Very, Very Strange Year at Uber," February 19, 2017. https://www.susanjfowler.com/blog/2017/2/19/reflecting-on-one-very -strange-year-at-uber.

Franklin, Sarah. 1995. "Science as Culture, Cultures of Science." *Annual Review of Anthropology* 24:163–184. https://www.jstor.org/stable/2155934.

Frehill, Lisa. 2007. "The ADVANCE Institutional Transformation Research in the Natural Sciences and Engineering: A Question of Content." In *Gender and Engineering: Strategies and Possibilities*, edited by Ingelore Welpe, Barbara Reschka and June Larkin, 225–242. Frankfurt: Peter Lang.

Frehill, Lisa, Carolyn Brandi, Amanda Lain, and Andrew Frampton. 2009. "Women in Engineering: A Review of the 2009 Literature." In *A Compendium of Women Engineers Annual Literature Reviews on Women in Engineering*, edited by Society of Women Engineers. Chicago: SWE Publishing.

Frickel, Scott, and Neil Gross. 2005. "A General Theory of Scientific/Intellectual Movements." *American Sociological Review* 70 (2): 204–232. https://doi.org/10.1177 /000312240507000202.

Fricker, Miranda. 2007. *Epistemic Injustice: Power and the Ethics of Knowing.* New York: Oxford University Press.

Garibay, Juan C. 2015. "STEM Student's Social Agency and Views on Working for Social Change: Are STEM Disciplines Developing Socially and Civically Responsible Students?" *Journal of Research in Science and Teaching* 52 (2): 1–23. https:// onlinelibrary.wiley.com/doi/full/10.1002/tea.21203.

Garvin-Doxas, Kathy, and Lecia Barker. 2004. "Communication in Computer Science Classrooms: Understanding Defensive Climates as a Means of Creating Supportive Behaviors." *ACM Journal of Educational Resources in Computing* 4 (1): 1–18.

Gibbons, Michael. June 2009. "Engineering by the Numbers." *American Society for Engineering Education Prism*, 10–49.

Ginorio, Angela B. 1995. *Warming the Climate for Women in Academic Science*. Program on the Status and Education of Women. Washington, DC: Association of American Colleges and Universities.

Ginsburg, Faye, and Rayna Rapp. 1991. "The Politics of Reproduction." *Annual Review of Anthropology* 20:311–343.

Ginsburg, Faye D. 1998. *Contested Lives: The Abortion Debate in an American Community*. Berkeley: University of California.

Ginsburg, Faye D., and Rayna Rapp. 1995. *Conceiving the New World Order: The Global Politics of Reproduction*. Berkeley: University of California Press.

Godfrey, Elizabeth, and Lesley Parker. 2010. "Mapping the Cultural Landscape in Engineering Education." *Journal of Engineering Education* (January): 5–22.

Gramsci, Antonio. 1971. *Prison Notebook*. New York: International Publishers.

Grassie, William. 1996. "Donna Haraway's Metatheory of Science and Religion: Cyborgs, Trickster, and Hermes." *Zygon Journal of Religion & Science* 31 (2): 285–304.

Greenberger, Marcia, Jocelyn Samuels, Ellen Eardley, and Jessica Manvell. 2005. *Tools of the Trade: Using the Law to Address Sex Segregation in Career and Technical Education*. Washington DC: National Women's Law Center

Greenwald, Anthony G., and Mahzarin R. Banaji. 1995. "Implicit Social Cognition: Attitudes, Self-Esteem, and Stereotypes." *Psychological Review* 102 (1): 4–27.

Gusterson, Hugh. 1997. "Studying Up Revisited." *PoLAR: Political and Legal Anthropology Review* 20 (1): 114–119.

Hacker, Sally L. 1981. "The Culture of Engineering: Woman, Workplace and Machine." *Women's Studies International Quarterly* 4 (3): 341–353. https://doi.org/10.1016/S0148-0685(81)96559-3.

Hacker, Sally L., Dorothy E. Smith, and Susan M. Turner. 1990. *Doing It the Hard Way: Investigations of Gender and Technology*. Boston: Unwin Hyman.

Hackett, Edward, and Diana Rhoten. 2011. "Engaged, Embedded, Enjoined: Science and Technology Studies in the National Science Foundation." *Science and Engineering Ethics* 17 (4): 823–838.

Hakken, David. 2003. *The Knowledge Landscapes of Cyberspace*. New York: Routledge.

Hakken, David, and Barbara Andrews. 1993. *Computing Myths, Class Realities: An Ethnography of Technology and Working People in Sheffield, England*. Conflict and Social Change Series. Boulder, CO: Westview Press.

Hamrick, Karen. 2019. *Women, Minorities, and Persons with Disabilities in Science and Engineering: 2019*. Alexandria, VA: National Science Foundation, National Center for Science and Engineering Statistics. https://www.nsf.gov/statistics/wmpd.

Haraway, Donna. 1988. "Situated Knowledges: The Science Question in Feminism and the Privilege of Partial Perspective." *Feminist Studies* 14 (3): 575–599.

Haraway, Donna. 1991. *Simians, Cyborgs, and Women.* 1st ed. New York: Routledge.

Harding, Sandra G. 1986. *The Science Question in Feminism.* Ithaca, NY: Cornell University Press.

Harding, Sandra G. 1991. *Whose Science? Whose Knowledge? Thinking from Women's Lives.* Ithaca, NY: Cornell University Press.

Harding, Sandra G, ed. 2004. *The Feminist Standpoint Theory Reader: Intellectual and Political.* New York: Routledge.

Harding, Sandra G. 2006. *Science and Social Inequality: Feminist and Postcolonial Issues.* Urbana: University of Illinois Press.

Harding, Sandra G. 2008. *Sciences from Below: Feminisms, Postcolonialities, and Modernities.* Durham, NC: Duke University Press.

Hartsock, Nancy C. M. 1998. *The Feminist Standpoint Revisited and Other Essays.* Feminist Theory and Politics. Boulder, CO: Westview Press.

Heckman, J. J. 1998. "Detecting Discrimination." *Journal of Economic Perspectives* 12 (2): 101–116.

Henwood, Flis. 1996. "WISE Choices? Understanding Occupational Decision-Making in a Climate of Equal Opportunities for Women in Science and Technology." *Gender and Education* 8 (2): 199–214. https://www.tandfonline.com/doi/abs/10.1080/09540259650038860 Herbers, Joan M., Heather E. Metcalf, and Rochelle L. Williams. 2019. "Identity-Based Harassment." ADVANCE Resource and Coordination Network workshop, Naperville, IL, July 21–23, 2019.

Hess, Abigail Johnson. 2019. "The 10 Highest-Paying College Majors of 2019, According to PayScale." *Work* (blog), *CNBC.com*, August 20, 2019. https://www.cnbc.com/2019/08/20/the-10-highest-paying-college-majors-of-2019.html.

Hess, David. 2007. "Crosscurrents: Social Movement and the Anthropology of Science and Technology." *American Anthropologist* 109 (3): 463–472.

Hewlett, Sylvia Ann. 2010. "The Sponsor Effect: Breaking Through the Glass Ceiling." *Harvard Business Review Research Report* (December): 5–7.

Hicks, Mar. 2017. *Programmed Inequality: How Britain Discarded Women Technologists and Lost Its Edge in Computing.* Edited by William Aspray. Cambridge, MA: MIT Press.

Hill, Catherine, Christianne Corbett, and Andresse Rose. 2010. *Why So Few? Women in Science, Technology, Engineering and Mathematics.* Washington DC: American Association of University Women.

Hing, Leanne, Ramona Bobocel, Mark Zanna, Donna Garcia, Stephanie Gee, and Katie Orazietti. 2011. "The Merit of Meritocracy." *Journal of Personality and Social Psychology* 101 (3): 433–450.

hooks, bell. 1990. *Yearning: Race, Gender and Cultural Politics.* Boston: South End Press.

hooks, bell. 2000. *All about Love: New Visions.* 1st ed. New York: William Morrow.

Howell, Nancy. 1988. "Health and Safety in the Fieldwork of North American Anthropologists." *Current Anthropology* 29 (5): 780–787.

Howell, Nancy. (1990). *Surviving Fieldwork: A Report of the Advisory Panel on Health and Safety in Fieldwork.* Washington, DC: American Anthropological Association.

Ilies, Remus, Nancy Hauserman, Susan Schwochau, and John Stibal. 2003. "Reported Incidence Rates of Work-Related Sexual Harassment in the United States: Using Meta-Analysis to Explain Reported Rate Disparities." *Personnel Psychology* 56 (3): 607–631. https://doi.org/https://doi.org/10.1111/j.1744-6570.2003.tb00752.x.

Jain, Sarah S. Lochlann. 2007. "Cancer Butch." *Cultural Anthropology* 22 (1). https://doi.org/https://doi.org/10.1525/can.2007.22.4.501.

Jorgenson, Jane. 2002. "Engineering Selves Negotiating Gender and Identity in Technical Work." *Management Communications* 15 (3): 350–380.

Katz, Cindi. 2001. "Vagabond Capitalism and the Necessity of Social Reproduction." *Antipode* 33 (4): 708–727.

Kelly, Alison. 1985. "The Construction of Masculine Science." *British Journal of Sociology of Education* 6 (2): 133–154.

Kemmis, Stephen, and Robin McTaggart. 2000. "Participatory Action Research." In *Handbook of Qualitative Research*, edited by Norman Denzin and Yvonna Lincoln, 567–605. Thousand Oaks, CA: Sage.

Keyes, Os. 2018. "The Misgendering of Machines: Trans/HCI Implications of Automatic Gender Recognition." *Proceedings of the ACM on Human–Computer Interaction* 2 (CSCW).

Kidder, Tracy. 1981. *The Soul of a New Machine.* Boston: Back Bay Books.

Klawe, Maria. 2012. "From 10 Percent to 40 Percent Female in Computer Science in Three Years." University of Washington CSE Distinguished Lecture Series, October 6, 2012, Seattle.

Koul, Parul, and Chewy Shaw. 2021. "We Built Google. This Is Not the Company We Want to Work For." *New York Times*, January 4, 2021. https://www.nytimes.com/2021/01/04/opinion/google-union.html.

Kraft, Philip. 1979. "The Industrialization of Computer Programming: From 'Programming' to Software Production." In *Case Studies on the Labor Process*, edited by Andrew S. Zimbalist, 1–13. New York: Monthly Review Press.

Kurtz, Annalyn. 2021. "The US Economy Lost 140,000 Jobs in December. All of Them Were Held by Women." *CNN Business*, January 8, 2021. https://www.cnn.com/2021/01/08/economy/women-job-losses-pandemic/index.html.

Latour, Bruno. 2004. "Why Has Critique Run out of Steam? From Matters of Fact to Matters of Concern." *Critical Inquiry* 30 (2): 225–248. https://doi.org/https://doi.org/10.1086/421123.

Lazowska, Ed. 2002. "Pale and Male: 19th Century Design in a 21st Century World." *SIGCSE Bulletin* 34 (2): 1–2.

Leacock, Eleanor Burke. 1981. *Myths of Male Dominance: Collected Articles on Women Cross-Culturally.* New York: Monthly Review Press.

Lerman, Nina E., Ruth Oldenziel, and Arwen Mohun. 2003. *Gender & Technology: A Reader*. Baltimore: Johns Hopkins University Press.

Leskinen, Emily A., Lilia M. Cortina, and Dana B. Kabat. 2011. "Gender Harassment: Broadening Our Understanding of Sex-Based Harassment at Work." *Law and Human Behavior* 35 (1): 25–39. https://doi.org/https://doi.org/10.1007/s10979-010-9241-5.

Level Playing Field Institute. 2011. *The Tilted Playing Field: Hidden Bias in Information Technology Workforce*. Oakland, CA: Kapor Center. https://www.smash.org/wp-content/uploads/2015/05/tilted_playing_field_lpfi_9_29_11.pdf

Lewis, Colleen M., Ruth E. Anderson, and Ken Yasuhara. 2016. "I Don't Code All Day: Fitting in Computer Science When the Stereotypes Don't Fit." *Proceedings of the 2016 ACM Conference on International Computing Education Research* (August): 23–32. https://dl.acm.org/doi/10.1145/2960310.2960332.

Lewis, Reina, and Sara Mills. 2003. *Feminist Postcolonial Theory: A Reader*. New York: Routledge.

Lie, Merete. 1995. "Technology and Masculinity: The Case of the Computer." *European Journal of Women Studies* 2 (3): 379–394.

Lie, Merete. 1997. "Technology and Gender versus Technology and Work: Social Work and Computers." *ACTA Sociologica* 40 (2): 123–141.

Litchfield, Kaitlin, and Amy Javernick-Will. 2015. "'I Am an Engineer AND': A Mixed Methods Study of Socially Engaged Engineers." *Journal of Engineering Education* 104 (4): 393–416.

Lohan, Maria. 2000. "Constructive Tensions in Feminist Technology Studies." *Social Studies of Science* 30 (6): 895–916.

Lohr, Steve. 2012. "The Age of Big Data." *New York Times*, February 11, 2012. https://www.nytimes.com/2012/02/12/sunday-review/big-datas-impact-in-the-world.html.

Loustaunau, Martha O., and Elisa Janine Sobo. 1997. *The Cultural Context of Health, Illness, and Medicine*. Westport, CT: Bergin & Garvey.

Lugones, Maria. 1989. "Playfulness, 'World'-Traveling, and Loving Perception." In *Women, Knowledge and Reality: Explorations in Feminist Philosophy*, edited by Ann Garry and Marilyn Pearsall, 419–435. Boston: Unwin Hyman.

Madison, D. Soyini. 2005. *Critical Ethnography: Method, Ethics, and Performance*. Thousand Oaks, CA: Sage.

Malcom, Shirley M. 1976. "The Double Bind: The Price of Being a Minority Woman in Science." AAAS Report No. 76-R-3, Conference of Minority Women Scientists, December 12–14, 1976, Arlie House, Warrenton, VA.

Malcom, Shirley M. 1999. "Fault Lines." *Science* 284 (5418): 1271–1272.

Malcom, Shirley M. 2011. "What Kinds of Skills Are Needed to Address the Challenges of the Future and How Do We Enable Students to Acquire These?" American Society for Engineering Education, Vancouver, BC.

Malcom, Shirley M. 2019. "400 Years and (Re) Counting." *Science* (6459): 1221.

Mann, Allison, and Thomas A. DiPrete. 2013. "Trends in Gender Segregation in the Choice of Science and Engineering Majors." *Social Science Research* 42 (6): 1519–1541. https://doi.org/10.1016/j.ssresearch.2013.07.002.

Manne, Kate. 2017. *Down Girl: The Logic of Misogyny*. Oxford: Oxford University Press.

Manne, Kate. 2020. *Entitled: How Male Privilege Hurts Women*. New York: Crown Random House.

Marcotte, Amanda. 2011. "Siri Is Sexist." *Forbes*, December 1, 2011. https://www.forbes.com/sites/kashmirhill/2011/12/01/siri-is-sexist/?sh=eb87db44b56f.

Margolis, Jane. 2008. *Stuck in the Shallow End: Education, Race, and Computing*. Cambridge, MA: MIT Press.

Margolis, Jane, and Allan Fisher. 2003. *Unlocking the Clubhouse: Women in Computing*. Cambridge, MA: MIT Press.

Margolis, Jane, Allan Fisher, and Faye Miller. 2000. "Caring about Connections: Gender and Computing." *IEEE Technology and Society Magazine:* (Winter): 13–20.

Marra, Rose, Kelly Rodgers, Demei Shen, and Barbara Bogue. 2009. "Women Engineering Students and Self-Efficacy: A Multi-Year, Multi-Institution Study of Women Engineering Student Self-Efficacy." *Journal of Engineering Education* 98 (1): 27–38.

Martin, Aryn, Natasha Myers, and Ana Viseu. 2015. "The Politics of Care in Technoscience." *Social Studies of Science* 45 (5): 625–641. https://doi.org/10.1177/0306312715602073.

Martin, Emily. 1992. *The Woman in the Body: A Cultural Analysis of Reproduction*. Boston: Beacon Press.

Martin, Emily. 1994. *Flexible Bodies: Tracking Immunity in American Culture from the Days of Polio to the Age of AIDS*. Boston: Beacon Press.

Massey, D. S. 1990. "American Apartheid: Segregation and the Making of the Underclass." *American Journal of Sociology* 96 (2): 329–357.

Maternowska, Catherine M. 2006. *Reproducing Inequities: Poverty and the Politics of Population in Haiti*. New Brunswick, NJ: Rutgers University Press.

Mayberry, Maralee. 1998. "Reproductive and Resistant Pedagogies: The Comparative Roles of Collaborative Learning and Feminist Pedagogy in Science Education." *Journal of Research in Science Teaching* 35 (4): 443–459.

McCall, Leslie. 2001. *Complex Inequalities: Gender, Class, and Race in the New Economy*. New York: Routledge.

McGee, Ebony O., and Lydia Bentley. 2017. "The Troubled Success of Black Women in STEM." *Cognition and Instruction* 35 (4): 265–289. https://doi.org/https://doi.org/10.1080/07370008.2017.1355211.

McInerney, Paul-Brian. 2014. *From Social Movement to Moral Market: How the Circuit Riders Sparked an IT Revolution and Created a Technology Market*. 1st ed. Palo Alto, CA: Stanford University Press.

McNeil, Maureen. 2007. *Feminist Cultural Studies of Science and Technology. Transformations*. New York: Routledge.

Merchant, Carolyn. 1980. *The Death of Nature: Women, Ecology and the Scientific Revolution*. San Francisco: Harper Collins.

Metcalf, Heather, Dorian Russell, and Catherine Hill. 2018. "Broadening the Science of Broadening Participation in STEM through Critical Mixed Methodologies and Intersectionality Frameworks." *American Behavioral Scientist* 62 (5): 580–599.

Metz, Cade. 2021. "Who Is Making Sure the A.I. Machines Aren't Racist?" *New York Times*, March 15, 2021. https://www.nytimes.com/2021/03/15/technology/artificial -intelligence-google-bias.html.

Microsoft. 2013. "Technical Recognition Awards." Advertisement. *The Seattle Times*, March 2013.

Misa, Thomas J., ed. 2010. *Gender Codes: Why Women Are Leaving Computing*. Edited by IEEE Computer Society. Hoboken, NJ: John Wiley and Sons.

Mohr, Rebecca I., and Valerie Purdie-Vaughns. 2015. "Diversity within Women of Color: Why Experiences Change Felt Stigma." *Sex Roles* 73:391–398. https://doi.org /https://doi.org/10.1007/s11199-015-0511-z.

Mol, Annemarie, Ingunn Moser, and Jeannette Pols. 2010. *Care in Practice: On Tinkering in Clinics, Homes, and Farms*. New York: Columbia University Press.

Molina, Nina, and Sammy Sussman. 2021. "Daily Investigation Finds Divergence in U-M, Outside Organization's Handling of Allegations against CSE Professor." *The Michigan Daily*, May 19, 2021.

Moody, JoAnn. 2004. *Faculty Diversity: Problems and Solutions*. New York: Routledge.

Moore, Henrietta. 1988. *Feminism and Anthropology*. Minneapolis: University of Minnesota Press.

Moore, Henrietta. 1994. *A Passion for Difference: Essays in Anthropology and Gender*. Cambridge: Polity.

Morley, Louise, and Rosemary Lugg. 2009. "Mapping Meritocracy: Intersecting Gender, Poverty and Higher Educational Opportunity Structures." *Higher Education Policy* 22:37–60.

Moss-Racusin, Corrine, John Dovidio, Victoria Brescoll, Mark Graham, and Jo Handelsman. 2012. "Science Faculty's Subtle Gender Biases Favor Male Students." *Proceedings of National Academy of Science* 109 (41): 1–6.

Mullings, Leith. 1997. "'Households Headed by Women: The Politics of Race, Class and Gender.'" In *Conceiving the New World Order: The Global Politics of Reproduction*, edited by Faye D. Ginsburg and Rayna Rapp, 122–139. Berkeley, CA: University of California Press.

Mullings, Leith. 2005. "Resistance and Resilience: The Sojourner Syndrome and the Social Context of Reproduction in Central Harlem." *Transforming Anthropology* 13 (2): 79–91.

Mullings, Leith, and Amy Schultz. 2006. "Intersectionality and Health: An Introduction." In *Gender, Race, Class and Health: Intersectional Approaches*, edited by Amy Schultz and Leith Mullings, 3–20. San Francisco: Jossey-Bass.

Mundie, C., and T. Hey. 2011. *Microsoft Research Connections Brochure*. Microsoft.

Murphy, Michelle. 2015. "Unsettling Care: Troubling Transnational Itineraries of Care in Feminist Health Practices." *Social Studies of Science* 45 (5): 717–737. https://doi.org/10.1177/0306312715589136.

Nader, Laura. 1972. "Up the Anthropologist: Perspectives Gained from Studying Up." In *Reinventing Anthropology*, edited by Dell H. Hymes, 284–312. New York: Pantheon Books.

Nader, Laura. 1996. *Naked Science: Anthropological Inquiry in Boundaries, Power and Knowledge*. New York: Routledge.

Nafus, Dawn. 2018. "Exploration or Algorithm? The Undone Science before the Algorithms." *Cultural Anthropology* 33 (3): 368–374. https://doi.org/https://doi.org/10.14506/ca33.3.03.

Nakano-Glenn, Evelyn. 1992. "From Servitude to Service Work: Historical Continuities in the Racial Division of Paid Reproductive Labor." *Signs: Journal of Women in Culture and Society* 18 (1): 1–43.

National Academies of Sciences, Engineering, and Medicine. 2018. *Sexual Harassment of Women: Climate, Culture, and Consequences in Academic Sciences, Engineering, and Medicine*. Washington, DC: National Academies Press.

National Academies of Sciences, Engineering, and Medicine. 2022. *Transforming Trajectories for Women of Color in Tech*. Washington, DC: National Academies Press.

Nelson, Jennifer. 2003. *Women of Color and the Reproductive Rights Movement*. New York: NYU Press.

Nelson, Robin G., Julienne N. Rutherford, Katie Hinde, and Kathryn B. H. Clancy. 2017. "Signaling Safety: Characterizing Fieldwork Experiences and Their Implications for Career Trajectories." *American Anthropologist* 119 (4): 710–722.

Nietfeld, Emi. 2021. "After Working at Google, I'll Never Let Myself Love a Job Again." *New York Times*, April 7, 2021. https://www.nytimes.com/2021/04/07/opinion/google-job-harassment.html#click=https://t.co/RObvwTavgL.

Noble, Safiya Umoja. 2018. *Algorithms of Oppression: How Search Engines Reinforce Racism*. New York: NYU Press.

Nora, Amaury, and Alberto Cabrera. 1996. "The Role of Perceptions of Prejudice and Discrimination on the Adjustment of Minority Students to College." *Journal of Higher Education* 67 (2): 119–148.

Obama, Barack. 2012. "Remarks at the White House Forum on Women and the Economy." The American Presidency Project, April 6, 2012.

Oldenziel, Ruth. 1999. *Making Technology Masculine: Men, Women and Modern Machines in America, 1870–1945*. Amsterdam: Amsterdam University Press.

O'Neil, Cathy. 2017. *Weapons of Math Destruction: How Big Data Increases Inequality and Threatens Democracy*. New York: Crown.

Ong, Maria. 2005. "Body Projects of Young Women of Color in Physics: Intersections of Gender, Race, and Science." *Social Problems* 52:593–617.

Ong, Maria, Carol Wright, Lorelle Espinoza, and Gary Orfield. 2011. "Inside the Double Bind: A Synthesis of Empirical Research on Undergraduate and Graduate Women of Color in Science, Technology, Engineering and Mathematics." *Harvard Educational Review* 81 (2): 172–208.

Parks-Stamm, Elizabeth, Madeline E. Heilman, and Krystle Hearns. 2008. "Motivated to Penalize: Women's Strategic Rejection of Successful Women." *Perspectives on Social Psychology Bulletin* 34 (2): 237–247.

Pawley, Alice L. 2011. "CAREER: Learning from Small Numbers: Using Personal Narratives by Underrepresented Undergraduate Students to Promote Institutional Change in Engineering." Poster presented at the Engineering Education and Centers PI meeting, Reston, VA, March 13–15, 2011.

Peterson, V. Spike. 2003. *A Critical Rewriting of Global Political Economy*. London: Routledge.

Pewewardy, Cornel, and Bruce Frey. 2002. "Surveying the Landscape: Perceptions of Multicultural Support Services and Racial Climate at a Predominantly White University." *Journal of Negro Education* 71 (1/2): 77–95.

Pinker, Steven. 2005. *The Stuff of Thought: Language as a Window into Human Nature*. New York: Penguin.

Plaut, Victoria. 2010. "Diversity Science: Why and How Difference Makes a Difference." *Psychological Inquiry: An International Journal for the Advancement of Psychological Theory* 21 (2): 77–99.

Posselt, Julie R. 2020. *Equity in Science: Representation, Culture, and the Dynamics of Change in Graduate Education*. Redwood City, CA: Stanford University Press.

Potter, Ellen F., and Sue V. Rosser. 1992. "Factors in Life Science Textbooks That May Deter Girls' Interest in Science." *Journal of Research in Science Teaching* 29 (7): 669–686. https://doi.org/https://doi.org/10.1002/tea.3660290705.

Procter, Paul. 1984. *Longman Dictionary of Contemporary English*. London: Longman.

Puig de la Bellacasa, Maria. 2011. "Matters of Care in Technoscience: Assembling Neglected Things." *Social Studies of Science* 41 (1): 85–106. https://doi.org/10.1177/0306312710380301.

Quinn, Beth A. 2002. "Sexual Harassment and Masculinity: The Power and Meaning of 'Girl Watching.'" *Gender and Society* 16 (3): 386–402.

Rabelo, Verónica Caridad, and Lilia Cortina. 2014. "Two Sides of the Same Coin: Gender Harassment and Heterosexist Harassment in LGBQ Work Lives." *Law and Human Behavior* 38 (4): 378–391. https://doi.org/10.1037/lhb0000087.

Rapp, Rayna. 1979. "Review Essay: Anthropology." *Signs: Journal of Women in Culture and Society* 4 (3): 497–513.

Rapp, Rayna. 1999. *Testing Women, Testing the Fetus: The Social Impact of Amniocentesis in America*. New York: Routledge.

Raver, Jana L., and Lisa Hisae Nishii. 2010. "Once, Twice, or Three Times as Harmful? Ethnic Harassment, Gender Harassment, and Generalized Workplace Harassment." *Journal of Applied Psychology* 95 (2): 236–254.

Reid, Roddey, and Sharon Traweek. 2000. *Doing Science + Culture: How Cultural and Interdisciplinary Studies Are Changing the Way We Look at Science and Medicine.* London: Routledge.

Reskin, Barbara F., Debra B. McBrier, and Julie A. Kmec. 1999. "The Determinants and Consequences of Workplace Sex and Race Composition." *Annual Review of Sociology* 25:335–361. https://doi.org/https://doi.org/10.1146/annurev.soc.25.1.335.

Richardson, Brian K., and Juandalynn Taylor. 2009. "Sexual Harassment at the Intersection of Race and Gender: A Theoretical Model of the Sexual Harassment Experiences of Women of Color." *Western Journal of Communication* 73 (3): 248–272. https://doi.org/https://doi.org/10.1080/10570310903082065.

Riley, Donna M. 2014. "What's Wrong with Evidence? Epistemological Roots and Pedagogical Implications of 'Evidence-Based Practice' in STEM Education." Presentation at the ASEE Annual Conference, June 15–18, 2014, Indianapolis, IN.

Riley, Donna. 2017. "Rigor/Us: Building Boundaries and Disciplining Diversity with Standards of Merit." *Engineering Studies* 9 (3): 249–265. https://doi.org/10.1080/19378629.2017.1408631.

Riley, Donna, Alice Pawley, Jessica Tucker, and George Catalano. 2009. "Feminisms in Engineering Education: Transformative Possibilities." *NWSA Journal* 21 (2): 21–40.

Roberts, Sarah T. 2019. *Behind the Screen: Content Moderation in the Shadows of Social Media.* New Haven, CT: Yale University Press.

Roos, Patricia A., and Barbara F. Reskin, ed. 1984. *Institutional Factors Contributing to Sex Segregation in the Workplace: Trends, Explanations, Remedies.* Washington, DC: National Academies Press.

Rosaldo, Michelle Zimbalist, Louise Lamphere, and Joan Bamberger. 1974. *Woman, Culture, and Society.* Stanford, CA: Stanford University Press.

Rosner, Daniela. 2018a. *Critical Fabulations: Reworking the Methods and Margins of Design.* Vol. 14. Cambridge, MA: MIT Press.

Rosner, Daniela K. 2018b. "Approaching Design as Inquiry: Magic, Myth, and Metaphor in Digital Fabrication." In *The Routledge Companion to Media Studies and Digital Humanities,* edited by Jentery Sayers, 511–520. Oxfordshire: Routledge.

Ross, Monique, Zahra Hazari, and Philip M. Sadler. 2020. "The Intersection of Being Black and Being a Woman: Examining the Effect of Social Computing Relationships on Computer Science Career Choice." *ACM Transactions on Computing Education* 20 (2): 1–15.

Rosser, Andrew. 2006. "The Political Economy of the Resource Curse: A Literature Survey." Working Paper 268, Institute of Development Studies, Brighton. https://opendocs.ids.ac.uk/opendocs/bitstream/handle/20.500.12413/4061/Wp268.pdf.

Rosser, Sue Vilhauer. 1995. *Teaching the Majority: Breaking the Gender Barrier in Science, Mathematics, and Engineering.* Athene Series. New York: Teachers College, Columbia University.

Rosser, Sue Vilhauer. 1998. "Group Work in Science, Engineering and Mathematics: Consequences of Ignoring Gender and Race." *College Teaching* 46 (3): 82–88.

Rosser, Sue Vilhauer. 2004. *The Science Glass Ceiling: Academic Women Scientists and the Struggle to Succeed*. New York: Routledge.

Rosser, Sue Vilhauer. 2012. *Breaking into the Lab: Engineering Progress for Women in Science*. New York: NYU Press.

Rosser, Sue Vilhauer. 2013. "Continuing Issues for Successful Academic Women Scientists and Engineers: Revisiting POWRE Awardees after a Decade." *Journal of Women and Minorities in Science and Engineering* 19 (4): 293–327.

Rossiter, Margaret W. 1998. *Women Scientists in America*. Baltimore: Johns Hopkins University Press.

Ruiz-Grossman, Sarah. 2022. "A New Billionaire Was Created Every 30 Hours during the Pandemic: Oxfam." *HuffPost*, May 22, 2022. https://www.huffpost.com/entry /billionaire-wealth-covid-pandemic-oxfam_n_6283e951e4b04353eb0a526d.

Sadowski, Jathan. 2020. *Too Smart: How Digital Capitalism Is Extracting Data, Controlling Our Lives, and Taking Over the World*. Cambridge, MA: MIT Press.

Sandberg, Sheryl. 2013. *Lean In: Women, Work, and the Will to Lead*. 1st ed. New York: Alfred A. Knopf.

Sandler, Bernice R., and Roberta M. Hall. 1986. *The Campus Climate Revisited: Chilly for Women Faculty, Administrators and Graduate Students*. Washington, DC: Association of American Colleges.

Sandoval, Chela. 2000. *Methodology of the Oppressed: Theory Out of Bounds*. Minneapolis: University of Minnesota Press.

Sanger, Pamela Chapman. 2003. "Living and Writing Feminist Ethnographies." In *Expressions of Ethnography: Novel Approaches to Ethnographic Methods*, edited by Robin Patric Clair, 29–45. Albany: State University of New York Press.

Sargent, Carolyn, and Carole Browner. 2005. "Globalization Raises New Questions about the Politics of Reproduction." *Anthropology News* 46 (3): 5–7.

Scheper-Hughes, Nancy, and Margaret M. Lock. 1987. "The Mindful Body: A Prolegomenon to Future Work in Medical Anthropology." *Medical Anthropology Quarterly* 1 (1): 6–41. https://www.jstor.org/stable/648769.

Schiebinger, Londa L. 1999. *Has Feminism Changed Science?* Cambridge, MA: Harvard University Press.

Schiebinger, Londa L. 2008. *Gendered Innovations in Science and Engineering*. Redwood City, CA: Stanford University Press.

Schiffer, Zoe. 2021. "Apple Employees Are Organizing, Now under the Banner #AppleToo." *The Verge*, August 23, 2021. https://www.theverge.com/2021/8/23/22638150 /apple-appletoo-employee-harassment-discord.

Schneider, Ava, and Laura Sydell. 2019. "Microsoft Workers Protest Army Contract with Tech 'Designed to Help People Kill.'" *NPR*, February 22, 2019.

Scott, Allison, Freada Kapor Klein, and Uriridiakoghene Onovakpuri. 2017. *Tech Leavers Study*. Oakland, CA: Kapor Center for Social Impact.

Seymour, Elaine, and N. M. Hewitt. 1997. *Talking about Leaving: Why Undergraduates Leave the Sciences*. New York: Avalon Publishing.

Sharma, Sarah. 2018. "Going to Work in Mommy's Basement." *Once and Future Feminist* (blog), *Boston Review*, June 19, 2018.

Sharp, Gwen, and Emily Kremer. 2006. "The Safety Dance: Confronting Harassment, Intimidation, and Violence in the Field." *Sociological Methodology* 36 (1): 317–327. https://doi.org/https://doi.org/10.1111/j.1467-9531.2006.00183.x.

Shriver, Maria. 2009. *The Shriver Report*. Washington, DC: Center for American Progress.

Siebel Newsom, Jennifer, and Jean Kilbourne. 2017. "VOCO's Sexist Ad Demonstrates That the Tech Industry Badly Needs Women." *The Daily Beast*, July 12, 2017. https://www.thedailybeast.com/vocos-sexist-ad-demonstrates-that-the-tech-industry-badly-needs-women.

Silliman, J., M. G. Fried, L. Ross, and E. R. Gutiérrez. 2004. *Undivided Rights: Women of Color Organize for Reproductive Justice*. Cambridge, MA: South End Press.

Simonite, Tom. 2018. "When It Comes to Gorillas, Google Photos Remains Blind." *Wired*, January 11, 2018. https://www.wired.com/story/when-it-comes-to-gorillas-google-photos-remains-blind/.

Singer, Natasha. 2019. "Amazon Is Pushing Facial Technology That a Study Says Could Be Biased." *New York Times*, January 24, 2019.

Sismondo, Sergio. 2010. *An Introduction to Science and Technology Studies*. 2nd ed. Malden, MA: Wiley-Blackwell.

Smith, Dorothy E. 1987. *The Everyday World as Problematic: A Feminist Sociology*. Northeastern Series in Feminist Theory. Boston: Northeastern University Press.

Smith, Dorothy E. 1990. *The Conceptual Practices of Power: A Feminist Sociology of Knowledge*. Northeastern Series Feminist Theory. Boston: Northeastern University Press.

Smith, Dorothy E. 2005. *Institutional Ethnography: A Sociology for People*. Lanham, MD: AltaMira.

Smyth, Frederick L., and Brian A. Nosek. 2015. "On the Gender–Science Stereotypes Held by Scientists: Explicit Accord with Gender-Ratios, Implicit Accord with Scientific Identity." *Frontiers in Psychology* 6 (415). https://www.frontiersin.org/articles/10.3389/fpsyg.2015.00415/full.

Society of Women Engineers. 2021. *SWE Fast Facts*. Chicago: SWE.

Solomonides, Tony, and Les Levidow. 1985. *Compulsive Technology: Computers as Culture*. London: Free Association Books.

Spaights, Ernest, and Ann Whitaker. 1995. "Black Women in the Workforce: A New Look at an Old Problem." *Journal of Black Studies: Sage Publications* 25 (3): 283–296.

Spiel, Katta., Ashley M. Walker, Michael A. DeVito, Jeremy P. Birnholtz, Pinar Barlas, Alex Ahmed, Jed R. Brubaker, Os Keyes, Emeline Brulé, Ann Light, Jean Hardy, Jennifer A. Rode, and Gopinaath Kannabiran. 2019. "Queer(ing) HCI: Moving Forward in Theory and Practice." Presentation at the CHI Conference on Human Factors in Computing Systems, May 4–9, 2019, Glasgow.

Star, Susan L. 1991. "Sociology of the Invisible: The Primacy of Work in the Writings of Anselm Strauss.'" In *Social Organization and Social Process: Essays in Honor of Anselm Strauss*, edited by Anselm Leonard Strauss and David R. Maines, 262–283. Piscataway, New Jersey: Transaction Publishers.

Steinpreis, Rhea, Katie A. Anders, and Dawn Ritzke. 1999. "The Impact of Gender on the Review of the Curricula Vitae of Job Applicants and Tenure Candidates: A National Empirical Study." *Sex Roles* 41:509–528.

Stewart, Heather, and Graeme Wearden. 2013. "Facebook's Sheryl Sandberg Attacks Gender Stereotypes at Work." *The Guardian*, January 25, 2013. http://www.guardian .co.uk/business/2013/jan/25/facebook-sheryl-sandberg-gender-stereotypes.

Strike, Beth, Bill Garner, Cynthia Witt, D. J. Corson, and Ann Feldmann. 2003. "The Survival Guide for Iowa School Administrators: Equity Vocabulary." School Administrators of Iowa. Accessed May 3, 2010. http://resources.sai-iowa.org/diversity/equity _vocabulary.pdf.

Subramaniam, Banu, Laura Foster, Sandra Harding, Deboleena Roy, and Kim Tall-Bear. 2017. "Feminism, Postcolonialism, Technoscience." In *The Handbook of Science and Technology Studies*, edited by Ullrike Felt, Clark Miller, Laurel Smith-Doerr, and Rayvon Fouchï, 407–434. Cambridge, MA: MIT Press.

Suchman, Lucy. 2012. "Configuration." In *Inventive Methods: The Happening of the Social*, edited by Celia Lury and Nina Wakeford, 48–60. Oxfordshire: Taylor and Francis.

Summers, Larry. 2005. "Remarks at NBER Conference on Diversifying the Science and Engineering Workforce," Cambridge, MA, January 14, 2005.

Swim, Janet, Kathryn Aikin, Wayne Hall, and Barbara Hunter. 1995. "Sexism and Racism: Old-Fashioned and Modern Prejudices." *Journal of Personality and Social Psychology* 68 (2): 199.

Táíwò, Olúfémi. 2020. "Being-in-the-Room Privilege: Elite Capture and Epistemic Deference." *The Philosopher*, May 20, 2020. https://www.thephilosopher1923.org /post/being-in-the-room-privilege-elite-capture-and-epistemic-deference.

Tam, Mo-Yin S., and Gilbert W. Jr. Bassett. 2006. "The Gender Gap in Information Technology." In *Removing Barriers: Women in Academic Science, Technology, Engineering, and Mathematics*, edited by Jill M. Bystydzienski and Sharon R. Bird, 108–122. Bloomington: Indiana University Press.

Tarnoff, Ben, and Moira Weigel. 2020. *Voices from the Valley: Tech Workers Talk about What They Do—and How They Do It*. New York: Farraer, Straus and Giroux.

Thomas, Suzanne, Dawn Nafus, and Jamie Sherman. 2018. "Algorithms as Fetish: Faith and Possibility in Algorithmic Work." *Big Data & Society* (January–June): 1–11.

Traweek, Sharon. 1988. *Beamtimes and Lifetimes: The World of High Energy Physicists*. Cambridge, MA: Harvard University Press.

Trower, Cathy, and Richard Chait. 2002. "Faculty Diversity: Too Little for Too Long." *Harvard Magazine* 104 (March–April): 33–37.

Turkle, Sherry, and Seymour Papert. 1990. "Epistemological Pluralism: Styles and Voices within the Computer Culture." *Signs: Journal of Women in Culture and Society* 16 (1): 128–157.

Urla, Jacqueline, and Alan Swedlund. 1995. "The Anthropometry of Barbie: Unsettling Ideals of the Feminine Body in Popular Culture." In *Deviant Bodies: Critical Perspectives on Difference in Science and Popular Culture*, edited by Jennifer Terry and Jacqueline Urla, 277–313. Bloomington: Indiana University Press.

Valian, Virginia. 1999. *Why So Slow? The Advancement of Women*. Cambridge, MA: MIT Press.

Vassallo, Trae, Ellen Levy, Michele Madansky, Hillary Mickell, Bennett Porter, Monica Leas, and Julie Oberweis. 2016. "The Elephant in the Valley." Panel discussion at South by Southwest (SXSW) Interactive 2016, Austin, TX, March 11–19. https://www.elephantinthevalley.com.

Viseu, Ana. 2015. "Caring for Nanotechnology? Being an Integrated Social Scientist." *Social Studies of Science* 45 (5): 642–664. https://doi.org/10.1177/0306312715598666.

Wajcman, Judy. 1991. *Feminism Confronts Technology*. Cambridge: Polity Press with B. Blackwell.

Wajcman, Judy. 2009. "Feminist Theories of Technology." *Cambridge Journal of Economics* 1:1–10.

Wakabayashi, Daisuke, Erin Griffith, Amie Tsang, and Kate Conger. 2018. "Google Walkout: Employees Stage Protest Over Handling of Sexual Harassment." *New York Times*, November 1, 2018. https://www.nytimes.com/2018/11/01/technology/google-walkout-sexual-harassment.html.

Walby, Kevin, and Seantel Anais. 2015. "Research Methods, Institutional Ethnography, and Feminist Surveillance Studies." In *Feminist Surveillance Studies*, edited by Rachel E. Dubrofsky and Shoshana Amielle Magnet, 208–220. Durham, NC: Duke University Press.

Watt, Helen M. G., and Jacquelynne S. Eccles. 2008. *Gender and Occupational Outcomes: Longitudinal Assessments of Individual, Social, and Cultural Influences*. 1st ed. Washington, DC: American Psychological Association.

Weeks, Kathi. 2011. *The Problem with Work: Feminism, Marxism, Antiwork Politics, and Postwork Imaginaries*. Durham, NC: Duke University Press.

West, Sara Myers, Meredith Whittaker, and Kate Crawford. 2019. "Discriminating Systems: Gender, Race, and Power in AI." *AI Now Institute*, April 2019. https://ainowinstitute.org/publication/discriminating-systems-gender-race-and-power-in-ai-2

Whittaker, Meredith, and Astra Taylor. 2020 "Demystifying Big Tech with Meredith Whittaker." In *The Dig*, September 25, 2020. Podcast, 2:08.54. https://thedigradio.com/podcast/demystifying-big-tech-with-meredith-whittaker/.

Williams, Joan. 2000. *Unbending Gender: Why Family and Work Conflict and What to Do About It*. Oxford: Oxford University Press.

Winner, Langdon. 2010. *The Whale and the Reactor: A Search for Limits in an Age of High Technology*. Chicago: University of Chicago Press.

Wisnioski, Mathew. 2012. *Engineers for Change: Competing Visions of Technology in 1960s America*. Cambridge, MA: MIT Press.

Wyer, Mary. 2009. *Women, Science, and Technology: A Reader in Feminist Science Studies*. 2nd ed. New York: Routledge.

Wylie, Alison. 2012. "Feminist Philosophy of Science: Standpoint Matters." Annual Meeting of the Pacific Division of The American Philosophical Society, April 6, 2012, Seattle.

Xie, Yu, and Kimberlee A. Shauman. 2003. *Women in Science: Career Processes and Outcomes*. Cambridge, MA: Harvard University Press.

Yoshino, Kenji. 2007. *Covering: The Hidden Assault on Our Civil Rights*. New York: Random House.

Zuboff, Shoshana. 2019. "Surveillance Capitalism and the Challenge of Collective Action." *New Labor Forum* 28 (1): 10–29. https://doi.org/https://doi.org/10.1177/1095796018819461.

Zweben, S., and B. Bizot. 2020. "2019 Taulbee Survey: Total Undergrad CS Enrollment Rises Again, but with Fewer New Majors; Doctoral Degree Production Recovers from Last Year's Dip." *Computing Research News* 32 (5). https://cra.org/crn/2020/05/2019-taulbee-survey/.

INDEX